Black Aliens

NEW SUNS:

RACE, GENDER, AND SEXUALITY

IN THE SPECULATIVE

Susana M. Morris and Kinitra D. Brooks, Series Editors

Black Aliens

Kinship in the Cosmic Diaspora

Joanna Davis-McElligatt

THE OHIO STATE UNIVERSITY PRESS
COLUMBUS

Copyright © 2026 by Joanna Davis-McElligatt.
All rights reserved.
Published by The Ohio State University Press.
Use of this material to train AI is prohibited without the express permission of the
  publisher and author.

Library of Congress Cataloging-in-Publication Data available online at https://
  catalog.loc.gov
LCCN: 2025051271
Identifiers: ISBN 9780814216088 (hardback); ISBN 9780814259771 (paperback); ISBN
  9780814284865 (ebook)

Cover design by Laurence J. Nozik
Text composition by Stuart Rodriguez
Type set in Palatino LT Std

∞ The paper used in this publication meets the minimum requirements of the
American National Standard for Information Sciences—Permanence of Paper for
Printed Library Materials. ANSI Z39.48-1992.

for august, nora, and jun
ad astra per aspera

CONTENTS

List of Illustrations   viii

Introduction   1

Chapter 1   History as Another Planet: Speculative Histofiction and Constellations of Black Alien Linealogy in *Kindred* and *These Ghosts Are Family*   14

Chapter 2   Black Skin, Human Masks, Alien Form: Narrative Physiognomy, Visual Phenomenology, and Image-Text Representations of (Extra)Terrestriality   57

Chapter 3   Black Alien M/other: Correcting the Intergalactic Archive   109

Chapter 4   "I Am Not of This Planet": The Making of Le Sony'r Ra's Cosmic Diaspora   153

Coda   Earth Is Ghetto   196

Acknowledgments   205

Bibliography   209

Index   217

ILLUSTRATIONS

Figure 1	Aliens departing a flying saucer while holding trash cans labeled DSNY	63
Figure 2	Barney and Betty Hill's renderings of an extraterrestrial spacecraft	65
Figure 3	Johann Kaspar Lavater's visual taxonomy from frogs to Roman gods in profile	71
Figure 4	Barney Hill's drawings of the aliens who abducted him and his wife, Betty	73
Figure 5	Johann Kaspar Lavater's visual taxonomy from frogs to Apollo	74
Figure 6	Lithograph of Banania advertisement, 1915	79
Figure 7	Arnus is recombinated into a human and taken in by his surrogate mother, Miriam	92
Figure 8	In his law office in Dakota City, Arnus contemplates his former life as an enslaved person	96
Figure 9	Arnus and Raquel are surrounded by S.H.R.E.D. police officers	101
Figure 10	Raquel and Arnus discuss Arnus's future superhero practices	107

INTRODUCTION

Let me set the scene. It is 1987, and we have returned from a regularly scheduled commercial break to an episode of *The Oprah Winfrey Show*. As applause fades in, the camera focuses in tightly on Oprah, who sits beside two middle-aged white women in armchairs, one dressed in a bright-pink pants suit, the other in a muted-gray business suit. There is nothing unusual about the women, nothing to indicate the strange topic of the show; in fact, the women's ordinariness—their mundane shoulder-padded Earthliness—is what makes the segment so surprising. As the applause fades out, Oprah directs her attention to the camera, summarizing for us the section's content: "I'm talking today to women who have been abducted by aliens from another planet. And you, you're going to describe to us what they looked like."[1] The audience immediately goes silent. Though there have been more than 1,700 reports of abductions by extraterrestrial aliens since 1961, when Barney and Betty Hill claimed they were taken in a spaceship one evening in New Hampshire, close encounters of the third kind, or direct physical contact with extraterrestrial aliens, are generally understood to be impossible, abductees labeled as frauds, liars, or grifters.[2] The details

---

1. OWN, "Thought of Black Aliens."
2. For an overview of alien abduction experiences, see Stuart Apelle, "The Abduction Experience: A Critical Evaluation of Theory and Evidence," *Journal of UFO Studies* 6 (1996): 29–78.

of their abductions—where the women were when the events took place, what happened to their bodies during the journey, where they wound up, what the spaceships were like—are less important here. What *really* matters to Oprah's audience is *what they looked like*; in the US, what someone (or something) *looks like* is often taken to be a sign of who (or what) they are, where they are from, what they can or will (or cannot) do. The woman in the gray business suit speaks first: "They're humanoid, as far as the body. Small frames, about three-and-a-half to four feet tall. And I found myself laughing to myself when I saw them, because—I just saw one being, actually—because the skin was very, very dark olive green, so dark it could be mistaken for black."[3] It is hard to know exactly *what* was so funny about the alien's skin to the woman, what could possibly have been so amusing that she felt compelled to laugh in the midst of contact. Was it that she believed extraterrestrial aliens are supposed to be light green or steel gray, not black, as is so commonly reported? Was she shocked to discover that an extraterrestrial alien could resemble Black Earthlings? Who, after all, would expect to encounter a *Black* alien?

Oprah would. Before her guest has a chance to finish her sentence, Oprah is already cheering: "Alright! *Alright!* We're in control of outer space! You know *I* believe you, girl."[4] Oprah's immediate identification with these Black extraterrestrials is not predicated on a shared national or planetary origin, or political allegiances, or a common ancestral homeland, but on what they both *look like* to another person, an entanglement in galactic relation by virtue of their apparent Blackness. *We're,* as in *Black folk*—not *you're,* as in *white folk*—in control of outer space, Oprah exclaims, as though she and these extraterrestrial aliens are kinfolk, relatives, old friends, family. In her enthusiasm, Oprah shifts the boundaries and confluences of Black belonging to include *everyone* or *anyone* Black wherever or whoever they might be—even space aliens from another planet. How do we make meaning of Oprah's eager identification of kinship with Black aliens? How do these off-Earth fantasies of belonging and unfettered freedom from the gravity of antiblackness extend the African diaspora into the stars? How have Black writers imagined themselves in genealogical, interpersonal, and intergalactic relation with extraterrestrial aliens in outer space—and *why*?

Black Aliens: Kinship in the Cosmic Diaspora examines extraterrestrial and interdimensional aliens who appear in Black speculative media and culture as representations of a cosmic diasporic experience and as charged

---

3. OWN, "Thought of Black Aliens."
4. OWN, "Thought of Black Aliens."

metaphors for Black fugitivity and escape. In other words, I take seriously Oprah's desire for intergalactic kinship with Black extraterrestrial aliens in a galaxy *we*—meaning *Black folk*—collectively control. Through a study of prose, poetry, film, record albums, comic books, illustrations and amateur drawings, art installations, and exhibition catalogues, *Black Aliens* traces how Black artists and visionaries—Octavia Butler, Maisy Card, Dwayne McDuffie and M. D. Bright, and Sun Ra—conceptualize extraterrestrial aliens who *appear to be* or *look* Black, and enter into visual, sociopolitical, experiential (phenomenological), embodied (ontological), and emotional (affective) relation with the terrestrial descendants of enslaved Africans. Stated another way, in this book I am interested in aliens whose bodies and beings are read, seen, and constituted as Black on Earth, and who make chosen kin-community with Black Earthlings. My definition of what constitutes an alien in this book is deliberately broad. Represented by the enslaved and their descendants, ghosts in the afterlife, time travelers and interstellar voyagers, extraterrestrial beings, space immortals, and alien abductees, the Black aliens I examine here are inherently disruptive figures—beings-on-the-move, out-of-joint in spacetime, typified by migration, flight, escape, with a bent toward navigation rather than stasis. Each of the Black aliens I explore comes from (and goes to) another planet or dimension—the past (*Kindred*), the afterlife (*These Ghosts Are Family*), Saturn and Jupiter (Sun Ra), and distant galaxies (*Icon* and *Xenogenesis*). And yet, as is so often the case in SF and speculative imaginaries, instead of contriving extraterrestrial and interdimensional aliens as threatening, dangerous Others, these creators construct the alien *relationally* as self, interspecial kin, and transgalactic community, fashioning alternative genealogies of belonging, new diasporic cartographies, and systems of interrelation for Black terrestrials and extraterrestrials alike.

As subjects entangled by spacetime in multiple locations all at once, Black aliens extend the Black Atlantic into the cosmos, and come to represent the machinations of removal, exile, and the impossibility of past return, the crisis of the present, and the inherent possibility and unknowability of the future. Black aliens can be defined by their estrangement from their homeplaces of origin and their ongoing alienation from the dominant structures, systems, and cultures in the spaces where they find themselves—yet, just as often, Black aliens resist, innovate, and revolt by creating new strategies for survival that foreground radical forms of communalism and collectivism. *Black Aliens* explores how Butler, Card, McDuffie and Bright, and Ra locate the Black alien as a subject whose experience of and entanglement in the African diaspora is both disjunctive and transgressive, tensions made manifest at the levels of plot, characterization, narrativization, and as narrative form itself. I analyze how these creators construct Black alien being in opposition to dominant modes of Western linear narratology by disrupting narrative spacetime through the use of critical fabulation, analepsis, prolepsis, fragmentation, gapping, paratext, and achronological serialization, among other strategies. To that end, I contend that Black aliens necessarily *recast narrative spacetime itself* in order to represent and reimagine Black entanglements, kinship systems, and histories as a cosmic diaspora.

Black Aliens contributes to discourses in and approaches to Black study advanced by Saidiya Hartman, Octavia Butler, Christina Sharpe, Hortense Spillers, Sylvia Wynter, Orlando Patterson, and Frantz Fanon, among others, that unsettle the category of the human, and examine how Black subjects have been excluded from and/or included in civic categories of terrestrial human being. As nonterrestrial entities from another planet or dimension, Black aliens are always-already cosmogenic and nonhuman—specially, sociopolitically, and/or spatiotemporally, as the case may be—and displace the human as the universal apex of evolution and interrelation, shifting our attention to categories of being and belonging beyond those enforced on Earth. The aliens I explore in this book are at certain times and spaces subject to the debasing death-politics of the antiblack US state because their bodies, again, *appear to be* or *look* Black—in their contacts with Earthlings they are interpellated as chattel slaves, dysgenic objects, subhuman monsters, animalized, incarcerated, and subject to physical pain, violence, and social and corporeal death, not because of their alienness but because of the surface of their Black(ened) being. In other words, extraterrestrial aliens who are "Black(ened)," Zakkiyah Iman Jackson explains, are constituted as animalized nonhuman (non)subjects via the same social, cultural, and political processes that "imagin[e] black people as an empty vessel, a nonbeing, a nothing, an ontological zero, coupled with the violent imposition of colonial myths and racial hierarchy."[5] Because the aliens I explore here are transformed to appear Black, dematerialized into Blackness or Black(ened) states of being, or are (re)materialized as Black subjects in alternative spacetimes, I follow Michelle Wright, who argues that Blackness must be understood "*when* and *where* it is being imagined, defined, and performed and in what locations, both figurative and literal."[6] *Black Aliens* makes the case that you do not need to be human in order to be Black. I frame Blackness as a marker of interstellar community—or, at times, terrestrial nonhumanity—in particular times and spaces, rather than an essential biological, racial, or

---

5. Jackson, *Becoming Human*, 1.
6. Wright, *Physics of Blackness*, 3.

special category of being. In this formulation, Black terrestriality itself can be seen as an alien subjectivity operating at productive odds with constructions of humanness on Earth. Following Wright again, I read (extra)terrestrial Blackness as "a construct (implicitly or explicitly defined as a shared set of physical and behavioral characteristics) and as phenomenological (imagined through individual perceptions in various ways depending on the context)."[7] Wright's explication of Blackness-as-construct and Blackness-as-phenomenological demands that we confront how "both modes comprise notions of space and time, or 'spacetime.'"[8] I approach Black life through the lens of "*epiphenomenal time,* or the 'now,' through which the past, present, and future are always interpreted."[9] Though the Black aliens I examine are subject to the strictures of antiblackness in particular times and spaces while on Earth, they are also bound up with and in off-planet galactic systems that reveal the violent provincialism of Earth hierarchies and gesture toward other uses and cultures of Blackness—and therefore other worlds, celestial affiliations, interstellar possibilities. In other words, *Black Aliens* attends to the many complex and fantastic ways Black folk imagine both on- and off-Earth constellations of (extra)terrestrial Blackness.

Black Aliens is a study of extraterrestrial alien entanglements with terrestrial being/s that generate new networks of kinship and relation—genealogical, reproductive, transspecial—and make survival possible for Black(ened) subjects on Earth and in the cosmos. Black aliens offer discursive, speculative, and galactic alternatives to the death-logics of terrestrial antiblackness, breaching constructions of Western Man as the human itself, as Sylvia Wynter has framed it, by moving Black kinship systems away from the planet Earth toward possibilities that might be found in extraterrestrial alien futures in outer space. Black aliens often find themselves, then, in an antagonistic relation with the very idea of terrestrial humanity itself, both because they are oriented toward and from an elsewhere, and because they are interpellated as dysgenic subhumans by racist, antiblack, and white supremacist Earth systems. And yet, because they signify an intergalactic origin and cosmic other-directionality, Black aliens are not bound to or by the confines of planetary spacetime, or the embodied, sociopolitical and terrestrial limitations of earthbound humanity—as we will see, each Black alien in this book possesses an extraspatial and transtemporal means of escape: aerial flight, time-hopping, transfiguration, dematerialization, transmolecularization, and/or space aviation. Black alien orientations in spacetime are therefore

---

7. Wright, *Physics of Blackness,* 4.
8. Wright, *Physics of Blackness,* 4.
9. Wright, *Physics of Blackness,* 4, italics in original.

always moving toward an *otherwise*, an interplanetary, transdimensional, or galactic *elsewhere*, a different cosmic reality where Earth's degradations of Blackness are in the mothership's rearview.

I therefore construct Black (extra)terrestrial aliens as speculative extensions of the *fugitive*, a subject position and moveable location in spacetime that Michelle Koerner argues "invokes a people [. . .][10] exterior to the state apparatus: a minor race understood as the 'unthought' of Western philosophy; a people who, from the perspective of the state model of thought and its existing ontologies, does not exist."[11] I argue that the Black alien is one such unthought presence—by occupying a position "exterior to" the constraints of terrestrial spacetime, Black aliens have the potential to enter into states of nonexistence made possible by their ability to escape into the cosmos; in other words, Black aliens do not *want* to exist on the antiblack planet, and they do what they can to get away from it. Following Gilles Deleuze and Félix Guattari, I construct Black alien fugitivity as a "line of flight,"[12] or a deterritorializing rupture and mode of relation that functions as an omnidirectional passageway to other worlds, planets, or dimensions. The *line of flight* can be understood as a speculative

> *map and not a tracing.* [. . .] The map is open and connectable in all of its dimensions; it is detachable, reversible, susceptible to constant modification. It can be torn, reversed, adapted to any kind of mounting, reworked by an individual, group or social formation. It can be drawn on a wall, conceived of as a work of art, constructed as a political action or as a meditation. [. . .] A map has multiple entryways, as opposed to the tracing, which always comes back "to the same."[13]

Black alien fugitivities shift the cartographic terrains of belonging, remap and reroute historicity and futurity, and generate new spaces of resistant representation; as Black aliens move along these lines of flight, they transform our relation to planet Earth, demanding alternative directions and novel ways to navigate spacetime. Each extraterrestrial in *Black Aliens* moves through, from, and beyond what R. Scott Heath has described as the "planetary south," or a speculative extension of the US South and "an archival technology that facilitates a collection of place-based time-sensitive cultural

---

10. Throughout the book, bracketed ellipses indicate an elision, while unbracketed ellipses are original to quotations.
11. Koerner, "Line of Escape," 178.
12. Deleuze and Guattari, *Thousand Plateaus*, 9.
13. Deleuze and Guattari, *Thousand Plateaus*, 11.

matter. It is a theoretical mechanism we can plug in . . . to variegate cartography. What we are about to do is take the flat, static map and explode it logistically."[14] By looking at the planet from the perspective of outer space, Heath reminds us that "north and south, as we have lived them, are rewritten as untenable effects, as are up and down. [. . .] From this mobile vantage, the entire earth is occasionally, possibly southern. It is an actually floating signifier."[15] According to this "postterrestrial futurist mode," the planetary south can be understood as a "hyperregion" that asks us to rethink and remap "spatiotemporal configurations among our souths, including our positionality relative to and irrespective of the constructed geography of our small planet."[16] In other words, in this book I explore Black alien fugitivities that imagine the planetary south as a critical line of flight, an open-ended mapping that is as infinite as the universe.

For these reasons, I argue that Black aliens reframe Black/Human and Human/Alien dialectics as a Black/Alien *trialectic*, or, as Edward Soja explains, a space of representation that is "radically open to additional othernesses, to a continuing expansion of spatial knowledge."[17] Following Soja, I make the case that the Black Alien trialectic introduces "an-Other term, a third possibility or 'moment' that partakes of the original pairing but is not just a simple combination or an 'in-between' position along some all-inclusive continuum. This critical thirding-as-othering is the first and most important step in transforming the categorical and closed logic of either/or to the dialectically open logic of *both/and also*."[18] The spacetime of *both/and also* introduces "a critical 'other-than' choice that speaks and critiques through otherness. That is to say, it does not derive simply from an additive combination of its binary antecedents but rather from a disordering, deconstruction, and tentative reconstitution of their presumed totalization producing an open alternative that is both similar and strikingly different."[19] The Black/Alien trialectic is a radical rethinking, revisioning, and remapping of boundaries of interrelated being; by bridging and collapsing the borders between Black(ened) being, humanness, and alienness, Black (extra)terrestrial aliens construct alternative fictive kinship structures and systems of

---

14. Heath, "Other Side of Time," 171.
15. Heath, "Other Side of Time," 171.
16. Heath, "Other Side of Time," 171.
17. Soja, *Thirdspace*, 6, emphasis mine.
18. Soja, *Thirdspace*, 60. Thirding-as-othering does not intend "to stop at three, to construct a holy trinity, but to build further, to move on, to continuously expand the production of knowledge beyond what is presently known" (61).
19. Soja, *Thirdspace*, 61.

interrelation, including chosen family, interspecial and/or transspatiotemporal biological family, lovers and friends, political allies and partners, cultural collectives, and individual self-fashionings or remakings of the self *as* alien. As Black aliens fuse spacetime with Black terrestrial beings, they extend the diaspora into the galaxy by devising new lines of flight—the Black/Alien trialectic emerges as a new genealogical, reproductive, spatiotemporal, futurist, and speculative mapping of *both/and also* relations between Black terrestrial and extraterrestrial aliens, or what I call a *cosmic diaspora*.

The Black Alien trialectic is yet-to-be, a speculative disruption, a gesture toward a critical unknown embodied in the *both/and also* of the cosmic diaspora—this is important because, as Octavia Butler reminds us, "at the moment there are no true aliens in our lives," only "the human alien from another country, culture, gender, race, ethnicity, religion class . . . This is the tangible alien whom we can hurt and kill."[20] For that reason, I argue that the alternative systems of relation and fugitivity represented by the cosmic diaspora are not mere escapist fantasy but speculative rejections of antiblackness, constructions of alternative possibilities of being, and attempts to conjure up what Rinaldo Walcott has described as *"glimpses of Black freedom,"* in which "freedom marks an individual and a collective desire to be *in common* and *in difference* in a world that is nonhierarchical and nonviolent. It marks, as well, the social, political, and imaginative conditions that make possible multiple ways of being in the world."[21] Neither is the cosmic diaspora an extension of what De Witt Douglas Kilgore has described as "astrofuturism," or SF and fantasy that conjures "visions of an American conquest of space [that] go hand in hand with thought experiments seeking some barely glimpsed alternative to the economic and political problems that dominated the twentieth century," in which outer space is structured as a "space frontier [. . .] where we can resolve the domestic and global battles that have paralyzed our progress on Earth."[22] Instead, I argue that Black aliens in the cosmic diaspora recast the "elsewhere and else*when* of outer space"[23] in order to reconstruct and reform the linear-historical cartography of Black life to a *then and there* in the afterlife of slavery. Following José Esteban Muñoz, I frame the cosmic diaspora as a "horizon," a mode-of-interrelating and "way of being in the world that is glimpsed through reveries in a quotidian life that challenges the dominance of an affective world, a present, full of anxiousness and fear. These future generations are [. . .] not

---

20. Butler, "Monophobic Response," 5.
21. Walcott, *Long Emancipation*, 2.
22. Kilgore, *Astrofuturism*, 4.
23. Kilgore, *Astrofuturism*, 2.

an identitarian formulation, but, instead, the invocation of a future collectivity, a queerness that registers as the illumination of a horizon of existence."[24] The cosmic diaspora is a meditation on the matter of "future generations," a mode of queer relation that is yet to come, but *will* come, and therefore a speculative embrace of the potential to imagine beyond the strictures and limits of the now.

I situate the cosmic diaspora as an extension of what Paul Gilroy has described as the "stereophonic, bilingual, or bifocal cultural forms originated by [. . .] blacks dispersed within the structures of feeling, producing, communicating, and remembering [. . .] called the black Atlantic world."[25] Whereas the Black Atlantic deconstructs "ideas of nation, nationality, national belonging, and nationalism," the cosmic diaspora additionally reframes conceptions of planetarity, humanity, terrestriality, and speciality. Black aliens in the cosmic diaspora participate both volitionally and compulsorily in the structures of the Black Atlantic world but reimagine its spatiotemporal trajectory by deterritorializing Earth as the singular system through which to apprehend Black life. *Black Aliens* therefore constructs the Black Atlantic world as a genealogical and collective entanglement between Black terrestrials and extraterrestrials, a relation that I read as a speculative attempt to exist in a condition of fugitivity with the antiblack Earth and move into an off-planet future. As Black aliens shift their entanglements in the Black Atlantic world to locations beyond the gravitational boundaries of the planet, they also reshape its temporality—their participation in the Black Atlantic world always signifies *another place and time*, necessarily designating alternative origins and homespaces. I follow Fred Moten and argue that the cosmic diaspora constructs "an ontology of disorder, an ontology of dehiscence [. . . that] gathers diaspora as an open set—or as an openness disruptive of the very idea of set—of accumulative and unaccumulable differences, differings, departures without origin, leavings that continually defy the natal occasion in general even as they constantly bespeak the previous."[26] I argue that the cosmic diaspora is a mode of belonging—genealogical, lineal, historical, social—that simultaneously enacts and disrupts, folds into and resists, and challenges and expands the very notion of belonging itself. At its most fundamental, the cosmic diaspora provides alternative histories and futures, offers new approaches for imagining the spacetime of diaspora and diasporic belonging, and ushers in new ways to circulate ideas in Black diasporic contexts.

---

24. Muñoz, *Cruising Utopia*, 25.
25. Gilroy, *Black Atlantic*, 3.
26. Moten, "Case of Blackness," 187.

Not enough attention has been paid to narrative form and the function of narratology in Black speculative fiction. For that reason, *Black Aliens* argues that thematic, figural, and metaphorical constructions of the Black alien trialectic *are also* evident as representations of narrative spacetime. In other words, I argue that Butler, Card, McDuffie and Bright, and Ra foreground what Heather Russell describes as an "African Atlantic narratology," or "formal contestations embodied in African Atlantic narratives [that] produce spaces, creating multivocal quiltings for new [. . .] diasporic possibilities."[27] African Atlantic narratological structures resist the linearity and historical mastery of Western grand narratives by attending to the "formal eruptions of the African Atlantic" that refute constructions of spacetime as "a single History."[28] For that reason, I argue that Black alien narrative spacetime engages Black life as material reality and mythos, as distinct and separate from linear constructions of spacetime that offer Black people no future, an uncertain present, and a closed past. For subjects who often have no access to ancestral family history and genealogies of deep time, alternative constructions of narrative spacetime and the creation of Black alien imaginaries are key tactics for representing complex and contradictory modes and methods of memory, futurity, and relation. The texts I explore in *Black Aliens* do this work in a variety of ways—via modes of analeptic or proleptic storytelling; critical fabulation and history work; the construction of serial narratives that cannot be contained in a single text; visual-narrative forms that resist sequentiality, including comic books and record albums; fragmented or partial narration; gaps and fissures in the narrative diegesis; and recursive or nonlinear narrative systems. In other words, I make the case that the cosmic diaspora is a representational, metaphorical, thematic, *and* narratological system.

Black Aliens comprises four chapters and a coda in which I move from more metaphorical and abstract constructions of Black alienness—for example, constructing history as another planet—to increasingly literal representations of Black alien being, such as the transmolecularization of Herman Poole Blount into the Saturnian extraterrestrial Le Sony'r Ra. This study is not designed to be an exhaustive exploration of the figure of the alien in Black speculative fiction—rather, I have selected texts and creators whose work represents the cosmic diaspora as a genealogical relation and offers innovative approaches to narrative spacetime. More importantly, I hope that *Black Aliens* will offer readers a critical hermeneutic for thinking through

---

27. Russell, *Legba's Crossing*, 4.
28. Russell, *Legba's Crossing*, 3.

and beyond constructions of the human, representing complex structures of diasporic belonging, and making sense of narratology, form, and structure. In chapter 1, "History as Another Planet: Speculative Histofiction and Constellations of Black Alien Linealogy in *Kindred* and *These Ghosts Are Family*," I read Octavia E. Butler's construction of history as another planet as a theoretical method for narrating and (re)constructing Black alien experiences in diaspora. By constructing history as another planet and approaching past peoples as aliens, simultaneously kin and strangers, Butler argues that we can better narrate the impossible stories of Black enslaved peoples and their descendants in diaspora. I use Butler's thinking here as a critical model for reading narratives I characterize as *speculative histofiction*, or texts that navigate Black alien genealogies beyond the constraints of Western temporal linearity. Speculative histofiction constructs history as another planet in order to historicize, emplot, and examine the genealogies of the Black enslaved and their descendants as aliens in their own right. I argue that speculative histofiction deforms the archive by materializing the past, conjuring new ways of being, and rememorying the world of the enslaved and their descendants as Black aliens in diaspora through the deployment of a complex of narrative strategies, including critical fabulation, re-presentation, gapping, paratextuality, generic overlapping, unnarration, and disnarration. I make the case that speculative histofiction constructs the enslaved as alien *to* and *from* the logics of Western linear genealogy in *Kindred* and Maisy Card's 2020 novel *These Ghosts Are Family* and explore how these novels reframe the exclusion of Black personhood from the genealogy of the human—and the concomitant construction of Black peoples as dysgenic aliens—by reimagining structures of Black kinship as a proliferate and endlessly regenerative relation.

In chapter 2, "Black Skin, Human Masks, Alien Form: Narrative Physiognomy, Visual Phenomenology, and Image-Text Representations of (Extra) Terrestriality," I theorize a cosmic Black diaspora as a relation forged out of visual and political intimacies between Black terrestrials and extraterrestrial aliens. Through a study of cartoons, advertisements, scientific illustrations, and amateur drawings, I argue that terrestrial and extraterrestrial aliens *become* Black via physiognomic strategies of *being, seeing, and being seen* in specific times, locations, and spaces, systems that often work to codify and contain terrestrial and extraterrestrial Others as Black *and* nonhuman. I contend that aliens who become Black draw our attention to the ways physiognomies of Blackness have been used to alienate subjects, while simultaneously engendering systems of collective and mutual survival from below. I explore how astrobiologists, race scientists, and cartoonists bring extraterrestrial, Black terrestrial, and nonhuman terrestrial animal embodiment into taxonomic alignment, specifically in cartoons and other drawings. Through a critical reading of Johann Kaspar Lavater's 1789 *Essays on Physiognomy* [*Essais sur la Physiognomie*], Rodolphe Töpffer's 1845 *Essay on Physiognomy*, and Frantz Fanon's *Black Skin, White Masks* [*Peau Noire, Masque Blanc*] (1952), I examine how these visual taxonomies are rooted in imperialist constructions of difference that frame Western Man as the most evolutionarily developed, beautiful, and morally and socially superior sentient lifeform in the universe, while structuring extraterrestrials aliens and Black terrestrials as lower-order organisms in intimate relation to one another. I conclude with an exploration of embodied intimacies between terrestrial and extraterrestrial aliens who are seen as Black and, over time, become Black in Dwayne McDuffie and M. D. Bright's comic series *Icon* (1993–97). Icon, an extraterrestrial alien named Arnus who lives on Earth in a recombinated Black terrestrial form, is forced to mask his alienness not as humanness but as Blackness, which constrains his superheroics and extraterrestrial powers—and yet be(com)ing Black ultimately makes possible the full expression of his alien abilities. In the end, I make the case that Arnus becomes Black through resistance to the antiblack state, but also through an enjoinment and entanglement of himself in Black community.

In chapter 3, "Black Alien M/other: Correcting the Intergalactic Archive," I examine Octavia Butler's essay "The Monophobic Response" in light of its contribution to Connie Samaras's 1994 art exhibition and catalogue *A Partial Correction to the Representations of Earth Culture Sent Out to Extraterrestrials on the United States 1977 Voyager Interstellar Space Probes*, which serves as a speculative critique and expansion of the planetary archive uploaded to the Golden Records and appended to Voyagers I and II. Framing humanity as a fundamentally genealogical and familial relation, Butler asks whether Earthling contact with "true aliens," or "supernatural beings or intelligences from the stars"—in contrast to "human aliens," or the aliens that we know we can hurt or kill—might prompt a re-evaluation of the nature of special belonging, urging human beings into new systems of family relation. I read Butler's *Xenogenesis* trilogy as an extended correction to the Golden Record archive that specifically interrogates the Black mother as human alien in relation to extraterrestrial true aliens at the axis of what Alexis Pauline Gumbs has described as "radical m/othering," a Black queer feminist praxis that insists on the survival of mothers and their children—and therefore all of society—in the face of world-ending cataclysm and the violence of the state. I demonstrate how Lilith's revolutionary m/othering praxis, informed by her experiences on Earth as a Black woman, and by long histories of radical, revolutionary, and resistant mothering strategies developed by chattel slaves and their descendants, emerges as a formal strategy for learning to mother aliens. Finally, I read the Oankali ability to perceive the interconnected lifeforms on scales ranging from microscopic to the galactic alongside Lilith's Black ancestral othermothering praxes, which I argue can be understood as an example of what Donna Haraway calls "sympoiesis," or the making of kin in complex networks of strangers. I contend that the trilogic narrative spacetime of *Xenogenesis* moves into an increasingly queer family system that includes an ever-widening circle of interspecial community, challenging us to rethink the limits and potential of reproductive kinship.

In chapter 4, "'I Am Not of This Planet': The Making of Le Sony'r Ra's Cosmic Diaspora," I frame Sun Ra's Black alien myth-making as a cosmic textual tradition through a reading of Ra's poetry, radical broadsides, poems, liner notes, and letters. I take Sun Ra at his word that he was not a human being but an alien from another planet, and I travel through his vision of the cosmic diaspora as a spacetime-bending, do-it-yourself politics, a fantasy of intergalactic space travel, and a movement toward a Cosmic Age where Black Earthlings and aliens are freed from the constraints of the planet in outer space. I frame Ra's desire for an off-Earth alter-destiny as an extension of what John Szwed describes as a "Black cosmic tradition" that emphasizes flight, escape, and mobility as central to Black liberation. I situate Sun Ra's celestial kinopolitics as an intellectual extension of Reverend A. W. Nix's Black cosmicism and Reverend Sutton E. Griggs's do-it-yourself radical Black textual futurist tradition and demonstrate how Ra's textual cosmic diaspora acts as a Black alien extension of early Afrofuturist and Afro-Baptist traditions. I offer a reading of Ra's work with Thmei Research, a secret society he founded with Alton Abraham while living in Chicago in the 1950s, and explore his vision of a cosmic diaspora, or his belief that Black people in the US were a cosmic amalgamation of galactic and spiritual beings, Indigenous Africans and their descendants, and ancient Egyptians and Ethiopians whose rightful alter-destiny was in the stars. I analyze several of Ra's broadsides and poems, many of which were composed in New York in the 1960s, and explore the development of what he called "Astroblackness," or his vision of a cosmic Black poetics that extends the diaspora into outer space, joining Black folk and aliens together in alternative spacetimes free from strictures of the antiblack Earth. I conclude by examining how Ra constructed Astroblackness as a sound-text-vibration that would lead Black people to their alter-destiny by locating them in an intergalactic future unfolding forever in the cosmo dark of outer space.

CHAPTER 1

History as Another Planet
Speculative Histofiction and Constellations of Black Alien Linealogy in *Kindred* and *These Ghosts Are Family*

In notes for a lecture on *Kindred* (1979), which she described as "My First Historical SF"[1] novel, Octavia Butler explained that her construction of the past "took a point of view that seemed right for a writer of science fiction: History as another Planet," a narrative model that imagined "historical worlds," or "other worlds known to be inhabited by people who are a lot like ourselves," but are importantly *not* ourselves. Butler was convinced that "humans of the past can make [the] best aliens—highly complex & sometimes incomprehensible. They help us to understand our origins better, to illustrate paths taken to avoid repeat consider those not taken."[2] *Kindred* follows Dana Franklin, a Black woman, as she is repeatedly transported

---

1. Butler, *Kindred*: speech, ca. 1993, box 154, OEB 3035, Octavia E. Butler Papers. In the summer of 2022, I spent a week at the Huntington Library, in Pasadena, California, exploring Octavia Butler's immense personal archive. This chapter could not have been—would not have been—written without Butler's critical historiography and the immense care and thought she put into collating, collecting, and preserving thousands of pages of manuscripts, letters, drafts of chapters, research papers, newspaper articles, speeches, poems, schoolwork, notes, diaries and journals, day calendars, letters and bills, periodicals, contracts, royalty statements, receipts, photographs, and drawings in more than three hundred separate boxes.

2. Butler, *Kindred*: speech, ca. 1993, box 154, OEB 3036, Octavia E. Butler Papers (hereafter Butler, *Kindred*: speech, OEB 3036, OEB Papers).

through spacetime from 1970s California, where she lives with her white husband, Kevin, to an antebellum plantation in 1800s Maryland. Dana eventually gleans that her travels are at the psychic behest of Rufus Weylin, the owner of the plantation and her "several times great grandfather,"[3] who summons her from the future on any occasion his life is endangered. After several visits to the past, Dana learns that she risks nonexistence unless she can keep Rufus alive, and make possible his enslavement and rape of her great-great-grandmother, Alice Greenwood, a free person of color, so that she can give birth to their child, Dana's great-grandmother, Hagar Weylin Blake.

Because Dana's "travels crossed time and as well as distance" (24), her present is always deferred and mitigated by the past and future. Spacetime in *Kindred* is so radically compressed that otherwise distinct states (then and now, here and there) become indistinguishable to her. Because Dana can only travel back to the future when she sustains life-threatening injury or believes her life is endangered, she must repeatedly provoke and withstand scenes of violence. Each time she returns to California she is in the throes of active, unresolvable trauma, often still bleeding from fresh wounds—and, in a recursive loop from which she cannot escape, is called back to the past before she has an opportunity to fully heal. When Dana returns to Maryland for the last time, she discovers that Hagar has been born, and Alice has committed suicide; in a final act of self-preservation and outrage, Dana stabs Rufus and kills him, trapping her arm underneath his body. Dana returns to her present after Rufus dies, but her arm fuses with the "cold and nonliving" (261) wall of her apartment as the (re)(de)corporealized past becomes foreclosed to her. I read this cycle of perpetual wounding and her subsequent disability as the afterlife of slavery enfleshed in/as Dana, her bodymind[4] a reminder of the way past traumas eventualize as generationally corporeal. For that reason, the narrative structure eschews linearity by beginning in a present that is also the novel's end. As Dana's loci repeatedly blur, and as she experiences her embodied reality in multiple distinct temporalities,

---

3. Butler, *Kindred*, 28. Further citations to this work appear in the text.
4. Sami Schalk explains that the concept of "bodymind" "insists on the inextricability of mind and body and highlights how processes within our being impact one another in such a way that the notion of a physical versus mental process is difficult, if not impossible to clearly discern in most cases." The term is specifically useful for approaching subjectivity in speculative fiction because "nonrealist possibilities of human and nonhuman subjects [. . .] often highlight the imbrication of mind and body." Following Schalk, I use this term here and elsewhere to emphasize the necessary interrelation between mind and body in and across spacetime, culture, and politics for Black diasporic peoples. See Schalk, *Bodyminds Reimagined*, 5.

the narrative's circular structure performs the disjunctions in spacetime that attend Black life in diaspora.

Contriving history as another planet spatiotemporalizes an inaccessible and unknowable past, constructing it as a locatable, yet alien place—*another planet, distinctly not our own*—where histories are terraformed into four-dimensional extraterrestrial domains with a scalable geography, origin made strange flesh. Reading *Kindred* as a critical genealogy of the Black alien, as I do here, requires rethinking the boundaries of spacetime, embracing varied and at times paradoxical approaches to narrative and embodied temporalities, and reconsidering what counts as historical evidence. I use Butler's thinking on *Kindred* as a model for reading narratives that I characterize as *speculative histofiction*, or texts that construct history as another planet in order to narrate the Black enslaved and their descendants as aliens. I make the case that speculative histofiction deforms the archive and materializes the past through a complex of narrative strategies, including fabulation, rememory, re-presentation, gapping, paratextuality, generic overlapping, unnarration, and disnarration. To that end, I examine how speculative histofiction constructs the enslaved as alien *to* and alienated *from* the logics of linear genealogy in *Kindred* and one additional recent work—Maisy Card's 2020 novel *These Ghosts Are Family*.

These Ghosts Are Family, like *Kindred,* is structured around a matrilineal family line, in this case headed by Florence, an enslaved woman in Jamaica whose present-day descendants have been scattered across the island, and to the US South and Global North. Card's Black alien genealogy deliberately disrupts traditional European heterosexist blood logics by including in kinship relation nonhuman entities and objects, such as ghosts, journals, written confessions, furniture, photographs, and buildings. For example, the novel's kinship network comprises Florence's great-great-grandson, Abel Paisley, who fakes his death while working in London, only to resurface in the United States as Stanford Solomon; Vera Paisley, Abel's Jamaican widow, who appears as a vengeful ghost eager to confront Abel in the afterlife; Bernard, Vera's yard boy and lover for more than twenty years, who is rejected by her family following her death; three nameless little girls, who leave with Bernard after he is removed from the family property, and become duppies, or eternal beings who exist in mythic time; Caren Solomon's couch, inherited from her grandfather Stanford, which becomes an instantiation of her mother, Estelle, after she dies on it; Harold Fowler, Florence's slave master, who exists only on the pages of a journal, but remains a material force in the world; and Louise Marie Paisley, Florence's daughter, whose written confessions help Abe Kincaid, Abel/Stanford's grandson, fill in some of the gaps in his family history. Rather than approach Black genealogy as a linear progression from the past to present, *These Ghosts Are Family* is instead horizontal and rhizomatic, constellating first-, second-, and third-person perspectives that move in, across, and out of time from the eighteenth century to an eternal afterlife.

I argue that *Kindred* and *These Ghosts Are Family* reframe the exclusion of Black people from genealogies of Western Man and concomitant constructions of Black peoples as dysgenic aliens by reimagining structures of Black kinship as an endlessly regenerative relation. By fabulizing narrative forms that simultaneously engage and exceed the archive, such as confessions, diary writing, personal stories, memories, myths, folktales, lies, hopes, and dreams, Butler and Card write history as another planet in order to (re)enflesh and reconstruct the linealogy of the enslaved alien. In the first section of this chapter, "Writing the Impossible: Speculative Histofiction and Black Alien Historiographies," I define speculative histofiction as a literary mode and describe the formal processes of narrating the impossible stories of the enslaved alien—those eclipsed or absented from the archive, forgotten, or erased—via radical acts of informed imagining. Through a consideration of Black speculative historiography and its intersections with what Saidiya Hartman has termed "critical fabulation," I construct speculative histofiction as a narrative process structured by overlapping and interconnected genres, and I examine how *Kindred* and *These Ghosts Are Family* approach speculative histofiction as emplotted metanarrative. In the next section, "Writing An-Other Planet: Black Alien Family Trees in Thirdspace," I draw on work by Hartman, Orlando Patterson, Edward Soja, Sylvia Wynter, and Hortense Spillers and explore the political ontology of Black alienness. I construct the Black enslaved subject as alien in three ways: as remanded from categories of the human and citizen; as a stranger without kin, imagined as having no structures for belonging; and as a subject occupying Thirdspace, an alien territory in an-Other spacetime altogether. I explore how the Black subject's excision from genealogies of Man was reflected in the family tree, which served not as a reflection of blood relation but as eugenic representations of white European fantasies of fitness and racial superiority, and I trace how Butler and Card reconstruct the eugenic family tree as a speculative Black alien linealogy.

Finally, in "'These People Are Our Family': Unnarration, Disnarration, and Structures of Black Alien Narrative Rememory," I argue that both *Kindred* and *These Ghosts Are Family* rememory Black alien kinship systems as always-already on an-Other planet radically outside European heteropatriarchal vertical genealogies. I define rememory as an inter-genre-al, intertextual, and trans-spatiotemporal process of remembering what has been forgotten, what cannot be forgotten, or what no one wants to forget; in other words, the work of rememory imaginatively fabulizes, materializes, and recovers the past as another planet. I argue that *Kindred*, on the one hand, rememories the linear spacetime of heteropatriarchal Western genealogy through strategies of unnarration, and by framing histories of Black kinship as circular, interconnected, and therefore anathema to vertical linealogy. On the other hand, *These Ghosts Are Family* rememories the genealogy of the enslaved alien as rhizomatic, and predicated on relation rather than blood through strategies of disnarration. In closing, I examine how Butler and Card construct Black alien linealogies in order to recover alternative structures of Black kinship.

Writing the Impossible: Speculative Histofiction and Black Alien Historiographies

Saidiya Hartman has argued that "*Kindred* offers a model for a practice," a way to "derang[e] the archive," and confront "the task of writing the impossible, (not the fanciful or the utopian but 'histories rendered unreal and fantastic')."[5] In notes on the writing of *Kindred*'s impossible story, Octavia Butler intentionally blurred the novel's genre by describing the text as a "historical novel," "the most autobiographical nvl I've written," a work of "personal history" and "family history,"[6] on the one hand, and as a work of "fantasy," on the other.[7] Hartman's description of Butler's speculative methodology—what she describes as "speculative history"—is designed to convolute the generic and intellectual boundaries between fiction and history, reality and invention. The "historiographical operation" of this mode of speculative narration "requires excavations at the margins of monumental history in order that the ruins of the dismembered past be retrieved, turning to forms of knowledge and practice not generally considered legitimate objects of historical inquiry or appropriate or adequate sources for history making and attending to the cultivated silence, exclusions, relations of violence and domination that engender the official accounts."[8] I call the literary-historical narrative system of these alternative "forms of knowledge

---

5. Hartman, "Venus," 13–14. See also Palmié, *Wizards and Scientists*, 97.
6. Butler, *Kindred*: speech, OEB 3036, OEB Papers.
7. Kenan, "Interview with Octavia Butler," 497.
8. Hartman, "Unnamed Girl"; Hartman, "Venus," 14; and Hartman, *Scenes of Subjection*, 11.

and practice" *speculative histofiction*,⁹ a composite narrative mode that takes up strategies of speculative fiction and historical archival work, in addition to those methods of narrating and remembering the past most immediately accessible to Black folk, such as received and personal memories, rumors, word-of-mouth stories, myths and folktales, lies, and dreams, alongside the entirely imagined and invented. Following Shelley Streeby, I derive this term from Butler's description of her "HistoFuturist archive,"¹⁰ which functions as a model for doing the work of *"archiving, constellating,* and *annotating"* the radical potential of Black life, and for protecting—and preserving—the too-often eclipsed knowledges of Black people. Because Butler "was an active agent in creating counter-histories and alternative futures by saving, organizing, connecting, and speculating on these disparate materials,"¹¹ I approach her archive as a system (and her *use* of the archive as a system) that moves beyond authoritative controls of history.

In a draft of her unfinished memoir *Positive Obsession*, Butler explained that her approach to speculative writing reconsidered "the present, the future, and the past," offered "alternative ways of thinking and doing," and considered "the possible effects of science and technology, of social organization and political direction," all while "stimulat[ing] imagination and creativity."¹² As a cover term for a wide range of genres—fantasy, science fiction, horror, utopian fiction, and alternative histories, among many others—speculative fiction embraces guesswork, possibility, and intentional breaks from accepted reality. Speculative histofiction can be identified by its "inter-genre-ality," or, as Amy J. Devitt defines it, narrative storytelling that thinks of genre as "overlapping forms," or intermingled generic discourses that consciously (and inevitably) "take up forms from the genres with which they inter-act."¹³ I frame speculative histofiction as an inter-genre-al

---

9. I use the neologism *speculative histofiction* not in opposition to the more familiar terms historical fiction, alternative history, historiographic metafiction, or speculative history, but rather as an alternative term intended to specifically highlight the generic imbrication and interdependence of history and fiction in this particular narrative mode. By combining the two descriptors into one single term, I emphasize the interconnection and inseparability of history and fiction as narrative genres, and I work to reinforce their concrete and meaningful generic differences while making the case that Black writers of speculative histofiction actively create a new, distinct generic form all its own.

10. Butler, Commonplace book, 1980, 1983, box 178, OEB 3221, Octavia E. Butler Papers.

11. Streeby, "Radical Reproduction," 720, emphasis in original; Streeby, "Radical Reproduction," 720.

12. Butler, Positive Obsession, ca. 1998, box 154, OEB 2346, Octavia E. Butler Papers.

13. Devitt, "Re-Fusing Form," 13.

constellation of speculative *history* and speculative *fiction* resulting in alternative re-presentations of Black life in diaspora.

Speculative histofiction imagines history as another planet, and therefore relies on what can be surmised, gathered from the margins, remembered but never recorded, invented or made new. Because archives eclipse the truth (or, at best, share a limited version of it), "reconstruction and fabulation," as Hartman puts it, are necessary tools for addressing relations of power that dictate whose stories can be narrated, who can narrate them, and how they can be narrated. Unfolding as an inter-genre-al narrative that is simultaneously *both and neither* true history and pure fiction, speculative histofiction deploys the tactics of critical fabulation, a narrative strategy that reconfigures dominant constructions of fictive and historical spacetime "by playing with and rearranging the basic elements of the story, by re-presenting the sequence of events in divergent stories and from contested points of view."[14] In setting aside linear and progressive emplotment, speculative histofiction antagonizes received histories, moves beyond accepted authorized accounts of the past, and imagines instead what *might have* been, *could have* happened, or *may have* been said. Speculative histofiction therefore makes possible the impossible task of recovering and re-presenting the world of the enslaved in ways that *must* exceed the archive. As Butler explained, narrating history as another planet can help readers "*feel* history instead of simply memorizing dates, wars/treaties, political leaders, court decisions, Big Impersonal Things."[15] Following Hartman, I argue that speculative histofiction operates in the conditional tense by "speculating about what might have been, imagining the things whispered in dark bedrooms, and amplifying moments of withholding, escape, and possibility."[16] In its re-presentation of past events, then, speculative histofiction intentionally fabulizes, dissembles, shifts terrain, imbricates spacetime, and channels memory.

It bears asking what it means to say that true history is a *real* re-enactment of past events, and fiction is singularly an *invention*—and on what critical ground rests speculative histofiction's inter-genre-al narrative form. In *Time and Narrative,* Paul Ricœur explains that "unlike novels, historians' constructions do aim at being *re*constructions of the past. Through documents and their critical examination of documents, historians are subject to what once was." Given that *re*constructions of the past are contingent upon "the documentary information available at a given moment," Ricœur argues that any attempt to find out what "really happened" is a "poetic operation" requiring

---

14. Hartman, "Venus," 11.
15. Butler, *Kindred*: speech, OEB 3036, OEB Papers, my emphasis.
16. Hartman, *Wayward Lives*, xv.

the historian to prefigure a narrative-historical terrain in advance: "The work of the historian thus consists in making narrative structure into a 'model,' an 'icon' of the past, capable of 'representing' it." In other words, "history is a construction." By blurring the boundaries between historical and fictional narrative process, Ricœur suggests that what we call history is always-already "a work of the imagination," precisely because "historians do not know the past at all but only their own thought about the past. [. . .] History is not possible unless historians know that they reenact a past that is not their own."[17] Operating from the assumption that re-presentations of the past are partial and interpretive, speculative histofiction takes history seriously as a poetics.

Though it may seem obvious, our inability to access any material spacetime beyond our immediate present means that critical fabulation is essential to foreclosing gaps between then and now, there and here. If the archive cannot recreate the real past—and if the past is not and can never be our own in the present—then it might instead be possible to construct an imagined rethinking of historical spacetime that, in fabulizing the past, "remain[s] something other than the past." As a self-consciously inter-genre-al form, speculative histofiction produces "something other than the past" by turning to history not for the purposes of *re*-enactment—an impossible task—but for *re*construction, *re*contextualization, and a *re*covery of speculative potential. Speculative histofiction therefore avoids taking the perspective that "understanding other people is the best analogue of historical understanding." Writers of speculative histofiction instead approach the past as another planet, and, in a "strategy of taking one's distance [. . .] practiced by those historians most concerned to repudiate the Western ethnocentrism of traditional history," re-present past peoples as a remote "alien psychic life."[18] By approaching the past and its people as profoundly different from us, Butler's *re*construction of history as another planet demands confronting one's ancestors as aliens, rather than as familiars.

Both Butler and Card construct speculative histofiction as a family matter, and describe its inter-genre-ality as a combination of memory and fantasy, archival research, personal and family history, (auto)biography, slave narrative, and Black historical experience. In the remainder of this section, I explore Butler and Card's inter-genre-al constructions of speculative histofiction, offering brief readings of the narrative form as emplotted metanarrative. Butler recalled that writing *Kindred* "was my first experience with

---

17. Ricœur, *Time and Narrative*, 142–43, emphasis in original, 152, 152, 144, 146.
18. Ricœur, *Time and Narrative*, 146, 148, 149.

on the spot research": "[The] idea of writing a historical novel scared me—didn't know how to research the past. Didn't know how to write about the past."[19] In order to fund a research trip to Maryland, Butler revised and sold *Survivor* (1978). While there, she stayed in a hotel "across the street from the M[aryland] Historical Society, around [the] corner from Enoch Pratt Free Library (much info) [and] down [the] street from Continental Trailways [CT], which took me to E[astern] Shore [E.S.] where I wandered. I wrote [the] final chapter of *Kindred* in CT's E.S. terminal."[20] Because she was new to the conventions of on-site archival research, however, Butler

> missed the tours of the old houses for that year, I didn't realize that they were not ongoing but seasonal. I went down to Washington, D.C. and took a Grayline bus tour of Mount Vernon and that was as close as I could get to a plantation. Back then they had not rebuilt the slave cabins and the tour guide did not refer to slaves but to "servants" and there was all this very carefully orchestrated dancing around the fact that it had been a slave plantation.[21]

Butler emplots these archival gaps in *Kindred*—Dana is likewise unable to locate any substantive evidence corroborating her experiences. After her final return to the present at novel's end, Dana and Kevin travel to Maryland to locate the site of Rufus's plantation, and visit the county archive to "skim newspapers, legal records, anything we could find" (263). They discover that nothing remains of the Weylin home—"the house was dust, like Rufus" (262). They ultimately locate only two paper records: a notice referring to Rufus's death in an accidental fire (incidentally set by Nigel, a fellow slave and Dana's friend, in order to cover up the scene of his killing); and a bill of sale for the slaves on Rufus's plantation, on which, with the exception of Nigel, his wife Carrie, and her ancestors Hagar and Joe, "everyone else was listed. Everyone" (263). Though Dana is desperate to know what happened to her ancestors and the others with whom she entered into relation on the plantation, the on-site archive is a critical dead-end for Dana—as Kevin notes, "you've found no records. You'll probably never know" (264).

---

19. Butler, *Kindred*: speech, OEB 3036, OEB Papers.
20. Butler, *Kindred*: speech, OEB 3036, OEB Papers. For a more extensive examination of Butler's research trip, see Jane Donawerth and Kate Scally, "'You've Found No Records': Slavery in Maryland and the Writing of Octavia Butler's *Kindred*," *Extrapolation* 58, no. 1 (2017): 1–19.
21. Butler, *Kindred*: speech, OEB 3036, OEB Papers.

Butler supplemented her archival research by scouring the shelves at the Pasadena public library, where she found "mainly slave narratives [. . .] and histories of the time."[22] Though these texts often failed to provide the level of specific detail she needed to construct Dana's world, she listed several titles that were essential to the writing of *Kindred*, including Eugene Genovese's 1974 *Roll, Jordan, Roll*, Kenneth Stampp's 1956 *The Peculiar Institution: Slavery in the Ante-Bellum South*, William Still's 1879 *The Underground Railroad Records: Narrating the Hardships, Hairbreadth Escapes, and Death Struggles of Slaves in Their Efforts for Freedom*, Frederick Law Olmstead's 1861 *The Cotton Kingdom: A Traveller's Observations on Cotton and Slavery in the American Slave States, 1853–1861*, and Eric McKitrick's 1963 *Slavery Defended: The Views of the Old South*, in addition to slave narratives by Harriet Tubman, Frederick Douglass, Solomon Northrup, and Harriet Jacobs. Dana also turns to the library to help her navigate the past, but the texts she finds do not contain the specific information she needs to survive in the past—for example, the language and format of a slave pass or an accurate geographical map of antebellum Maryland.

Butler eventually turned to her own personal and family history to fill in gaps, and to verify historical accounts. In her construction of Dana's menial slave labor, for example, she noted that

> little things create problems in the novel-writing. What people eat, how they cook, what they wore, how they wash clothes . . . That last stopped me. How were my antebellum Marylanders likely to wash clothes? Wash boards? River & rock? After long library hunt, I found that peo[ple] were likely to beat & boil clothes clean outdoors in huge kettles. I was so relieved, I mentioned the method later to my mother. She said, oh yes, I remember my mother doing that. [. . .] Sometimes things take far too long to change.[23]

Butler's inter-genre-al mode of speculative histofiction mitigates gaps in the archive by turning to family memory and intergenerational experience as legitimate and legitimating forms of historical documentation. Butler's entanglement of family memory, personal history, and generational legacy in the afterlife of slavery—her observation that the legacy of poverty and lack of access to modern technologies remained the same for enslaved and their descendants following emancipation—is a central structural logic in *Kindred*, mirrored in the novel's recursive form and time-travel conceit.

---

22. Butler, *Kindred*: speech, OEB 3036, OEB Papers.
23. Butler, *Kindred*: speech, OEB 3036, OEB Papers.

And yet, Butler tempered her understanding that many aspects of Black life in the afterlife of slavery had remained unchanged by addressing the stark cultural and experiential differences between her grandmother, her mother, and herself:

> My mother's life and my grandmother's life and the little bit I know of her ancestors' lives were very hard and terrible. These were not lives that I would have wanted to live. [My mother] was born in 1914, so she was a child quite a long time ago. Her mother chopped sugar cane, and she also did the family laundry, not just her own family but the white family for whom they worked. She washed clothes in the big iron pots with paddles and all that. That was hard, physical labor. It's no wonder she died at fifty-nine, after having a lot of children and working her life away. This is the kind of life that she had no choice but to live. [. . .] I wanted to take a character, when I did *Kindred*, back in time to some of the things that our ancestors had to go through, and see if that character survived so very well with the knowledge of the present in her head.[24]

These intergenerational differences form the basis of Butler's construction of the historical past and are central to her understanding of past peoples as aliens. Unlike her ancestors who performed hard physical labor, Butler lacked the skills to cook, clean, garden, mend, and build. Neither does Dana's education and writing career help her perform slave labor; in fact, her ability to read and write more often than not directly imperils her survival. Butler's turn to speculative histofiction is therefore also informed by what she described as the use of one's "ignorance"[25] as an antiarchival mode of not-knowing, nonmastery, and guesswork. Rather than adopt of a pose of narrative omniscience, *Kindred* instead deploys limited knowledge of the past as a way of narrativizing the rift between past and present (and therefore between generations) as a splintering that has resulted in the impossibility of ancestral intimacy. In other words, Butler imagines Dana as doubly alienated, as she is both *excluded from* and a *stranger to* the past.

These Ghosts Are Family also adopts an inter-genre-al narrative structure. As a credentialed librarian and trained researcher, Card turned to historical archives to research her novel, specifically by reading the Jamaican slave owner Thomas Thistlewood's papers, which describe in lurid detail the sexual abuse and torture of enslaved persons on his plantation over the

---

24. Butler and Rowell, "Interview," 50.
25. Butler, *Kindred*: speech, OEB 3036, OEB Papers.

course of forty years.[26] Thistlewood's diary offered Card a narrative model for Harold Fowler's journal—Fowler owned the novel's oldest ancestral matriarch, Florence, and possibly fathered her child, Louise Marie Paisley, Abel/Stanford's direct ancestor—and the opportunity to narrate how white power maintains itself by violently suppressing knowledge of all interracial linealogies borne out of the system of enslavement. Card explains that *These Ghosts Are Family* traces how "the lineage of the victims and the perpetrators sometimes become very entangled. I think what the Paisley family is struggling with in the present day is a kind of erasure of the truth of their history that just keeps repeating itself across time."[27] Indeed, when David Fowler, Harold Fowler's oldest living white descendant, bequeaths the journal to his youngest daughter, Debbie Norgood, encouraging her to "be the historian"[28] for the family, he commands her to keep the text to herself, in spite of its immense value to their present-day Black kin, or the "hundreds of [Black] cousins" (107) around the world whose existence Debbie verifies on a DNA testing website.

Overwhelmed by the responsibility to protect "a piece of history, the likes of which she was used to seeing in an archive or a museum" (109), Debbie makes arrangements to give the diary to a professor of history in Harold Town, Jamaica, a small village named after her ancestor, and peopled by many of his Black descendants, including Abel/Stanford's son, Vincent Paisley, who is incidentally hired to be her driver. Debbie's desire to be free from her genealogical complicity in slavery's violence manifests as a mounting obsession with the journal, which she begins to think of as a transubstantiated object-version of Fowler himself, a nonhuman embodied thing, as though by writing the text he had, in some way, remained alive through and in it. Debbie's investments in the affordances of white supremacy, however, are ultimately stronger than her desire to bring the incomplete history of her ancestor's brutality to light and acknowledge her family's Black kin. Rather than donate the diary to the university, as the horrified professor looks on Debbie rips the book to pieces and drops its pages in a shallow creek, a violent erasure of the archive she describes as "killing" (129) Fowler's object-body, thereby ridding herself of the responsibility to confront the text's representation of history and her own personal responsibility to acknowledge her Black kin as kin. After Debbie's trip to Jamaica, she and Vincent

---

26. The Thomas Thistlewood papers (1748–1792) have been digitized and are fully available online at Beinecke Rare Book and Manuscript Library at Yale University at https://hdl.handle.net/10079/fa/beinecke.thistle.

27. Card and Mania, "Living with Our Ghosts."

28. Card, *These Ghosts*, 108. Further citations to this work appear in the text.

marry—though Debbie wonders briefly if "Harold own[ed] his great-great-great-great-grandfather," or "rape[d] his ancestor" (124), which he most certainly did, she remains willfully unable to verify their lineal connection.

The Thistlewood papers, however, also facilitated for Card a counterarchival reading of the past that elevated the experiences of enslaved women; she explains that "even reading from the point of view of the slaveholder, you get a sense of the ways [. . .] women resisted. [. . .] They were victims of course, but [. . .] as brutalized as they were, many of them still found the strength to disobey."[29] In a late section of the novel, Abel/Stanford's grandson, Abe Kincaid, is performing anthropological research in the Harold Town archives, hoping to gather enough data to write a master's thesis using his family's lineal history as a case study. In the archives, Abe locates the written confessions of his ancestor, Louise Marie Paisley—Florence's daughter—who was convicted of arson and the attempted murder of William MacDaniel, a white slave owner who took on the role of her adoptive father after Florence's death. Though MacDaniel raised Louise (and may even be her biological father) once she comes of age he announces his plan to marry her. Abe discovers in her confessions that Louise valiantly resisted sexual violence, the coercive logics of heteropatriarchy that compel marriage, and the strictures of slave ownership by attempting to burn down MacDaniel's home with him in it. Unlike Butler and Card's archival findings, which yield very little first-person information about Black life, in *These Ghosts Are Family* Louise writes her own confessions, in her own voice, on her own terms, for her descendant to find.

Card explains that her novel narrates "this hazy quality to the past and to my family history that no amount of research can clarify."[30] *These Ghosts Are Family* performs the impossibility of closing these gaps in historical spacetime by refusing to settle on any single lineal narrative, alternating instead—at times intentionally unevenly—between various narrative points of view, perspectives, locations, and temporalities, including those of both the enslaved and slave masters, their descendants, and their broader communities. *These Ghosts Are Family* is written as an entanglement of blood kin, intimate friends, acquaintances, ghosts, and lovers moving in nonchronological sequence *in* spacetime, rather than simply straightforwardly *through* it. Card clarifies that *These Ghosts Are Family* "mirrors the way I learned about my family history, through stories told by relatives, filled with truths and untruths. Those stories are just bits of a narrative that will never be

---

29. Meinhardt, "Maisy Card."
30. Meinhardt, "Maisy Card."

complete."[31] For example, Card turned to Ancestry.com and familysearch.org for genealogical information about her ancestors, as did Debbie Norgood; though Card was able to trace her father's family back to 1834, the year her paternal great-great-great-grandfather was born, and the year the slave trade to Jamaica ended, she struggled to locate any information about her mother's ancestors because "their last name, Golburn, is the same as many plantation owners."[32] Like Butler, Card turned to family memories, her own personal imagination, incomplete stories, and mythlore, specifically about her deceased grandmother, in order to shape the narrative past. In that way, speculative histofiction for Card is a critical imbrication of history and fabulation in radical confluence and contradistinction.

As I discuss in greater depth in the following section, Card's fragmented and nonlinear construction of the Paisley family genealogy as paratext becomes a visual-narrative metaphor for the "absence of a complete historical record" for the enslaved alien in diaspora: "I wanted the family tree to acknowledge the way that slavery and colonialism have made it virtually impossible to make a complete family tree. I wanted it to have question marks, I wanted it to be complicated."[33] And, indeed, enslaved alien linealogy *is* complicated and incomplete, its narration made possible by paying close attention to gaps, fissures, lies, and memories in and of Black life, narrativizing the unknown and inconceivable, and refusing to anneal Black diasporic being into a seamless totality. This impossible narration is effectuated at every level of *These Ghosts Are Family*—from the novel's multiple narrative perspectives, including first, second, and third person, to the narrative plot's performance of imbricated temporalities, including both deep time and eternity. As we see from Butler's and Card's descriptions of their writing processes and narrative emplotments of the form, speculative histofiction is not a model of narrative completeness or so-called historical accuracy but is instead an inter-genre-al system that engenders contradiction, complexity, and unfettered speculative imagining.

Writing An-Other Planet: Black Alien Family Trees in Thirdspace

In the prologue to *Lose Your Mother: A Journey Along the Atlantic Slave Route*, Saidiya Hartman repeatedly describes herself as an extraterrestrial alien. As

---

31. Meinhardt, "Maisy Card."
32. Meinhardt, "Maisy Card."
33. Card and Mania, "Living with Our Ghosts."

a self-described "slave baby"[34] from the United States traveling in Ghana, Hartman hoped that she would be recognized as being *from* there; and yet, as she walks through the Elmina Castle grounds, she is called an *obruni*[35] by children "tickled to have spotted some extraterrestrial fall to earth in Ghana." Alienness is an embodied experience defined from without, in tension with how Hartman wishes to be seen; in Africa, she remains "a stranger. A foreigner from across the sea. [. . .] I imagined myself in their eyes: an alien wrapped in the skin of a blue rain slicker, the big head bursting from its navy pod." Hartman's alienation is both embodied and spatiotemporal: "I was the proverbial outsider. [. . .] My customs belong to another country. [. . .] Old and new worlds stamped my face, a blend of peoples and nations and masters and slaves long forgotten. In the jumble of my features, no certain line of origin could be traced. Clearly, I was not Fanti, or Ashanti, or Ewe, or Ga. [. . .] A black face didn't make me kin." Unable to salvage a lineal identity at the level of ethnic affiliation, embodied memory, or historical record—a consequence of "the catastrophe of our past," as she describes it—Hartman configures herself and is configured not only as nonfamily, but as an alien from another planet altogether.

The conditions of statelessness, rootlessness, and alienness define Black life in diaspora. Hartman argues that "the most universal definition of the slave is stranger. Torn from kin and community, exiled from one's country, dishonored and violated, the slave [. . .] is the perpetual outcast, the coerced migrant, the foreigner, the shamefaced child in the lineage." Having lost any memory of kin or homeplace, descendants of the enslaved remain unmoored from the lineal flows of progressive spacetime that have provided for people a measure of belonging to deep time and futurity. Rather than force the slave to function within impossible-to-attain structures of familial and social belonging, Hartman connects the slave and their descendants to an alien

---

34. Hartman, *Lose Your Mother*, 4.
35. Bayo Holsey explains that the Akan word *obruni*—or

> *oburoni* [. . .] has become a bone of contention between Ghanaians and blacks in the diaspora, who, having been told that *oburoni* means "white man," find themselves to their dismay called by this term. In actuality *oburoni* means "those who come over the horizon." This is not a racial label then but rather a demonstration of the ways in which Ghanaians often identify people by the places from which they come, in quite literal terms. Indeed, the American-ness of African Americans is quite significant from the point of view of Ghanaians. For them, African American and white tourists sometimes occupy the same mental space; they are all privileged foreigners.

Hartman is clear that she reads the term not as a racial marker but rather as a marker of fundamental disaffiliation and nonbelonging. See Holsey, *Routes of Remembrance*, 220.

otherworldliness, to another planet, to outer space, to a cosmic diaspora. If the violence of forced exile from the known world was for Black folk "both an end and a beginning,"[36] then this alien positionality emerges as a distinctly cosmic diasporic spatiotemporal location, a way of being, knowing, and experiencing the Black subject's exclusion from loci of belonging.

The slave trade depended upon a severing of African genealogies and geographies, but bondage was maintained through the forced erasure of familial bonds for Black peoples. Black subjects in diaspora experienced what Orlando Patterson describes as "natal alienation," or "the loss of ties of birth in both ascending and descending generations," resulting in an "extraordinary shallowness of their genealogical and historical memory." Natally alienated enslaved peoples were not only denied legal or social ties to blood relations—at any moment, families could be and were violently separated—but also to any other peoples not otherwise mandated by the slave master, including kinship ties to the master himself. Enslaved peoples were also unable to determine their genealogical futures—they could not exact custodial control over their children, protect the sanctity or legality of their marriages, or determine the scope and context of their social relationships. As a consequence, slaves suffered "social death," or an inability to belong to legitimizing social or political orders. Configured as the categoric property of their masters, denied a deep ancestral past, and prevented from realizing the potential of future relation, as Patterson makes clear,

> the slave was denied all claims on, and obligations to, his parents and living blood relations but, by extension, all such claims and obligations on his more remote ancestors and on his descendants. He was truly a genealogical isolate. Formally isolated in his social relations with those who lived, he also was culturally isolated from the social heritage of his ancestors. He had a past, to be sure. But a past is not a heritage. Everything has a history, including sticks and stones. Slaves differed from other human beings in that they were not allowed freely to integrate the experience of their ancestors into their lives, to inform their understanding of social reality with the inherited meanings of their natural forebears, or to anchor the living present in any conscious community of memory.[37]

As an erasure of the past's lineal value, a form of "genealogical isolat[ion]" in the present, and an obliteration of any successional future, natal alienation

---

36. Hartman, *Lose Your Mother*, 3, 3, 4, 4, 6, 8.
37. Patterson, *Slavery and Social Death*, 7, 6, 5.

was first and foremost a family matter. Unable put to use systems of ancestral memory and structures of belonging, slaves had a "history," but were denied "heritage." Enslaved peoples and their descendants, in other words, remained alienated from the spatiotemporal stuff of humanity, reduced instead to "sticks and stones," or objects that may exist or do things, but are, in the relation of slavery, disconnected from systems of related living.

Africans and their descendants were consequently made radically alien—their embodiment deemed foreign and grotesque, their flesh made vulnerable to the violent depersonalization of commodification—and forced to occupy what Sylvia Wynter has termed an "archipelago of Human Otherness," inhabited by Black subjects imagined to be "dysselected by Evolution." In her reworking of W. E. B. Du Bois's color line, Wynter argues that "the struggle of our new millennium will be one between the ongoing imperative of securing the well-being of our present ethnoclass (i.e. Western bourgeois) conception of the human, Man, which overrepresents itself as if it were the human itself, and that of securing the well-being, and therefore the full cognitive and behavioral autonomy of the human species itself/ourselves." These processes, Wynter argues, were "made possible only on the basis of a colonizer/colonized relation that the West was to discursively constitute and empirically institutionalize on the islands of the Caribbean, and, later, on the mainlands of the Americas." In this imperialist-capitalist relation, whereas white Western Man was categorized as "selected by Evolution," and therefore fully human, Black people were "dysgenic or dysselected-by-Evolution," positioned as antitheses to very idea of the human itself. Ordered by the principle of "nonhomogeneity of substance," or the "ontological distinction between the supralunar and the sublunar, heaven and earth," as a consequence of their "dysgenicity,"[38] Black diasporic subjects were constructed as unassimilable aliens who existed outside of the genealogy of Man itself, imagined to be as different from the human as night from day, as sea from land.

And yet Black people in diaspora zealously organized their *own* kinship structures, and worked hard to both make and protect generations. Patterson explains that "when we say that the slave was natally alienated and ceased to belong independently to any formally recognized community, this does not mean that he or she did not experience or share informal social relations."[39] These informal relations were often clandestine, occupying alternative spaces and places within and beyond the scope of plantation

---

38. Wynter, "Unsettling the Coloniality of Being," 321, 316, 260, 318, 325, 274, 323.
39. Patterson, *Social Death*, 6.

powers. I argue that one way to better understand how Black folk have moved beyond, outside, around, and through the subjection of natal alienation is to consider how writers of Black diasporic speculative histofiction make use of the figure of the alien as an embodied metaphor for genealogical isolation and spatiotemporal cataclysm. The *Oxford English Dictionary* (*OED*) defines an alien as a subject "from elsewhere," "born in [. . .] a foreign country," "of a different species," "strange, unfamiliar, different," a "being from another planet."[40] The *OED* also, however, defines an alien as "a person who does not belong to a particular family, community, country, etc.; a foreigner, stranger, an outsider," "a person who is separated or excluded *from* a particular community, country, custom, etc.," as well as "a person who or thing which is opposed, repugnant, or unaccustomed *to* a specified person or thing; a stranger *to*."[41] Aliens "excluded *from*" are codified as fundamentally not-belonging, foreign and strange, their exclusion essential to the founding of the nation-state and empire. Aliens can also be "a stranger *to*" a community in which the directionality of estrangement is reoriented *toward* the subject's location, and away from the conditions that make the alien excluded *from*. The alien's doubleness—both *excluded from* and a *stranger to*—anchors my reading of Black alien subjectivity.

Rather than fix the Black alien at the boundary line between the present genre of the human and its construction of Black subjects as nonhuman, I situate the alien enslaved in what Edward W. Soja has described as "Thirdspace," in which a "critical strategy of thirding-as-Othering [. . .] open[s] up our spatial imaginaries to ways of thinking and acting politically that respond to all binarisms, to any attempt to confine thought and political action to only two alternatives, by interjecting an-Other set of choices." In Soja's conception of "critical thirding," the original binary formation—in this case, human/alien—is "subjected to a creative process of *restructuring* that draws selectively and strategically from two opposing categories to open new alternatives." Given that Black folk are peripheral to the concerns of US sociopolitical life, Soja argues that Black writers and culture workers have theorized Thirdspace "as a space of radical openness, a context from which to build communities of resistance and renewal that cross the boundaries and double-cross the binaries of race, gender, class, and all oppressively Othering categories."[42] Black alienness is a binary-destroying position, deliberately strange, intentionally outside dualist constructions of

---

40. *OED Online*, "alien, adj. and n."
41. *OED Online*, "alien, adj. and n.," emphasis mine.
42. Soja, *Thirdspace*, 5, 5, 84.

nonhuman/human, in an-Other terrain altogether, a mode of being, in Butler's terms, encompassed by life both on and from "another planet."

Black diasporic alien genealogies have always emerged from a contested Thirdspace. François Weil observes that in the late eighteenth century, British imperialists sought to transform noble pedigree into an "Atlantic dominated colonial genealogy" in order to secure permanent rights to land via heritable descendancy through colonial marriage, and by counting as family subjects who might have been previously excluded from inheritance, such as mixed-blood children. At the same time in the US, concerns about the nation-state's burgeoning identity fueled the notion that genealogy ought to be a legitimate pursuit for every American, rather than reserved for the well-born and powerful. Inscribed in family Bibles, embroidered, or illustrated, family trees—or pedigree charts, as they are also often called—were developed as a form of republicanist quasi-resistance to aristocratic European genealogies that sought to redefine belonging to the nation-state as a matter of democratic heritage. In different ways and to different ends, Free Persons of Color, elite African Americans, and the white European migrant middle class "viewed genealogy as a science that would help them reinforce their sense of self and the significance of the family as a moral, civic, and social unit."[43]

This push for these democratized genealogies did not, however, "completely displace the colonial taste for status-based pedigree." White European Americans who could establish their descendancy from early settler colonial families adjudged themselves to be originary Anglo-Saxons, and therefore racially, culturally, and socially superior to all other white and nonwhite people. More generally, Western genealogies left out so-called illegitimate children, people with disabilities, slave kin, and other undesirables. For that reason, antebellum genealogies redeployed these exclusory hierarchies as a stratified relation to Blackness, among other things. In the postbellum era, as formerly enslaved peoples were ostensibly transformed from property into citizens, genealogies became tangled up in the logics of eugenics and evolutionary heredity as the search for pedigree became an expression of a newly mobilized "racialized genealogy." Over time, pedigree charts were transformed into putatively genetic histories that were designed to "promote race betterment [. . .] by choosing or excluding a potential mate on what was considered a scientific basis." Because eugenicists believed that social and moral traits were transmitted through bloodlines, family trees "help[ed] identify those families that were considered bad breeders, or

---

43. Weil, *Family Trees*, 5, 6.

'dysgenic,' and endangered the future of the country."[44] Black people were always-already dysgenic. Under no conditions could an enslaved person improve a family genetic profile, including their own.

Because enslaved Africans were not included in these new American conceptions of genealogy, and, as property, were unable to "preserve the memory of their ancestors in their time of bondage," they developed alternative "kin-related genealogical practices."[45] Black people traced lineaologies on their own terms, particularly in the decades after Reconstruction as the formerly enslaved searched for and made contact with their loved ones. As Patterson explains, the vast majority of Africans and their descendants "throughout the New World slave systems [. . .] tenaciously held on to the strong valuation of kinship and to the fundamental West African social tendency to use kinship as the idiom for the expression of all important relationships and rankings. [. . .] Slaves who survived the trauma of the crossing redefined themselves in fictive kinship terms as ship brothers and sisters, and this extended to their progeny."[46] Systems of fictive kinship generated an-Other space for enslaved peoples to create and maintain networks of belonging in spite of and in direct opposition to systems that sought to render them kinless. Enslaved Black kinship structures therefore tended to emphasize forms of intimacy typically unacknowledged in root-to-branch pedigree charts, such as othermothers and adopted children, play cousins, foster children, neighbors, lovers, and intimate friends.

Indeed, as Hortense Spillers notes, "it seems very clear [. . .] that 'Family,' as we practice and understand it 'in the West'—the *vertical* transfer of a bloodline, of a patronymic, of titles and entitlements [. . .] becomes the mythically revered privilege of a free and freed community." Spillers argues that Black peoples were instead required to take up modes of

> *horizontal* relatedness of language groups, discourse formations, bloodlines, names, and properties by the legal arrangements of enslavement. [. . .] It is probably truer than we know at this distance [. . .] that the captive person developed, time and again, certain ethical and sentimental features that tied her and him, *across* the landscape to others, often sold from hand to hand,

---

44. Weil, *Family Trees*, 78, 6, 123, 123.
45. Weil, *Family Trees*, 5. Weil notes that small numbers of wealthy African Americans in the late nineteenth century deployed eugenic genealogical research as markers of non-dysgenicity, respectability, and success in order to "fight the idea, common among whites in the racial context of the period, that all blacks were indistinguishable from one another" (140). For the most part, however, genealogical research was unavailable to the formerly enslaved and offered them no basis for national belonging.
46. Patterson, *Rituals of Blood*, 27.

of the same and different blood in a common fabric of memory and inspiration. [. . .] We might choose to call this connectedness "family," or "support structure," but that is a rather different case from the moves of a dominant symbolic order, pledged to maintain the supremacy of a race.[47]

As Spillers articulates so clearly here, the Black family cohered beyond the boundaries of white supremacist rule by establishing kinship systems that functioned *across* space and time, and in *horizontal*, rather than *vertical*, relation. Even as the function of genealogy shifted and changed over time, especially for Black Americans—to prove genetic descent, remember kin, or validate claims to humanity—Black kinship restructured Western heteropatriarchal modes of belonging, all while repurposing, redefining, and reimagining genealogic possibility.

As independent networks that operated beyond and in spite of enslavement, these alternative horizontal systems of Black alien kinship do not often appear in the archives of enslavement. And yet, as Black people transitioned from location to location—compulsorily and voluntarily—their horizontal fictive kinship structures strained against blood logics and eugenic reason. These deeply intimate and personal connections between chosen kin were necessarily located in the Thirdspace of plantation life, their entanglement sustained by way of individual family record-keeping, mythlore, and memory, and inclusive of both blood and nonbiological kin. As a consequence, Black enslaved kinship structures were flexible, capacious, and idiosyncratic. I suggest that speculative histofiction's commitment to fabulizing historical spacetime re-presents these horizontal attachments by giving them voice, and providing context for radical Black alien kinship in slavery's afterlife. In different ways, Butler and Card take up the spatiomateriality of the enslaved alien family tree at the level of narrative emplotment, and, for Card, additionally at the level of paratext. *Kindred* and *These Ghosts Are Family* are structured around and simultaneously exceed a matrilineal Black alien family line, and, as works of speculative histofiction, fabulize the enslaved alien's family tree by constructing history as another planet. Whereas Card literalizes the historical world of the enslaved alien family tree as introductory paratext in the form of an intentionally truncated pedigree chart constructed by Abe, Abel/Solomon's grandson, Butler approaches these historical worlds through Dana's circular and recursive time travel, or what Denise Ferreira da Silva calls her "traversality."[48] Both Butler and

---

47. Spillers, "Mama's Baby, Papa's Maybe," 74, emphasis in original; 75, emphasis in original.

48. Ferreira da Silva, *Unpayable Debt*, 109.

Card, however, trace the slave's alienation *from* the genre of the human, and construct Black kinship structures as alien *to* Western vertical linealogy by re-presenting Black genealogy as a horizontal relation—again, Butler's as recursive, Card's as proliferative.

In *Kindred*, Dana's engagements with her ancestral kin are informed by informal systems of record-keeping that were central to constructions of Black alien linealogy. Dana first discovers her ancestral connection to the Maryland plantation after Rufus Weylin tells her his surname during her second trip to the past, a name she immediately recognizes as having been recorded in her family Bible:

> If the child before me was real and was telling the truth, maybe he was one of my ancestors. Maybe he was my several times great grandfather, but still vaguely alive in the memory of my family because his daughter had bought a large Bible in an ornately carved, wooden chest, and had begun keeping family records in it. My uncle still had it. Grandmother Hagar Weylin. Hagar Weylin, born in 1831. Hers was the first name listed. And she had given her parents' names as Rufus Weylin and Alice Green-something Weylin. (48)

The Franklin family records made no mention of the specific nature of Rufus's connection to Alice and Hagar. For that reason, though Dana recognizes Rufus's name, she only learns by visiting the past that he took possession of his own kin. Centered as they were on Black alien intimacies, Black genealogies relied on knowledges that often could not be corroborated with archival or other documentary evidence, including memory, hearsay, stories and lore, and informal personal records, such as those kept in the family Bible. Even in the aftermath of the master's denial of kinship, Black folks registered their own systems of belonging intentionally outside of official repositories of Western genealogical systems.

Benjamin Robertson argues that *Kindred* might be seen as a "story of the flesh," particularly given that "being a black woman opens Dana's body, her flesh, to stories of marginalization."[49] And yet it is the safety, security, and preservation of Rufus's white male embodiment that remains responsible for Dana's shifts in time, as she is called back to him when he is in danger of death by injury—Rufus nearly drowns twice, sets his room on fire, breaks his leg, is severely beaten, and contemplates suicide; at every juncture, save for the last when she kills him, Dana is compelled by the weight

---

49. Robertson, "'Some Matching Strangeness,'" 369–70.

of her own existence to intervene. Dana's enfleshment, in direct contrast to Rufus, must be repeatedly imperiled if he is to survive—she experiences vertigo, displacement, whippings, beatings, isolation, starvation, intense fear and anxiety, sexual assault, and a complete destabilization of spacetime. Because Dana's time travel is the result of her entanglement with Rufus, her encounters with slavery are inextricably bound to questions of lineage. By transforming the present dead to "vaguely alive" persons, and yet again into embodied flesh, Dana's time travel transubstantiates her textual family tree. That said, given that the precise nature of Rufus's relation goes unarticulated in her family's archive, the vertical family records are of limited utility to Dana. As Dana comes to know her ancestors as people to and from whom she is alienated, their collective spatiotemporal disrupture, ongoing fragmentation, and thoroughgoing natal alienation do not stand in the way of kinship, but rather become its foundation; in other words, their alienation forms the basis for their relation.

Maureen Barr suggests that, in this way, the figure of "the alien other" is made new by Butler; in *Kindred*, "Black women [. . .] who are alien to patriarchal society, alter fiction's depiction of the alien" as hostile, given that they "join with or are assisted by the aliens they could be expected to view as epitomizing the very opposite of humanness. These female characters, who are themselves the Other, do not oppose the Other."[50] Indeed, though Dana understands the past to be an "alien, dangerous place" (190) and an "alien time" (220) populated by people whom she cannot fully comprehend, she shares both a physical resemblance and emotional resonance with her ancestors, particularly with Alice (more than once the two women are described as appearing to be sisters who look like "two halves of the same whole"; 228), in their collective desire for freedom, the forms of self-liberation that arise through education, and an impulse to survive and engender the survival of their kin. Lisa Yaszek links "Dana's recognition of black women like herself as the alien others of American history" to Dana's position "as the alien other of American history."[51] Dana is made alien by patriarchy and the logics of white supremacy, in both her present and in the past, conditions that are transtemporal and transhistorical. Dana is likewise estranged by the manifold divergencies in spacetime she experiences as a result of her time travel. In every moment Dana visits—past, present, and future—she must navigate the "double jeopardy" of being a Black woman, defined by Frances M. Beal as the means by which capitalism engenders itself at the intersection

---

50. Barr, *Lost in Space*, 98–99.
51. Yaszek, "A Grim Fantasy," 1063.

of misogyny and antiblackness.[52] Dana understands herself to be the "worst possible guardian for [Rufus]—a black to watch over him in a society that considered blacks subhuman, a woman to watch over him in a society that considered women perennial children" (68). Though Dana's complex and often uneven entanglements with her Black kin make their survival possible, not least because their relation ensures her own, she at times uses her alienness to gain access to spheres of influence and power absolutely denied to her Black kin. For example, Dana relies on the direct intervention of white men—her husband, Kevin, as well as Rufus—to escape some forms of quotidian violence meted out to other slaves. This is perhaps what makes Dana most alien in the past: she is the singular Black subject in the novel with the agentic potential to manipulate the fissures inherent in the logics of white power to engender her own survival.

Given that *Kindred*'s temporal paradox demands that Dana protect her white kin at the expense of her Black kin, her alienness also requires her to make decisions that are at times not in the best interest of her Black ancestors. Though Dana is interpellated as a slave, she is simultaneously so removed from the experience of the enslaved that it is Rufus with whom she believes she shares a "matching strangeness" (29). This multidimensional alienation is reflected in the novel's narrative point of view; Dana's first-person perspective makes it clear that, unlike her ancestors, *she* is the one inserted into *their* past-world, and therefore the true alien outsider. By conceiving of history itself as another planet, comprising past and present peoples in horizontal and recursive relation, peoples alien to one another in their own right, Butler decenters Western conceptions of linear space-time that might suggest we could (and should) imagine ourselves in a line of seamless (and therefore timeless) transgenerational familiarity with our ancestors, our histories, our pasts.

Card's representation of the Black alien cosmic diaspora destabilizes the logics of Western linear genealogy by deconstructing the textual family tree itself. *These Ghosts Are Family* features a representation of a vertical matrilineal pedigree chart as paratext, one page before the narrative begins. Gérard Genette defines paratext as a marginal, transitional space that does often disregarded work—it is a "threshold," "an undecided zone between the inside and the outside," "a zone of [. . .] transition," "a zone of [. . .] transaction," a "fringe," "a border," and "a strategy." For that reason, paratext is best understood to as an "empirically composed [. . .] assorted set of

---

52. Beal, "Double Jeopardy," 166.

practices and discourses."[53] Beth A. McCoy argues that paratext is a "territory important, fraught, and contested. More specifically, its marginal spaces and places have functioned centrally as a zone transacting ever-changing modes of white domination and of resistance to that domination." Spaces deemed marginal or unimportant by white people were routinely reappropriated by Black folks as opportunities to reclaim space for themselves; in that way, as Black diasporic peoples "diagnosed paratextual space as one way through which white supremacy could be channeled, they also saw that space as offering possibilities for resistance."[54] The paratextual family tree in *These Ghosts Are Family* is a critical response to logics of blood that were denied (and resisted) by Black peoples, occupying the terrain of an imagined representation of spatiality, an-Other space on another planet.

The paratextual family tree in *These Ghosts Are Family* is a reduplication of Abe Kincaid's incomplete notes on his family history. As a graduate student working toward a degree in library science, Abe spends his days "drawing a family tree" (250), and conducting anthropologic and autoethnographic archival research for his thesis, an evaluation of "the best electronic resources for studying Caribbean genealogy, using his own family as the subjects" (246). As Abe "combed database after database of scanned newspapers, slave registers, wills, and letters, getting a picture of life on the plantation" (246), his efforts are frustrated by the limits of the archive, which contain few concrete details about his distant family history. Because his uncle Vincent married Debbie Norgood, Abe knows that she is Harold Fowler's descendant but has no way of knowing if they are distantly related to one another through him. Debbie offers Abe her notes on Harold's journal, which contain "the names of slaves she jotted down. [. . .] That was where he first saw the name Florence, next to a date, 1817" (249). Her destruction of Harold's journal, however, makes it impossible for Abe to extend his vertical linealogy—indeed, "there is no information about anyone before Florence" (250). Abe's inability to locate information about Louise Marie Paisley's father or partner is an uncertainty that permeates the entire paratext, and therefore the entire novel.

Every aspect of Abe's genealogic research is complicated by his grandfather's lifetime of deceit. While working in a shipyard in London as a young man, Abel Paisley's friend, Stanford Solomon, also from Jamaica, is crushed by a shipping container. When their co-workers incorrectly identify the dead man as Abel, he chooses not to correct them, assumes Stanford's identity,

---

53. Genette and Maclean, "Paratext," 261, 261.
54. McCoy, "(Para)Textual Condition," 156, 159.

and moves to the United States. Abel/Stanford justifies abandoning his wife, Vera, and two children, Vincent and Irene—Abe's mother—because he had taken out an insurance policy. As Stanford, Abel purchases a brownstone in Harlem, opens a restaurant, and marries a woman named Adele, who gives birth to a daughter, Estelle; additionally, some years later, he sires with another woman yet another daughter, Ruthie, whom he does not raise. Abe's truncated family tree is a reflection of his own descendental alienation, both distant and past; he never knows his grandfather, does not have a relationship with his father, and has no intimate connection to his family in Jamaica.

Abel Paisley's abandonment of his Jamaican kin is a recursion and extension of the natal alienation that attended his ancestors in slavery—it is a self-imposed generational and historical void, a doubled and doubling alienation that functions as a repetition of Black alien genealogical isolation. And yet Abel/Stanford's desertion simultaneously induces Abe's family tree to a complex transverse relation, one that includes family outside the limits of known heritable descent. Abel's transition to Stanford disrupts the family tree's vertical linearity. In Abe's pedigree chart, the = sign signifies his placement on the tree (Abel = Stanford), shifting the family's vertical structure to a horizontal relation that includes biologic and nonbiologic kin, so-called legitimate and illegitimate children, speculative ancestors and unknown kin. Riddled with elision, gaps, and ruptures, Abe's family tree also represents the impossibility of the enslaved alien ameliorating their linealogy into a single, vertical root system. Card's paratext deliberately produces its history as narrative. By describing Black kinship as a proliferative assemblage, the family tree as paratext creates an-Other space of horizontal relation, one that challenges the eugenic function of the pedigree chart as a marker of heritable descendancy by highlighting the real complex nature of Black relation.

As I make more clear in the final section of this chapter, the novel overextends Abe's family tree by fleshing out biologic and nonbiologic kinship structures in rhizomatic relation, including neighbors, close friends, ghosts, duppies, and lovers, as well as nonhuman things, such as graves, animals, water, the shadowy world of the afterlife, apartment buildings, photographs, and texts; these beings and objects bind the family's kinship system together outside the blood logics of Western heteropatriarchy, as the gaps and fragments in Card's paratext are enfleshed and transcended by and in the text itself. I read Abe's family history, even emplotted in the incomplete form of the family tree, as a comment on the failure of vertical linealogies to ever fully apprehend the complexity of Black kinship structures. Alienation becomes a narrative structure of possibility for Card; to be a Black alien is to be opened up to multiplicity, change, chance, interdimensional communication, and new modes of resistance. To become kindred is to approach the alien as an alien—even, or perhaps especially, in spite of what is not known or cannot be known.

"These People Are Our Family": Unnarration, Disnarration, and Structures of Black Alien Narrative Rememory

I have so far argued that *Kindred* and *These Ghosts Are Family*, as inter-genre-al works of speculative histofiction, narrate history as another planet by fabulizing Black alien linealogies that move within and beyond the archive into narrative terrains of speculation and memory-work. In doing so, Butler and Card construct the Black subject as alien *to* and alienated *from* eugenic Western linear exclusory genealogies that seek to deny and control their belonging, all while imagining and tracing divergent complex Black alien kinship systems in Thirdspace. In this final section, I offer an explication of two specific narrative strategies—unnarration and disnarration—that Butler and Card employ in order to emplot Black alien belonging, and I examine how each novel extends vertical root-to-branch genealogies into a Thirdspace of Black alien relation. By constellating linealogies of the enslaved alien, *Kindred* and *These Ghosts Are Family* construct narrative counterlogics—*Kindred* circularly, *These Ghosts Are Family* rhizomatically—that reject vertical root-to-branch kinship structures and embrace systems of Black alien kinship that shift the loci of affiliation from blood to other forms of relation. Finally, I examine how Butler and Card emplot structures of belonging as meditations on the Black alien's lineal self-fashioning and their entanglements in alternative configurations of kinship.

Because Butler and Card construct speculative histofiction in ways too numerous for me to discuss in this chapter, I want to specifically highlight their use of *rememory* as a narrative strategy that explores the complexity of Black alien kinship. As a concept, rememory is derived from Toni Morrison's *Beloved* (1987); the novel's protagonist, Sethe, describes the term as follows:

> Some things go. Pass on. Some things just stay. I used to think it was my rememory [. . .] but it's not. Places, places are still there. If a house burns down, it's gone, but the place—the picture of it—stays, and not just in my rememory, out there, in the world. What I remember is a picture floating around out there outside my head. I mean, even if I don't think it, even if I die, the picture of what I did, or knew, or saw is still out there. Right in

the place where it happened. [. . .] Someday you be walking down the road and you hear something or see something going on. So clear. And you think it's you thinking it up. A thought picture. But no. It's when you bump into a rememory.[55]

Both *Kindred* and *These Ghosts Are Family* turn to narrative rememory in order to create alternative locations of diasporic belonging. Rememory functions as a noun, verb, material location, and immaterial impression—you can rememory spacetime; possess a rememory in the form of a "thought picture"; touch or "bump into a rememory"; or visit a rememory "out there, in the world." Angelyn Mitchell describes rememory as a "liberatory narrative construct" that "functions [. . .] as an imaginative recovery of the historical past." Rememory can be seen as a materialization of a past that "stays," both as a floating picture-memory and as a literal place. In its emphasis on the simultaneity of forgetting and remembering, rememory interconnects the past with all other possible temporalities in a radical multiplicity of potential action—past events are permanent both in the world and in memory, experienced again and again in different ways at different times by different people. As Jeong-eun Rhee explains, turning to rememory as a way of imagining spacetime ushers in a "different way of being/knowing/doing that recollects our [. . .] connections, relations, and connectivity across geographies, culture, time, and language."[56] Rememory therefore operates as a material constellation of memories, "things," "places," and people, blurring the boundary between memory and reality, space and time.

Kakali Bhattacharya observes that "rememory work [. . .] includes not only what was lived, remembered, and forgotten in the past; it is also the work that connects time, space, matter, and histories, including creating memories of the future. In this way the linearity of past, present, and future is disrupted when we go in and out of that which we think is tangible and that which we know and feel in our spirits, bodies, and minds." As an embodied location, rememory "is or becomes the place forever transcending the temporality of past, present, and future." As a way of knowing, being, and doing in the world, narrative rememory in *Kindred* and *These Ghosts Are Family* "generates different relationships between you, me and place (time/space)"[57] by cohering Black alien kinship as an assemblage of affectual, object, and social relations. In order to show *how* these texts narrate history

---

55. Morrison, *Beloved*, 43.
56. Mitchell, *Freedom to Remember*, 12; and Rhee, *Decolonial Feminist Research*, 20.
57. Bhattacharya, "Methodology Is Connectivity," x–xi; Rhee, *Decolonial Feminist Research*, 2; and Bhattacharya, "Methodology Is Connectivity," xii.

as another planet, I first examine how Butler rememories Dana's enslaved alien linealogy via strategies of *unnarration,* in which her alienation to and from the antebellum past is a mimetic emplotment of the Black alien's fragmented and incomplete history. I conclude with an exploration of the way Card rememories the Paisley family history via strategies of *disnarration,* in which Black alien belonging is represented as an endlessly horizontal kinship network entangling people, places, and things.

Kindred is structured by Dana's cycles of departure and return. She travels to 1800s antebellum Maryland from 1976 California six times, each chapter representing either a location or event where Rufus was harmed, such as "The River" or "The Fall." Dana's departures to the past are plotted along a linear timeline, which is to say that each time she departs from the present to the Maryland plantation, its people have grown older. This linearity is a feature of the novel's emplotment of vertical genealogy. Dana *must* exist within the borders of Rufus's linear genealogic time in order to make possible Hagar's birth, or cease to exist herself. That said, Dana remains out of joint with linear time; as she moves back and forth and through the past and present-future in a loop, she is repeatedly alienated from her ancestors and contemporary kinfolk alike. The discrepancies between Rufus's linear genealogic time and Dana's circular alien time become particularly clear as she returns to the past over and over again without appearing to have aged. Upon her fifth arrival at the Weylin plantation, six years have passed by since her fourth departure—only a matter of hours for Dana in 1976. Rufus's father, Tom Weylin, inquires about a scabbed-over wound on her face, observing that she "look[s] as young as you ever did" (199). When Dana explains that *he* had given her the abrasion during a vicious beating shortly before her fourth return, Tom insists in a rage that "six years for me is six years for you!" (200). But, of course, as Nadine Flagel explains, time in *Kindred* is variable:

> Duration is not synchronous between the 1800s and 1976 [. . . but] there is a consistent ratio: ten minutes in the nineteenth century takes a few seconds in 1976, several months take a few hours, and so forth. History is compressed; the past takes up less time in the present. And while duration may be proportional, occurrence is unpredictable: Dana cannot predict when in 1976 she will be called to the 1800s, and once there, she cannot predict when she will be called back to 1976.[58]

---

58. Flagel, "'Almost Like Being There,'" 220.

The second time Dana returns to the past, after Rufus sets his curtains on fire, Kevin tells her that she was gone "almost three minutes [. . .] but it seemed to be longer" (44). Prompted to go back to the present-future after being physically and sexually assaulted by a slave patroller, Dana arrives in physical pain, emotional distress, and with a "sickening dizziness" (58). The shorter duration of Dana's dematerialization in her present-future and the longer duration of her enfleshment in the past can be read as a kind of chronotopicity, in which, according to Mikhail Bakhtin, "spatial and temporal indicators are fused into one carefully thought-out concrete whole. Time, as it were, thickens, takes on flesh, becomes artistically visible; likewise, space becomes charged and responsive to the movements of time, plot, and history."[59] These cycles thoroughly discombobulate Dana by blurring her experience of spacetime, a confusion that is narrated from her first-person point of view. The chronotope of Black alien lineagly in *Kindred* is re-presented as Dana's (dis)embodied and (un)enfleshed entanglement in and across spacetime, as she is repeatedly brought into kinship networks only to become alienated from them in a recursive loop, a circularity that is *also* evident in the novel's narratological structure.

Upon returning to California following her second departure, Dana awakens to find Kevin looming over her. In the moment, she confuses Kevin with the slave patroller, scratching his face and drawing blood. Though she gradually becomes reoriented to the present, she continues to suffer from pain and lingering exhaustion: "I had been gone for hours and I knew it. But at that moment, I couldn't have argued it. [. . .] The surge of strength that helped me to fight when I thought I was fighting for my life was gone" (44). Dana's embodied and emotional registers—her spent strength and residual "pain and weariness" (44)—collapse spatiotemporal boundaries, exceeding triadic temporality, or past, present, and future, in and as Dana's flesh. Dana's conflation of Kevin with the slave patroller heightens the effects of this collapse by drawing a parallel to (and distinction between) Dana's uneasy relation to the structures of white supremacist heteropatriarchy. During Dana's fourth departure, Kevin travels with her; while in Maryland, they attempt to mask their married kinship as a master-slave dynamic. When Dana is prompted to return to California, Kevin remains behind in the antebellum world for five years. When he returns home to California with Dana, she observes a shift in his personality—he "sound[s] a little like Rufus and Tom Weylin," and, in a moment of frustration, she observes "an expression on his face [. . .] like something [. . .] I was used to seeing on Tom Weylin.

---

59. Bakhtin, *Dialogic Imagination*, 84.

Something closed and ugly" (194). Kevin is and remains Dana's chosen family—her "kindred spirit" (57), as she describes him—and yet these dislocations in spacetime alienate her from him (and him from her) by bringing into sharp relief intimacies between past and present constructions of white masculinity. Though Dana feels "safe" (44) with Kevin, her momentary inability to distinguish his care from the patroller's violence reorients her relation to him once more, requiring her to confront the persistence of white supremacist and white masculinist violence in her present, and to rethink her white husband's complicity in its perpetuation across spacetime.

Dana's position outside of history—again, she exists circularly, rather than linearly—is also a paradoxical re-presentation of her inability to fully inhabit triadic temporality; when she is in her present's past of antebellum Maryland, she is always oriented toward her present-future in 1976, unpredictably wavering between an uncertain now, which is always moving into the future, and a permanently foreclosed past. Dana notes that even as she and Kevin "were watching history happen around us" (98), "I couldn't do anything to change history" (141). Dana's slippages in spacetime, marked by her inability to exist anywhere singularly, can be read as a narrative re-presentation of the Black alien's positionality. Dana's unending embodied present—her fleshy persistence in spite of the manifold gaps and intervals of seconds, minutes, days, years, decades, centuries—is a recursive (re)doubling of the slave's natal alienation, re-presented as an inability to belong to any vertical linealogy. These ruptures and incongruities in Dana's experience of spacetime, or what Ferreira da Silva describes as her "violation of sequentially,"[60] create gaps in her experience of reality and memory, alienating her from the flow of linear genealogic spacetime. Dana's first-person past-tense perspective reinforces these gaps in perception, highlighting what she knows, what she cannot know, and what she will never know about the past or any temporality she does not immediately inhabit.

As if to reinforce this point, in the novel's prologue we learn that Dana narrates these cycles of departure and return from a position of backward-lookingness following her "last trip home" in the wake of Rufus's death, after she has "lost about a year of my life and much of the comfort and security I had not valued until it was gone" (9). I frame this narrative perspective of looking backward and the novel's circular emplotment of spacetime as an example of narrative rememory, in which boundaries between then, there, here, and now have fundamentally collapsed. And, indeed, on her first return home Dana reverts to this narrative mode: "I went back to the

---

60. Ferreira da Silva, *Unpayable Debt*, 86.

beginning, to the first dizziness, and remembered it all for him [Kevin]—relived it all in detail" (15). The recursion of remembering and forgetting creates fissures in Dana's experience and recall of her lived experiences. For example, even as she "relive[s]" the memory of the past in her present-future, after Dana spends a few days in California, she notes that she "had forgotten" the past was "a hostile place," because, in her "time-distorted reality" "it didn't look alien any longer" (126–27). As Dana grows more comfortable navigating the antebellum past, she begins to feel increasingly like she is "losing my place here in my own time" (191). These gaps and slippages in memory are a terrifying effect of her time travel; following her first return, Dana explains to Kevin that "as real as the whole episode was, as real as I know it was, it's beginning to recede from me somehow. It's becoming like something I saw on television or read about—like something second hand" (17). Dana's cycles of forgetting and remembering rememory Black alien positionality by enfleshing fragments of diasporic history.

Even as Dana moves through spacetime, her narrative point of view delimits the scope of her experience. It may seem obvious, but Dana cannot narrate what she does not see, know, or remember. For that reason, most of the antebellum past is unnarratable. Gerald Prince broadly defines unnarratability as "that which, *according to a given narrative,* cannot be narrated or is not worth narrating because it transgresses a law (social, authorial, generic, formal) [. . .] defies the powers of a particular narrator (or those of any narrator) or [. . .] falls below the so-called threshold of narratability (it is not sufficiently unusual or problematic)."[61] These forms of unnarration govern much of *Kindred*'s tellability. For example, Dana and Kevin cannot tell their friends and family in 1976 about their time-travel experiences without opening themselves up to medical or carceral intervention, a form of self-imposed silence that is exceeded only in the course of Dana's narrative retelling. Dana also chooses not to recount memories that are too painful, too quotidian, or too personal—her sexual intimacy with Kevin, for example, or many of the more mundane aspects of slave life.

Prince highlights another aspect of unnarration, one not eclipsed from the narrative by repression or choice, but instead found in

> all the frontal and lateral ellipses found in narrative and either explicitly underlined by the narrator [. . .] or inferable from a significant lacuna in the chronology or through a retrospective filling-in: given a series of events, e_1, e_2, e_3 . . . e_n occurring at time t or at times t_1, t_2, t_3 . . . t_n respectively, one of

---

61. Prince, "Disnarrated," 2.

the events goes unmentioned. In *this* case, something is not told (at least for a while) not so much because of a narratorial incapacity, a tellability imperative, a "legal" imposition, but because of some narrative call for rhythm, characterization, suspense, surprise, and so on.[62]

This form of unnarration occurs repeatedly between travels in *Kindred* for what might seem, at first glance, to be singularly intended to build tension and suspense. I argue that these unnarratable gaps can also be seen, however, as the work of narrative rememory. As I noted above, following Dana's third return to California, Kevin remains behind in the antebellum past. Dana is prompted to return during a vicious beating from Tom, who catches her teaching another slave, Nigel, to read. This chapter of the novel—"The Fall"—ends with Dana positioned at some physical distance from Kevin: "I saw Kevin, blurred, but somehow still recognizable. I saw him running toward me in slow motion, running. Legs churning, arms pumping, yet he hardly seemed to be getting closer. Suddenly, I realized what was happening and I screamed—I think I screamed. He had to reach me. Had to! And I passed out" (107). Dana's unconsciousness serves as a pivot point between a receding past and insurgent future, but it is also a critical gap in her rememory of spacetime. This strange sense of embodied time is reinforced when, at the beginning of the following chapter—"The Fight"—she unnarrates the events immediately following her unconsciousness, offering instead an extended history of her romantic relationship with Kevin and thereby reinforcing her lineal alienation from her ancestors in the past, and from her chosen kin in the present. Dana's meditation on her relationship with Kevin highlights their mutual interdependence and emotional intimacy, in stark contrast to her relationships with Tom and Rufus, which are structured by violence, manipulation, and control. And yet, when Kevin is stuck in the past, he is as dead as Tom or Rufus in the present; her separation from him reinforces her genealogic isolation, even from those kinship structures she chooses. As I discussed in the first section of this chapter, in the novel's epilogue, which takes place some weeks after her final return, Dana and Kevin circle back to Maryland where they find very little corroborating evidence about their time travel, and even less information about the fate of her ancestors. Though Dana and Kevin remain a committed family at the novel's end, their future relation goes unnarrated. These strategies of unnarration frame Dana's lineal history as another planet, which is to say they offer up new ways to rememory the complex histories of the enslaved

---

62. Prince, "Disnarrated," 5.

and their descendants. As Dana cycles through time, the novel resists closure, operating as an open-ended narrative set. Though we have no way of knowing precisely which direction Dana is headed when the novel ends, we do know she will never go back to the constraints of the past.

Rather than approach history as another planet *circularly*, *These Ghosts Are Family* resists the logics of Western narrative genealogical linearity *rhizomatically* through strategies Prince describes as "disnarration," or,

> most generally, terms, phrases, and passages that consider what did not or does not take place [. . .] whether they pertain to the narrator or their narration [. . .] or to one of the characters and his or her actions [. . .] [these] constitute the disnarrated. [. . .] I am thus referring to the alethic expressions of impossibility or unrealized possibility, deontic expressions of observed prohibition, epistemic expressions of ignorance, ontologic expressions of nonexistence, purely imagined worlds, desired worlds, or intended worlds, unfulfilled expectations, unwarranted beliefs, failed attempts, crushed hopes, suppositions and false calculations, errors and lies, and so forth.[63]

The entire plot of *These Ghosts Are Family* is constellated around various modes of disnarration, beginning with Abel Paisley's death, an event that did not take place. As I discussed in the previous section, Abe Kincaid's incomplete vertical genealogy is likewise structured by disnarration, both in its representation of what is not known about the Paisley family genealogy, and in its re-presentation of the possibility of Black diasporic belonging. In the remainder of this chapter, I explore how *These Ghosts Are Family* rememories Black alien linealogy as a horizontal, rhizomatic relation through strategies of disnarration.

Gilles Deleuze and Félix Guattari explain that the rhizome, as an organizational system, represents "connection and heterogeneity"—"any point of a rhizome can be connected to anything other, and must be. This is very different from the tree or root, which plots a point, fixes and orders." Rhizomatic structures insist on "multiplicity" in order to produce modes of relation that Deleuze and Guattari describe as an "assemblage," or "an increase in the dimensions of a multiplicity that necessarily changes in nature as it expands its connections. There are no points or positions in a rhizome, such as those found in a structure, tree, or root. There are only lines."[64] Whereas the novel's paratextual family tree features an incomplete vertical genealogy

---

63. Prince, "Disnarrated," 3.
64. Deleuze and Guattari, *Thousand Plateaus*, 7, 8.

of the Paisley family, its narrative structure is rhizomatic, drawing lines of connection between biological and nonbiological kin, their environments, and the animals and things in their worlds. Édouard Glissant, whose theory of relation is informed by Deleuze and Guattari's construction of the rhizome, clarifies that

> the root is unique, a stock taking all upon itself and killing all around it. In opposition to this [Deleuze and Guattari] propose the rhizome, an enmeshed root system, a network spreading either in the ground or in the air, with no predatory rootstock taking over permanently. The notion of the rhizome maintains, therefore, the idea of rootedness but challenges the idea of a totalitarian root. Rhizomatic thought is the principle behind what I call the Poetics of Relation, in which each and every identity is extended through a relationship with the Other.[65]

These Ghosts Are Family rememories Black alien kinship structures as a "Poetics of Relation," in which heteropatriarchal blood logics are replaced by rhizomatic systems of interconnection. What Glissant describes as "relation identity," then, "is produced in the chaotic network of Relation and not in the hidden violence of filiation; [it] does not devise any legitimacy as its guarantee of entitlement, but circulates, newly extended; [and] does not think of land as a territory from which to project toward other territories but as a place where one gives-on-and-with rather than grasps."[66] I argue that this deterritorialized, nonfilial system of relation engenders alternative forms of Black belonging by constructing horizontal relation as an antithesis to vertical logics of blood.

This is immediately apparent in the multiply perspectival first chapter of the novel, "The True Death of Abel Paisley," set in Harlem in 2005, when Abel/Stanford is an elderly widower; his wife, Adele, passed away a month before the novel's action begins. Feeling that his own death is imminent, Abel/Stanford gathers together his daughters, Irene Paisley and Estelle Solomon, and his granddaughter, Caren Solomon, in order to tell them the truth about his double-identity. Estelle and Caren believe that he is Stanford, a Jamaican immigrant who owns a small restaurant and a bit of property in New York. Irene, an immigrant from Jamaica herself and hired by Abel/Stanford as a home health-care aide, believes that her father, Abel, died in London when she was a small child. Also present, albeit unseen and

---

65. Glissant, *Poetics of Relation*, 11.
66. Glissant, *Poetics of Relation*, 144.

unheard, is Vera Paisley, Abel's deceased wife—"a dead woman, six years on the other side" (12)—who exists in an immaterial "other place" (13) as a ghost who cannot speak to or be seen by the living. As the women gather around him, the second-person narrator shifts from Abel/Stanford, to Irene, to Estelle, to Caren, before concluding with Vera. In each instance, the narrator implores the reader to inhabit the position of the narrative subject; for example, "Let's say you are a sixty-nine-year-old Jamaican man called Stanford, or Stan for short, who once faked your own death" (1) or "Now let's say that you are a dead woman [. . .] whose husband let you believe he was dead" (12). The novel begins by structuring the family as an assemblage, drawing them together as kin in horizontal relation with one another—siblings and half-siblings, husband and wife, the living and the dead.

The narrator's use of second-person perspective as a form of disnarration also re-presents the Paisley/Solomon kinship relation as inherently rhizomatic. Matt DelConte explains that second-person is "a narrative mode in which a narrator tells a story to a (sometimes undefined, shifting, and/or hypothetical) narratee—delineated by *you*—who is also the (sometimes undefined, shifting, and/or hypothetical) principal actant in that story." Rather than emphasize the singular "voice/narrator," second-person narration is instead "based on the triad of narrator, protagonist, and narratee (these three corresponding to the elements of the traditional rhetorical model: speech, text, and audience)." *These Ghosts Are Family* deploys what DelConte describes as "non-coincident narration," or "a narrative in which the narrator, narratee, and protagonist functions are all discrete."[67] In the first section of *These Ghosts Are Family*, the omniscient second-person narrator assumes a position outside spacetime, offering the narratee more information about the protagonists than the protagonists know about themselves. The use of non-coincident narration is clearest in Caren Solomon's section, as the narrator offers the narratee information about Caren that she does not yet know: "Say you are an eighteen-year-old college student named Caren who lives in a Harlem brownstone with your mother, who is a heroin addict, and your wheelchair-bound Jamaican grandfather who faked his own death, *but you won't know it for a few hours*" (9, emphasis mine). Just as Abel draws his descendants together in order to usher them into a new system of relation, so too does the second-person narrative entangle the narratee, the protagonists, and the narrator together as kin.

Following Michelle Wright, I argue that *These Ghosts Are Family* rejects the "linear progress narrative [. . . that] gives us hierarchies that prize certain

---

67. DelConte, "Why *You* Can't Speak," 207–8, 210, 211.

bodies over others, draws firm, biological boundaries around racial collectives that do not really exist." Instead, the novel embraces what Wright describes as a "nontraditional form of diaspora [. . .] that operates in a snarl, eschewing fixed hierarchies," a mode of belonging that asks us to rethink diasporic kinship as a poetics of relation and entanglement of self with "all the people and 'things' that surround and impact us."[68] Caren and Estelle's relationship, for example, is dictated by their relation with objects, or what might be understood as a material diaspora; indeed, Anna Pechurina explains that "objects, whether they are real or imagined, lost or forgotten, act as powerful symbols of migrant and diasporic belonging."[69] In the segment "Estelle's Black Eye," set in 2020 in Harlem, fifteen years after Abel/Solomon's death, we learn that Caren was bequeathed Abel/Stanford's Harlem brownstone, instead of her mother, Estelle, an artist and lifelong heroin addict. Narrated from Caren's first-person past-tense point of view, this chapter serves as Caren's remembrance of her mother after she dies of a heroin overdose. Caren's possession of the property circumvents the traditional progression of inheritance; by cutting Estelle out of the lineal property order, Abel/Stanford functionally disowns her. Caren observes that "though she [Estelle] hated living there when my grandparents were alive, she expected them to leave it to her, but they left it to me instead. They raised me, so in a way, I became more their daughter than she was. [. . .] I was grateful to them . . . but I understood now how they sometimes used me to control and punish my mother" (178). As an object representing the Solomon family's line of heritable descent, the brownstone (re)defines the family's kinship structure. As Caren explains, the brownstone is evidence that she was "more [the] daughter" than her mother, functioning as a mechanism to "control" the Solomon linealogy by excising the dysgenic element (Estelle) from the traditional progression of lineal descendancy.

In spite of their social and emotional alienation from one another, Caren provides Estelle with a key to the brownstone so that she has a safe place to sleep, and a place to safely rob when she is in need of money. Caren's offer of a house key is made all the more meaningful because, after repeated robberies, Abel/Stanford refused to grant Estelle access to any part of the brownstone beyond its unfinished basement; Estelle's inability to enter the family quarters of the brownstone can be read as a sign of her dysgenicity, or of Abel/Stanford's refusal to include her in the vertical family tree. Caren maintains ownership of the property, but her willingness to share the living

---

68. Wright, "Diaspora and Entanglement," 226, 237.
69. Pechurina, "Diasporic Objects," 669.

spaces of the brownstone and her possessions reconfigures the vertical lineal bond. The brownstone serves as an additional poetics of relation, shifting the emphasis away from blood to other modes of belonging. Estelle and Caren's kinship relation is structured around entering into and exchanging objects; Caren most frequently encounters her mother only when she needs money, "her body slouching under the weight of my belongings" (170–71). Their interactions are exclusively codified around an assemblage of things—the brownstone, the house key, or the battered white mink coat which is always the first sign that Estelle has arrived.

Much of this chapter's disnarration concerns a well-known self-portrait of Estelle, entitled *Estelle's Black Eye*. The photograph, featuring a close-up of Estelle's bruised face, "was the piece of art that got her started" (173)—Abel/Stanford kept the framed original in a position of prominence over the fireplace, a sign of both his pride in her and his outrage at her drug addiction. Caren had "always hated it" because it reminded her of her mother's absence, "that she was out there somewhere, hurting herself" (173). As a disnarrated representation of Estelle's self-destruction, the photograph is a symbol of her grandfather's uncommunicated love for his daughter, and a talisman that reinforces her absence from Caren's life. The photograph also functions as way for Caren and Estelle to communicate with one another. Caren sells the original print and destroys the negatives but, because she knows her mother dislikes it, keeps a print above the fireplace "like putting up a crucifix to ward off a vampire" (173). Estelle, in turn, makes a point to remove the print and hide it "behind the couch" (172) each time she enters the brownstone. This object-oriented tête-à-tête continues until Estelle's death of an overdose on that same couch, when she is metaphorically transformed from person to thing: "When they took Estelle away, I sat on the royal blue velvet sofa. It smelled of her, of drugs, of death. I had inherited it from my grandparents too" (179). In the midst of Caren's grief, the couch becomes indistinguishable from her mother, so she decides to remove it; after placing it on the curb, "hop[ing] someone would take it" (180), her downstairs tenants move it back into the brownstone. As an object-version of her relation with her mother, the couch's return to the brownstone also represents Estelle's return to the family system. To that end, Caren and Estelle's interobject relation can also be seen as a horizontal assemblage that exceeds vertical linealogy, a system in which nonhuman things become kin and enable kinship relation.

By including nonbiological kin, ghosts, and mythic beings in the Paisley family linealogy, *These Ghosts Are Family* narrates (and disnarrates) kinship systems that cannot be verified or disputed because they exist entirely outside the boundaries of traditional genealogical spacetime. For example, we learn that shortly before Abel/Stanford's death in England, Vera Paisley begins a clandestine decades-long affair with her sixteen-year-old yard boy, an orphan named Bernard; their relationship lasts more than thirty years until her death. As her lover, helper, and sometimes confidant, Bernard had "invested his entire future in Vera" (62), giving up the opportunity to have a family of his own or with her—Vera has three abortions while they are lovers, refusing to acknowledge him as anything other than her servant. Though their relationship is Bernard's sole kinship affiliation, Vera's children, Irene and Vincent, regard him as "property that [. . .] they] had no wish to inherit" (61), despite his faithful service to the family for their entire lives. On the day of the funeral, in a welter of grief, Bernard barricades himself inside Vera's room, a sacred space that must be kept untouched until purified lest the former inhabitant become a duppy, or ghost, which, we have already learned from the novel's opening section, does indeed happen. After Bernard is forcibly removed from Vera's bedroom shortly before her interment, Vincent pulls him aside "and whisper[s]: 'That foolishness you did have with me mother nuh mean nuttin. You nuh family'" (81). In an instance of disnarration, we learn that Vincent had always been aware of Vera's relationship with Bernard, and that his rejection of their kinship rests on his understanding of family as a hereditary bloodline.

In this chapter, the narrative shifts between Bernard's perspective, narrated via third-person free indirect discourse, and the first-person perspective of "we visitors," a collection of "relatives" (53) from Jamaica and the United States who have assembled to attend to the rites and rituals of Vera's homegoing. Unlike Bernard, who was forced to sleep in an outdoor shed, and on only one occasion in thirty years slept inside the home, "we visitors" sleep inside on pallets made by Bernard, are shuttled to-and-fro from the airport to the home by Bernard, eat the provisions purchased by Bernard, view Vera's body after it was prepared by Bernard, and watch her interred in a grave dug by Bernard, into which he climbs after her coffin is placed in it. In spite of the evidence of his "real grief" and his years of service to the family, we visitors insist that it was "no matter if we were Vera's grandnieces or grandnephews, her uncle's cousin by marriage, her son's school friend's brother, we all had more claim to Vera [. . .] than Bernard" (59). Even as they frame their entitlement to Vera's property as a matter of horizontal relation inclusive of nonbiological kin—"cousin[s] by marriage" and a "school friend's brother"—their entanglements are still predicated on blood relation: "Vera's grandnieces or grandnephews," "her uncle," "her son."

The singular exception to this can be found in a collective known as "three little girls" (60)—"no more than six, no younger than four. [Bernard] didn't know which visitor they belonged to" (70)—who develop a fascination with him; when he leaves the Paisley family property after Vera's burial, they follow him into the bush. Though all of what happens next is disnarrated, given that we are left to speculate about the course of events, I read their collective disappearance as a murder-suicide, predicated on Bernard's belief that, in death, the three little girls will live with him and Vera forever:

> As he led them through the bush, Bernard told the girls that Vera would fly above them, whispering to God, and get them everything they ever wanted. He told them that they belonged to Vera now, just as he did. He told them not be afraid to walk into the bush; Vera had promised him, as he was lying in her grave, that she would protect them always. He told them not to pity their mothers and fathers because they were fools; they were probably still standing there [...] believing that Vera was still that thing that they had just covered with dirt. (83)

By bringing the three little girls and Vera's ghost into a nonbiological system of "belong[ing]," Bernard constructs an alien kinship structure that entangles the living and the dead, the stranger and the familiar. Bernard's disnarrated act of violence reorients the Paisley's and we visitors' desire for a heritable family structure toward a new poetics of relation, one that paradoxically brings him into permanent relation not only with the Paisleys/we visitors, but also the broader community of Harold Town: "Where were the yard boy's people? Where would he take them? Not a soul knew. We had thought the man was no one to know or remember. [...] Now we find ourselves whispering his name in our beds at night, reciting it like a prayer, hoping one day he will forgive and have mercy on us" (84). We visitors' configuration of their relation to Bernard functions as a rememory, in which the community's unarticulated hopes, their collective burden to remember, and concomitant desire to forget, form the basis for a new (even if grotesque) linealogy in which even the missing or the dead must be accounted for.

Though Bernard more or less vanishes from the narrative after his disappearance, the three little girls return at the novel's end as "strange" (259), ravenously hungry, blood-drinking *soucouyants* who exist in eternal, mythic time. As Giselle Anatol explains, the soucouyant is often typified as a "frightening old hag, skin-shredder, bloodsucker, fly-by-night," a woman who is "perceived as suffering from excess body and excess flesh." The soucouyant is most often "an elderly woman who has the ability to cast away her skin, fly about in the form of a ball of flame, and invade the homes of neighbors to drain them of their life-blood." In general, the soucouyant represents "transgressed borders—whether those are the boundaries of one's property or of one's physical, corporeal body when its fluids are drained." As a Caribbean cultural tradition, the soucouyant figure worked "to establish a strong sense of ethnic community,"[70] binding listeners together in their fear of the potentially destructive nonhuman alien entity in their midst. That said, communities could—and often did—live alongside and with soucouyants in relative peace and harmony. The final section of the novel traces the (re)emergence of the three little girls and their entanglements with community members of Harold Town. Importantly, none of the protagonists in this final section are blood kin, and Abel/Solomon's genealogy fades away from the plot—rather, the community's kinship network coheres around their entanglement with the three little girls, with one another, in the space and place of Harold Town, and the world beyond it. The final multiply perspectival chapter—an echo of the novel's first chapter—is told from the point of view of the three little girls, alongside several members of the Harold Town community, including Norma Montague, a woman who developed a close childhood friendship with the three little girls, and occasionally let them suck her blood; Augustus Monroe, who the three little girls attack ("break me skin and nearly draw blood"; 257) in a welter of starvation; Philomena Randolph, who watches the three little girls steal her baby, so they can drink its blood; and Birdie Wemberley, who catches the three little girls drinking the blood of her chickens, and instead offers herself to them, even going so far, for a time, to "raise them like them my own family" (268). The community members initially regard the three little girls as merely "feral [. . .] isolated and left to fend for themselves for a while before they found this town" (266), and so, like Birdie, they collectively take them in, attempting to develop alternative kinship structures by providing the children with "family." Over time, as the three little girls approach adolescence, their insatiable hunger alienates them from the community as they wreak havoc by attacking Augustus, locking Birdie in her chicken coop for three days, draining the blood of thirty chickens at once, biting and lashing out. As a result, they are "never formally adopted" but instead "bounced from house to house in Harold Town, taking scraps like stray dogs" (269). After the three little girls devour Philomena's baby, the community collectively rescinds its agreement to provide the three little girls with care and kinship, and, in a scene that is disnarrated as rumor and speculation, they kill the three little girls once again, burying them deep in the bush surrounding Harold Town. This communal-ritual murder does indeed eliminate the increasing threat from the

---

70. Anatol, *Things That Fly*, 37, 40, 42, 37.

three little girls; as a consequence of the horror of their collective violence, and their inability to bring the three little girls into loving, living kinship with them, the community is cohered around a new and terrible kinship structure, one not predicated on blood relation or even a presumption of intimacy but rather the logics of secret, shameful rememory, as they work to forget what they did in the midst of a ceaseless recursion of remembering.

Among the actors in this final section is Astor Graham, a Black private investigator hired by the parents of three little girls to recover their bodies, who functions as an "insider/outsider" (259) in the community. From his perspective, "the girls had been missing for just over eight years, after being led away from a funeral by their cousins' gardener. A man they called Bernard. I say *called* because we later found that the man had no birth certificate, no record he'd ever been born; he was a ghost" (258). Bernard's ghostliness is a reflection of his kinlessness, and an additional mirror of the three little girls' ghostly kinlessness, a sign of their collective inability to be brought into meaningful relation in their communities; as aliens—Bernard a familyless yard boy, the three little girls as wandering soucouyants—their relation is destabilizing to vertical root-systems.

Because Birdie remembers all too well the destruction wrought by the three little girls, she begs Astor not to exhume their bodies, though she shows him the clearing where they are buried. Astor digs their bodies out of the ground with his bare hands, leaving soon after they are exhumed to alert the authorities; when he returns shortly thereafter with the police, the three bodies are missing, only footprints left behind that "led out of the clearing [. . .] they disappeared and were replaced by smaller prints, like those of little animals" (269). Unable to move forward with the investigation without the bodies, Astor believes the community must suffer from a "mass hallucination"—and yet he registers that "none of the people I talked to seemed a bit surprised. They really believed. The whole town believed" (268–69). This belief is substantiated by the narrative—we see the three little girls learn to "feel the sun on their skin after so much time" because their bodies were "stiff, petrified" (268). Though they remember that the community members killed them, "they weren't angry, they were glad, for they had learned that for girls like them, dying was part of growing up" (269)—and, indeed, the three little girls are no longer unable to provide for themselves. After warming their bodies, they shed their skins, clean them in a stream, and lay them out to dry, discovering that they have become adult women when they put them back on. Together they walk to Birdie's home to convince Astor to drop the investigation and leave them be. Though Astor, who chooses to believe he is still dreaming, argues that Harold Town has effectively become "your prison," insisting that the three women have not been and will never be considered kin, they respond emphatically that "We are home. [. . .] This is our home. [. . .] These people are our family" (270). When Astor refuses to listen, the three women bite and frighten him into silence.

According to Astor's root-based logic, the three women belong exclusively to their blood kin, and are therefore fatally out of step with structures of vertical belonging. And yet the community members and the three women see themselves as entangled in a complex and eternal relation—the three women now belong to mythic time, an indefinitely repeatable nonlinear spacetime. In other words, the three women and their community exist outside of what K. A. Nuzum has termed "historic time," a genealogic time zone that "proceeds in linear fashion, so that each of its events is a unique, one-time experience."[71] As a consequence, the three women become permanently entangled with the Harold Town community as unchanging myth, and enfleshed entities. The novel concludes with Birdie's disnarrated warning that, should anyone come across a woman covered in blood, "her sisters a lay wait you. Is not her blood on her. Is fi yuh blood"—rather, you should "bring a hen. Leave it at the boundary line before you drive on. One hen is enough. Them three girl is older now. Them learn restraint. Them will let you pass through" (271). The three women's eventual entanglement in their Harold Town community is a form of eternal Black alien kinship; they are fed by their community, and in turn show restraint in what they take from them, each working together in a new Thirdspace of relation. As the novel's re-presentation of Black kinship transitions from the vertical lineal family tree to a rhizomatic relation that moves between, across, among, and around people, ghosts, objects, biological, and nonbiological kin, the novel reveals its structure as necessarily nonlinear and horizontal, and as fundamentally alien as the three soucouyants themselves. In its embrace of Black alien kinship, *These Ghosts Are Family* suggests that becoming entangled with one's family in the cosmic diaspora is to enter into strange alternative systems of relation, structures of belonging that constellate, aggregate, and move outward and across, expanding forever and ever.

---

71. Nuzum, "Historic Time," 209.

CHAPTER 2

Black Skin, Human Masks, Alien Form
Narrative Physiognomy, Visual Phenomenology, and Image-Text Representations of (Extra)Terrestriality

In scientific taxonomies of organisms in the West, Black terrestrials have been cast as zoologically alien, or, according to Sylvia Wynter, as "Untrue Human Others to the 'true' human that is Man." According to Wynter, Black folk are "made to occupy the nadir, 'n——r' rung of being human," classed as subrational beings whose natal inferiority is evident everywhere: in the body, the mind, the blood, the gene, and, in particular, the "alien features of the Negroid physiognomy."[1] As I discussed in chapter 1, these taxonomies hierarchize Black people as evolutionarily dysselected, positioning them as genealogical isolates beyond the boundaries of related human being. The science of physiognomy, or the process of ordering humans and nonhuman animals according to their physical characteristics, extends the logics of vertical eugenic genealogy into the domain of the visual. Physiognomists organize individual organisms around differences that surface on the body—skin color, the shape and size of noses, lips, eyes, skull shape, and musculature. In the process, Black flesh is transformed into an observable index of sheer, incomprehensible alterity. As I explain in greater detail in the first two sections of this chapter, distinctions between the normative white Western human and the dysgenic Black (extra)terrestrial alien have been and

---

1. Wynter, "Coloniality of Being," 318–19, 261–62, 319.

continue to be produced through physiognomic systems circulated globally via narrative and image-text. In other words, I argue that Black folks are remanded to the category of the sub- or nonhuman Other via processes of *seeing* and *being seen*.

Michelle Wright reminds us, however, that Blackness, which *cannot* be located on or in the body, "operates as a construct (implicitly or explicitly defined as a shared set of physical and behavioral characteristics) and as phenomenological (imagined through individual perceptions in various ways depending on the context)." Blackness is "not a scientific discovery, but an economic and political argument" that frames and controls living and being in specific spatiotemporal contexts. As a category of (non)belonging, Blackness transforms social beings into fungible objects, which, as Shannon Winnubst explains, "in both its economic and legal meanings, is to have all distinctive characteristics hollowed out." Blackness is therefore a paradoxical ascription: determined by corrupt fantasies of blood kinship; immutable yet malleable; a marker of both dysgenicity and suprahumanity; an irrecoverable absence (of light, of humanity, of reason) and yet also a powerful signifier of cultural and social collectivity, affiliation, and community. Be(com)ing Black is not, however, merely or only felt; in the antiblack universe being and being seen as Black in certain locations and times can be deadly. Wright observes that Blackness functions both as "a matter of perception [. . . and] made up of moments of performance in which performers understand their bodies to be Black."[2] For that reason, I argue that physiognomic perceptions of Black (extra)terrestrial aliens can, paradoxically, make space for subjects who both perform and resist performance, are seen and resist being seen, are interpellated and simultaneously masked.

Black terrestrials have long served as models for imagining life on other planets, most evidently in the way taxonomic systems designed to register the optic Otherness of Black bodies on Earth are speculatively mapped onto the universe. In scientific and popular imaginaries, extraterrestrial aliens are frequently collectivized and homogenized, rarely possessing distinctive characteristics.[3] Due to their spectacular strangeness, Ursula K. Le Guin argues that in SF the "racial Alien," or "the Alien everybody recognizes as

---

2. Wright, *Physics of Blackness*, 4, 2; Winnubst, "Many Lives of Fungibility," 104; and Wright, *Physics of Blackness*, 3.

3. For more information on representations of extraterrestrial aliens in science fiction, see George Edgar Slusser and Eric S. Rabkin, *Aliens: The Anthropology of Science Fiction* (Carbondale: Southern Illinois University Press, 1987); and Jenny Wolmark, *Aliens and Others: Science Fiction, Feminism, and Postmodernism* (Iowa City: University of Iowa Press, 1994).

alien," is routinely epitomized as inherently threatening—in other words, "the only good alien is a dead alien." These depictions have grave consequences for writers and readers of speculative fiction, considering that in SF imaginaries that transform the alien "into a thing [. . .] the only possible relationship is a power relationship." In their constructions of "a permanent hierarchy of superiors and inferiors," writers of American SF, Le Guin argues, are often responsible for reimagining the global empire as a galactic enterprise by projecting the "Age of Queen Victoria" into the stars.[4]

Nicholas Hauman agrees that "when astronomers look out into space, they find difference, hierarchy, and biological determinism," and, in doing so, bring the extraterrestrial alien into the same taxonomic sightlines that define the bodies and beings of Black terrestrials. In constructions of extraterrestrial life by writers of speculative fiction, astrophysicists, and astrobiologists, one finds "constant slippages, moments where the terrestrial and the extraterrestrial are conflated. [. . .] Behind the extraterrestrial, this unidentifiable subject of science, it is seen there are real human beings, colonial subjects, obfuscated to a trace by projections of the colonial subject into space."[5] For that reason, rather than treat extraterrestrial aliens as metaphors for Black being in this chapter, I instead examine spectacular intimacies between extraterrestrials and Black terrestrials by tracing slippages in their visual and narrative representation. I argue that these visual (extra)terrestrial intimacies reimagine the limits and potential of Blackness, humanness, and alienness, and challenge Western white supremacist desires to colonize the cosmos through the use of antiblack speculative taxonomies.

Black terrestrial and extraterrestrial alienness, Matthew David Goodwin claims, are both "relative concept[s]" and "relational concept[s] [. . .] about how one being sees another being. The 'alien' part [. . .] is about one being seeing another as different in some way, strange, foreign, and the like. It is not an essential quality, but one that is attributed to another being."[6] These relative and relational concepts ask us to consider how Black terrestrial and extraterrestrial alienness alternately expand and destabilize conceptions of the human, how Black and alien bodies are imagined to be visually alike, and how be(com)ing Black is a perceptual process that interpellates the body as an object, and yet simultaneously makes space for collective sociopolitical action and individual self-determination. I argue here that aliens, like Black folk, are made—not born—by *being seen*, or by becoming subject

---

4. Le Guin, "American SF and the Other," 209, 209, 210.
5. Hauman, "Heavenly Bodies," 126, 126.
6. Goodwin, *Latinx Files*, 13.

in particular spacetime to visual systems that fix and overdetermine their embodiment, movement, and social being.

In this chapter, I theorize a spectacular Black cosmic diasporic relation forged through aesthetic and political intimacies between embodied and representational forms of terrestrial and extraterrestrial life. I examine what W. J. T. Mitchell has termed "image-texts," or works that "designat[e] *relations* of the visual and verbal,"[7] including cartoons, advertisements, scientific illustrations, and amateur drawings. My purpose here is to explore how terrestrial and extraterrestrial aliens *become* Black via physiognomic strategies of *being, seeing, and being seen* in specific times, locations, and spaces, tactics that codify terrestrial and extraterrestrial Others as enfleshed Black bodies *and* as nonhuman aliens. For that reason, I argue that subjects need not be human in order to be(come) Black. Though aliens who become Black draw our attention to the many ways physiognomies of Blackness are used to alienate and destroy, I argue that be(com)ing Black can also engender systems of collective and mutual survival from below by fomenting radical acceptance of Black looks, Black community, and Black futures. In the first section, "Hierarchical Schemas: (Extra)terrestrial Physiognomy, Lines of Animality, and Embodied Form as Image-Text," I explore how astrobiologists, race scientists, alien abductees, and cartoonists turn to physiognomic methodologies in order to draw extraterrestrial, Black terrestrial, and nonhuman terrestrial animal embodiment into taxonomic alignment, specifically as image-text in cartoons and other drawings. I argue that visual constructions of interplanetary special difference are central to evolutionary discourses that attempt to fix organic life in racial categories. Through a critical reading of Johann Kaspar Lavater's 1789 *Essays on Physiognomy* [*Essais sur la Physiognomie*], arguably the most popular historical treatise on the science of physiognomy, I examine how these visual taxonomies are rooted in colonialist, imperialist, and racist constructions of hierarchized difference in which Western Man is represented as the most evolutionarily developed and aesthetically beautiful, and therefore morally and socially superior, sentient lifeform in galactic existence. Hovering between nonhuman animals and Western Man, I explore how physiognomists visually schematized aliens and Black terrestrials as lower-order organisms in contradistinction to and in intimate relation with one another.

In the second section, "Being, Seeing, and Being Seen: Racialization and the Spectacular Logics of Cartoon Physiognomy," I examine how these physiognomic taxonomies interpellate (extra)terrestrial subjects as Black

---

7. Mitchell, *Picture Theory*, 89, emphasis in original.

through systems of being, seeing, and being seen that Karen E. and Barbara J. Fields describe as "racecraft," or the often invisible structures that govern how, why, when, and where subjects can interact and co-exist. Through an analysis of Frantz Fanon's *Black Skin, White Masks* [*Peau Noire, Masque Blanc*] (1952), I explore how *techniques of seeing* interpellate subjects as objects who must navigate spacetime within the parameters of *being seen* as Black, and therefore as dysgenic non- and subhuman Others. I suggest that this visual phenomenological system is both an affective and aesthetic tentacularity that pervades all visual representation but is particularly evident in new global media technologies, such as caricature and cartoons. I frame the medium of cartooning as an intrinsically physiognomic art, and, through a reading of Rodolphe Töpffer's 1845 *Essay on Physiognomy,* the first treatise on cartoon grammar and syntax, demonstrate how systems of seeing and being seen form the foundation for social perceptions of spectacular difference.

Finally, in the final section, "Black Skin, Human Masks, Alien Form: Constructing Black (Extra)terrestrial Cartoon Counterpublics in Milestone's *Icon* (1993–1997)," I explore embodied intimacies between Black terrestrials and Black extraterrestrials in the comic series *Icon*. Icon, an extraterrestrial named Arnus who lives on Earth in a recombinated Black terrestrial form, is forced to mask his alienness not as humanness but as Blackness, which constrains and overdetermines public expression of his extraterrestrial being—and yet be(com)ing Black ultimately engenders and makes possible full expression of his alien abilities. I argue that Arnus becomes Black not only through interactions with (and resistance to) the antiblack carceral state and its systems of control, but also through an enjoinment and entanglement of self with Black community. If being seen as Black locates Arnus at the nadir of human existence as a consequence of antiblackness, it also equally enjoins him in a generative and resistant Black community *in spite of* that antiblackness. In other words, over time Arnus comes to identify with and foment Black collective liberation, using his extraterrestrial powers in service of Black life and in opposition to the violence of the antiblack state. Through the processes of be(com)ing Black by experiencing and resisting intense ontological and psychoaffective violence, *Icon* makes evident how Black communities cohere around collective politics of resistance, survival, and care. I argue that *Icon* also stages the process of becoming Black as an entanglement of self with physiognomies of Blackness, animality, and alienness, represented narratively as a preoccupation with the body—its fleshy strangeness and extraordinariness—as resistance to carceral logics, and as political identification with other Black terrestrials. I conclude by demonstrating how *Icon* reframes traditional superhero narratives by generating alternative reading strategies and cartoon counterpublics that encourage and reflect a Black gaze in opposition to depersonalizing physiognomic sightlines.

Hierarchical Schemas: (Extra)terrestrial Physiognomy, Lines of Animality, and Embodied Form as Image-Text

In the summer of 1950 at the Los Alamos National Laboratory in New Mexico, Enrico Fermi sat down for a late lunch with two other physicists, Edward Teller and Herbert York, and the nuclear scientist Emil Konopinski. The conversation gradually turned to the current national obsession with aliens and space ships, fueled by the uptick in UFO sightings in the US since 1947. In June of 1947, pilot Kenneth Arnold spotted a fleet of objects moving "like saucers across a pond" (the event that coined the term "flying saucers"), and, in July, rancher William "Mack" Brazel reported one of his fields in Roswell, New Mexico, so strewn with purple metallic debris his livestock could not graze.[8] Konopinski drew their attention to Alan Dunn's recent *New Yorker* cartoon (see figure 1).[9] The cartoon features extraterrestrial aliens on their home planet, signified by two suns hovering in the sky, unloading trash cans labeled DSNY (for the City of New York Department of Sanitation) from their fleet of three-wheeled spaceships. Dunn's extraterrestrial aliens are bipedal gray-white humanoids with heads shaped like teardrops, large oval-shaped eyes, two slits for a nose, and simple line-drawn smiles. Their embodied sameness belies no specific gender, although their shirtlessness, antennaed hats, black shoes, and being at work encourage us to read them as a kind of nonhuman man. Fermi observed that Dunn's comic, which framed the disappearance of municipal trash cans in New York City as an alien abduction, could be said to account for both the increased reports of flying saucers and NYC's missing bins.

---

8. Webb, *Where Is Everybody?*, 37, 37. Mack Brazel believed that the debris was likely due to a military operation originating from the Roswell Army Air Field (RAAF) four hours away. Though military personnel argued that the debris was from a weather balloon, early media reports that the detritus glowed purple and contained an alien script took hold in the popular imaginary. For more information about the Roswell Incident, see Kevin D. Randle, "A Grounded Theory Update on the Roswell UFO Incident," *Journal of Scientific Exploration* 36, no. 2 (2022): 264–88.

9. In April and May of 1950, hundreds of DSNY trash receptacles went missing from locations throughout the city. The receptacles were located in a Manhattan warehouse, and it was eventually determined that their removal was the result of a large-scale prank. See Staff, "First of Stolen Trash Baskets Recovered; 6 Men Face Various Charges as Aftermath," *New York Times* (New York), May 16, 1950.

FIGURE 1. Aliens departing a flying saucer while holding trash cans labeled DSNY. *The New Yorker*, May 20, 1950, Alan Dunn.

As the conversation shifted to the probability of locating extraterrestrial alien life, Fermi looked around the empty dining hall and asked, "Where is everybody?"[10] Though he was referring to his fellow Earthlings at Los Alamos, his lunchmates initially presumed he was speaking about extraterrestrials. According to legend, Fermi quickly performed a sequence of calculations and concluded that Earth should have been visited by aliens many times over *and* long ago. This discussion led to what is known as the Fermi paradox, or the disjunction between the overwhelming statistical likelihood that intelligent life exists somewhere in the universe and our lack of conclusive evidence of that existence. For that reason, the Fermi paradox might be said to owe as much to cartooning as to astrophysics.

Resolutions to the Fermi paradox are organized into three primary categories: we have never seen aliens because they do not exist—Earth's lifeforms are cosmically anomalous; intelligent aliens are "out there," but we have yet to find them; or aliens have already been to (or currently are on)

---

10. Webb, *Where Is Everybody?*, 21.

Earth. As space exploration expanded and Earthlings arrived on the moon in the decades following the lunch at Los Alamos, astronomers and physicists began to more seriously consider the possibility that life existed on other planets, research that gradually culminated in the field of astrobiology, which endeavors still to locate cosmic biosignatures and construct taxonomies of potential alien lifeforms.[11] Though in 1992 the National Aeronautics and Space Administration (NASA) briefly inaugurated a program dedicated to the search for extraterrestrial intelligence (SETI) using radio astronomy, global disinvestment in space exploration and technological limitations have rendered SETI largely philosophical, politically fringe, and entrenched in stratified Earth logics, particularly those concerning extraterrestrial alterity, social advancement, and alien biopower. For example, the Kardashev scale, developed by Nikolai Kardashev in 1964, consists of a three-tiered system (type I–III civilizations) that classifies worlds according to their technological development and energy consumption. Carl Sagan's 1970 revision shifted the scale to highlight a civilization's capacity for communication, but retained the original investments in stratification and hierarchy.[12] These cosmic "hierarchical schemas," as Hauman describes them, and their "speculative typologies of alien lifeforms" emerge from and are reinforced by processes of "racialization," imperialism, and colonialism that cannot be divorced from constructions of being on Earth.[13]

SETI research has always been driven by anxieties about extraterrestrial embodiment, made perhaps most clearly manifest in reports of alien abduction from the 1960s and 1970s. In 1961 Barney and Betty Hill, an interracial couple, claimed to have been stalked by an unidentified flying object and abducted by aliens while driving their car one night in New Hampshire.[14] The Hills alleged to have seen and touched extraterrestrial lifeforms—and,

---

11. For more on the current field of astrobiology, see Mark Voytek, Linda Billings, and Aaron L. Gronstal, *Astrobiology: A History of Exobiology and Astrobiology at NASA* (NASA Astrobiology Program, 2022). See also NASA's website, https://astrobiology.nasa.gov.

12. Kardashev argued that Type I civilizations consumed only terrestrial sources of power, Type II would be able to harness the energy of its own star, and Type III would be capable of using energy at a galactic scale. See Robert H. Gray, "The Extended Kardashev Scale," *The Astronomical Journal* 159, no. 228 (2020): 1–5; and Carl Sagan, *The Cosmic Connection: An Extraterrestrial Perspective* (Cambridge: Cambridge University Press, 2000).

13. Hauman, "Heavenly Bodies," 125.

14. Barney Hill was a Black man, and his wife, Betty, was white. For more on the Hill abduction, see Matthew Bowman, *The Abduction of Betty and Barney Hill: Alien Encounters, Civil Rights, and the New Age in America* (New Haven: Yale University Press, 2023); and Jonathan Jacob Moore, "Starships and Slave Ships: Black Ontology and the UFO Abduction Phenomenon," *Qui Parle* 31, no. 1 (June 2022): 143–58.

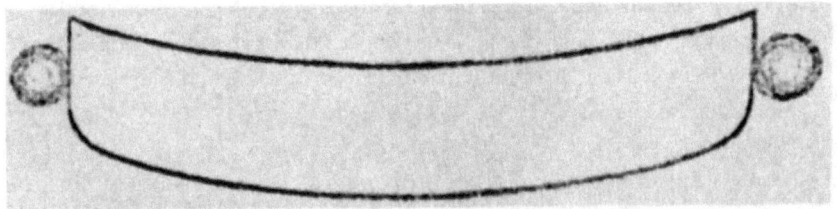

UFO as seen by Betty Hill in first encounter
From sketch by Betty Hill

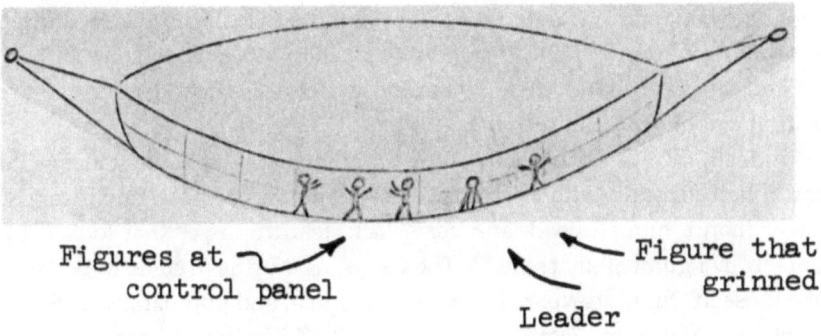

UFO as seen by Barney Hill showing figures, "fins," and red lights
From sketch by Barney Hill

FIGURE 2. Barney and Betty Hill's renderings of an extraterrestrial spacecraft. Drawings appear in *The Interrupted Journey: Two Lost Hours Aboard a Flying Saucer*, by John Fuller.

after undergoing medical hypnosis, drew and described them. Barney Hill's drawing of the UFO that abducted him (see figure 2), with its round, flat shape and circular bank of windows, closely resembles Dunn's illustration, as does his narrative description of alien embodiment:

> The men [ETs] had rather odd-shaped heads, with a large cranium, diminishing in size as it got toward the chin. And the eyes continued around to the sides of the heads, so that it appeared that they could see several degrees beyond the lateral extent of our vision. [. . .] And something [else] that I remembered [. . .] is the mouth itself. [. . .] But it was much like when you draw one horizontal line with a short perpendicular line on each end. [. . .] The texture of the skin [. . .] was grayish, almost metallic looking. I

didn't notice any hair—or headgear for that matter. Also, I didn't notice any proboscis; there just seemed to be two slits that represented the nostrils [. . .] so it looked as if the mouth had almost no opening and as if they had practically no nose.[15]

As John F. Moffitt explains, Barney's image-text depictions of the "distinctive physiognomy" of the alien as gray-skinned, large-eyed, big-headed, triangle-faced humanoids "would prove central to all forthcoming [. . .] canonical ET iconography." Textual descriptions combined with drawings or sketches are similarly fundamental to representations of extraterrestrial embodiment—Moffitt notes that, given the lack of photographic evidence, alien "physiognomy is only made known to us visually in the medium of *grissaille* drawings."[16] Hill's image-text depiction of aliens remains the earliest and most successful attempts to physiognomically taxonomize extraterrestrial embodied form.

Indeed, the "Generic Alien," Toby Smith explains, is "a humanoid, four and a half feet tall, with a large hairless cranium, flat nose, small ears set lower than a human head, and coal-black, teardrop eyes that looked like slots from a gumball machine."[17] The Grays, as they have come to be called, like those in Dunn's cartoon, Barney's image-text, and popularized in Steven Spielberg's 1979 film *Close Encounters of the Third Kind*, are the most recognizable and widely reported alien lifeform.[18] These extraterrestrial image-texts are not politically neutral, however. Our collective imaginings of extraterrestrial alien embodiment and so-called intelligence are tied to constructions of ecological difference on Earth, and therefore frequently reproduce arguments that maintain the joint biological supremacy of the human and the white European (male). Goodwin explains that "race has often been correlated with biological concepts [. . .] and therefore correlates with the species difference between humans and space aliens. [. . .] The use of race to construct the space alien renders the figure [. . .] a particularly potent tool because the space alien fixes racial difference as biology and essence"—and, moreover, in popular descriptions of extraterrestrial embodiment, "race-color is [. . .] almost always connected in some way to an essentialized vision

---

15. Fuller, *Interrupted Journey*, 49. Written in conjunction with the Hills, Fuller's text is an authoritative exploration of their abduction experience.
16. Moffitt, *Picturing Extraterrestrials*, 150, 164.
17. Smith, *Little Gray Men*, 113–14.
18. For more information on our perceptions of alien lifeforms, see Don Lincoln, *Alien Universe: Extraterrestrial Life in Our Minds and in the Cosmos* (Baltimore: Johns Hopkins University Press, 2013); and Neil Badmington, *Alien Chic: Posthumanism and the Other Within* (London: Routledge, 2004).

of racial difference."[19] Barney and Betty were most compelled by their captors' flesh and skin, evidenced by Betty's description of their dark pigmentation, a distinction that functioned for her as a marker of their combined biological, special, and racial difference: "Their complexions were of a gray tone; like a gray paint with a very black base; their lips were of a bluish tint. Hair and eyes were very dark, possibly black."[20] This description of "very black base" of their skin, a sign of their dysgenicity and fleshy strangeness, draws them into phenotypical (and therefore racial) alignment with other very Black terrestrial bodies—including Barney's.

The Hills's understanding of extraterrestrial form was informed by a lecture delivered by Harvard anthropologist Carleton S. Coon; their captors, Barney explained, closely resembled Coon's description of "group of Indians" who lived near the Magellan Straits, "where there was little oxygen. [. . .] They had Oriental sort of eyes."[21] In his virulently racist 1962 tome *The Origin of the Races*, Coon hierarchically ordered human life in five categories based on visible differences by situating Indigenous Africans at the lowest possible rung of human evolutionary development. Coon supported these claims, David Drysdale explains, "with photographs of African persons in close proximity to photographs of lemurs, chimpanzees, and gorillas." By turning to an astrobiological physiognomy rooted in colonialist and imperialist taxonomies of human life, and by aligning extraterrestrials at the bottom of a racialized chain of being in which they are both sub- and nonhuman, Drysdale argues that "the Hills reproduce [. . . a] raciological discourse of skin and bone" and advance an "epidermal schema"—a dermopolitics—that "attests to the persistence of scientific racism and biopolitics."[22] In other words, the Hills's image-text accounts of extraterrestrial embodiment render aliens radically Other by bringing them into taxonomic complicity with imperialist constructions of special and organismic difference on Earth.

The Hills and Coon were not, of course, alone in their deployment of a dermopolitical hierarchy of (extra)terrestriality. At the end of the nineteenth century and the start of the twentieth century in Europe and the US, eugenicists and scientific racists, including Francis Galton, August Weismann, Comte Joseph-Arthur de Gobineau, Vacher de Lapouge, Madison Grant, and Lothrop Stoddard, among many others, developed theories of special variation and evolution that were designed to confirm the biological supremacy of white northern and western Europeans, and affirm the

---

19. Goodwin, *Latinx Files*, 16–17.
20. Fuller, *Interrupted Journey*, 298.
21. Fuller, *Interrupted Journey*, 262.
22. Drysdale, "Alienated Histories, Alienating Future," 105, 113.

endemic inferiority of the colonial Other. Central to these eugenic claims were constructions of "hard heredity" that framed so-called congenital characteristics, including race, sex, geography, intelligence, and physical ability, as unalterable predictors of individual potential. The Hills's conflation of extraterrestrial alien embodiment with Coon's "Indians" is an example of hard heredity in action; according to their eugenic evolutionary logics, aliens, Indians, and Black folk are products of an "inherited racial essence"[23] that no shift in spacetime or genetics could alter. Proponents of hard heredity advanced negative eugenics campaigns that encouraged people of European descendancy to avoid mixing their bloodlines with inferior stock, or to sterilize (or outright eliminate) subjects whose difference was deemed too endemic to be bred out.

Smith observes that the desire to know "what [. . .] an alien really look[s] like" has pervaded scientific and popular discourses—in particular, the "alien's color and physical characteristics have been all-consuming." I argue that this is at least in part due to the emphasis in eugenics on "directly sensed evidence."[24] Even as scientists turned their attention to microscopic phenomena, such as cells, seeds, or atoms, their obsession with visually identifiable traits as an essential loci of special existence persisted as visual logics used to classify, represent, and organize sentient life. This preoccupation with seeing, rendering, and ordering (extra)terrestrial embodiment cannot be separated from a dermopolitics that places, again, *observable* difference at the center of scientific inquiry into race, evolution, and ability. I situate these efforts in the optic logics of physiognomy, the eugenic race science popularized by the late eighteenth-century Swiss intellectual Johann Kaspar Lavater, and further instrumentalized by scientific racists in the late nineteenth and twentieth centuries. Physiognomy and phrenology, a related science, were once deemed legitimate and effective approaches to codifying special difference, and have therefore influenced scientific understandings of race and the body. I turn to Lavater not only because physiognomy concretizes hard heredity as an optic politic, but because it additionally functionalizes racial and special difference as a spectacular phenomenon.

In *Essays on Physiognomy* [*Essais sur la Physiognomie*] (1789), Lavater describes physiognomy as a science that correlates an individual's "visible superficies" with their character and ability, or "invisible contents."[25] Lavater insists that "all men (this is indisputable) [. . .] estimate all things, whatever, by their physiognomy, their exterior [. . .] superficies," and from

---

23. Drysdale, "Alienated Histories, Alienating Future," 70.
24. Smith, *Little Gray Men*, 2; and Drysdale, "Alienated Histories, Alienating Future," 68.
25. Lavater, *Essays on Physiognomy*, 10. Further citations to this work are in the text.

them "draw [. . .] conclusions concerning their internal properties" (10–12). In other words, physiognomy formalizes a process for determining a person's moral and intellectual capabilities based on an analysis of the structures of their appearance. According to the physiognomist, a subject's body shape, size, and musculature, facial features and composition, and skull shape and size are external manifestations of an endemic internal capability: "Every thing in man [. . .] is congenital: form, stature, complexion, hair, skin, veins, nerves, bones, voice, walk, manner, style, passion, love, hatred. [. . .] He has a determinate sphere in which his powers and sensations are allowed, within which they may be freely exercised, but beyond which he cannot pass" (180). As an optic model predicated on the eugenic logic of hard heredity, physiognomy holds that physical form is destiny, that all organic special difference observable on the skin is also bone deep, as intrinsic as marrow. In Lavater's view, no "Ethiopian can change his skin, or the leopard his spots" (227).

Physiognomy foments a dermopolitical gaze by ranking sentient beings according to physical characteristics observed on the surface of their bodies. To that end, physiognomists examine

> the gradations of form in men and animals, and regularly [. . .] systematize and define, in a physiognomically-mathematical manner, the peculiar and absolutely fundamental lines [. . .] delineating the transition from brutal deformity to ideal beauty, from satanical hideousness and malignity to divine exaltation; from the animality of the frog or the monkey, to the beginning humanity of the Samoiede [Indigenous people of Siberia] and thence to that of a Newton and Kant. (493–94)

This interspecial taxonomy does not offer different scales for embodied forms. Frogs and monkeys, colonial subjects, and European intellectuals are aesthetically linked, even as they are brought into radical biological contradistinction with one another. Lavater's physiognomic scale simultaneously reinforces and challenges the idea of special isolation, and, though this does not lessen the violence of physiognomy, it offers up space for understanding why, for example, the Hills's representations of alien embodiment are intimately bound up in visual constructions of colonial subjects, Black bodies, and nonhuman animals.

This hierarchical progression of aesthetic embodiment from the nonhuman animal to "the Apollo" is centrally predicated on "the form of the skull and bones"—these, Lavater insists, constitute a "magical mirror" which "shows us [. . .] the depression and elevation of our internal power" (494).

Lavater ranks nonhumans, subhumans, humans, and gods according to "*angles of the lines of the countenance*" constituted by a measurement of "the angle of the profile [. . .] which extends either from the closing of the teeth to the cavity of the ear, and the utmost protuberance of the forehead; or the extreme end of the nose to the outer angle of the eye, and the corner of the mouth" (494, emphasis in original). Between the seventieth and eightieth degree are "all creatures which we comprehend as man" (495). Unsurprisingly, the "most beautiful European" is fixed at the highest degree, only exceeded by the countenances of "divinities and heroes" above the eightieth degree, who are decidedly something other than human. At seventy degrees, Black people represent the lowest possible angle of the human, after which any "further diminution soon loses all trace of resemblance to humanity," as is evidenced in the immediate declension from "negro" to orangutan, tailed ape, dog, frog, bird, and, finally, insect (495).

Closer to the animality of the frog and monkey than the humanity of the European or suprahumanity of Apollo, "the negro" serves as a racial-special hinge between the animal and the human, emerging, Joshua Bennett argues, as "a subgenre of the human, always already positioned in fraught proximity to animal life." Though configured as distinct from nonhuman animals in important ways, Black people remain "a lower order of organism,"[26] congenitally incapable of creating civilization, inventing new things, having novel ideas, or navigating the stars; indeed, Isaac Newton, Lavater's shorthand for the apex of intelligent European Man, could never "have invented the theory of life, residing in the head of a negro," just as no amount of "education can arch the skull of the negro like that of the star-conversant astronomer" (272). Black people, like animals, are "sociolegal *nonpersons*," "co-constructed as living flesh but never as *bodies*," or rather as nonhuman objects that are meant to be put to use.[27]

Physiognomy squarely locates these co-constructions as image-text, represented by Lavater as eighty line illustrations featuring caricatures of real and imagined peoples, and hierarchical gradations of sentient being. Lavater believed that "drawing is the first, most natural, and most unequivocal language of physiognomy; the best aid of the imagination, the only means of preserving and communicating numberless peculiarities, shades, and expressions, which are not by words, or any other mode, to be described" (66). His artistic style was influenced by European artists such as Albrecht Dürer and Raphael, and by other naturalists, scientists, and philosophers, including Johann Joachim Winckelmann, Samuel Thomas von Sömmering,

---

26. Bennett, *Being Property Once Myself*, 4–5, 9.
27. Bennett, *Being Property Once Myself*, 9, emphasis in original.

FIGURE 3. "Plate LXXVIII" and "Plate LXXIX." Johann Kaspar Lavater's visual taxonomy from frogs to Roman gods in profile. *Essay on Physiognomy*, Johann Kaspar Lavater, 1853.

and Georges-Louis Leclerc, Comte de Buffon, who were similarly invested in classifying sentient life based on visible racialized characteristics.[28] The drawings in *Essays on Physiognomy* bear this out directly (see figure 3). Lavater includes a sequence of illustrated plates that feature "a gradual transition from the head of a frog to the Apollo" (496), in which colonial subjects, nonhuman animals, and Black bodies are brought into taxonomic uniformity. Represented by images 1–4, frogs are "the swollen representative of disgusting bestiality" (496), among the lowest forms of nonhuman animal life given their bulbous eyes, and flat foreheads and jaws. Though image 5 is still a lower-order organism, its lines of animality indicate that it "is no longer a frog" (496). Lavater here enters into an entirely speculative realm by taxonomizing embodied forms that do not exist among Earth organisms.

28. For more on eighteenth-century race science, see Bronwen Douglas, "Notes on 'Race' and the Biologisation of Human Difference," *The Journal of Pacific History* 40, no. 3 (2005): 331–38; Nicholas Hudson, "From 'Nation' to 'Race': The Origin of Racial Classification in Eighteenth-Century Thought," *Eighteenth-Century Studies* 29, no. 3 (1996): 247–64; Londa Schiebinger, "The Anatomy of Difference: Race and Sex in Eighteenth-Century Science," *Eighteenth Century Studies* 23, no. 4 (1990): 387–405; and Roxann Wheeler, *The Complexion of Race: Categories of Difference in Eighteenth-Century British Culture* (Philadelphia: University of Pennsylvania Press, 2000).

Images 5–11 instead represent an imaginary liminal racialized species visually aligned with the frog but something else altogether, an organism that is becoming by literal degrees more human and less animal, but that remains neither. Halfway through Lavater's speculative morphology, immediately following "the line of the countenance of the orang-outang," at image 12 we arrive at "the lowest degree of humanity" representing "the negro," whose "very projecting nose and defined lips decisively indicate commencing humanity" (496). By occupying the precise middle between the frog and the Apollo, the "negro" is visually aligned with the nonhuman and speculative animal, configured as a being yet-to-approach humanity, and as a dysgenic human. Neither fully nonhuman animal nor terrestrial human, Black folk are visually (and therefore racially, specially, morally) closest to Lavater's speculative species that is not quite nonhuman animal but not yet Man.

As Zakiyyah Iman Jackson makes clear, Lavater's physiognomy evidences how "anxieties about conquest, slavery, and colonial expansionism provided the historical context for [. . .] the emergence of a developmental model of [. . .] a newly consolidated generic 'animal' that would be defined in both nonhuman *and* human terms. In this context, discourses on 'the animal' and 'the black' were conjoined and are now mutually reinforcing narratives in the traveling racializations of the globalizing West." Lavater's image-text makes plain how "black(ened) people are the living border dividing forms of life such that 'the animal' is a category that may apply to animals and some humans"—in other words, the construct of the "animal" "crosses lines of species." In this physiognomic model, Black people "qualify as human but only tentatively so, given their purported physical or mental similarity to nonhuman animals and vice versa." As a consequence, the "animal" emerges as a transspecial racializing category of embodiment and enfleshment in which *"blackness [. . . is] defined as the emblematic state of animal man, as the nadir of the human."* In this system, "discourses on nonhuman animals and animalized humans are forged through each other; they reflect and refract each other for the purposes of producing an idealized and teleological conception of the human."[29] I argue that discourses amalgamating nonhuman animals and animalized humans also invoke the embodied form of the extraterrestrial alien. As the extraterrestrial alien is brought into physiognomic intimacy with animalized humans inherently inferior to Western Man, so too is the alien framed as a kind of animal, a racialized Black(ened) being who, like Lavater's negro, is, again, not quite a nonhuman animal and not yet Man.

---

29. Jackson, *Becoming Human*, 14; 22; 22, emphasis in original; 23.

Barney Hill, under hypnosis, drew the above sketch of the "leader" of the alleged abductors. Later, while listening to the tape recording of his own account of the incident, he seemed to go into a trancelike state and drew the below more-finished sketch. The eyes were elongated, he said, and the lips appeared to have no muscles.

FIGURE 4. Barney Hill's drawings of the aliens who abducted him and his wife, Betty. Drawings appear in *The Interrupted Journey: Two Lost Hours Aboard a Flying Saucer,* by John Fuller.

FIGURE 5. "Plate LXXX." Johann Kaspar Lavater's visual taxonomy from frogs to Apollo. *Essay on Physiognomy*, Johann Kaspar Lavater, 1853.

Dunn's cartoon and Barney Hill's drawing of his alien abductor (see figure 4) make this connection visually clear. According to Lavater's frontal scale (see figure 5), the frog is represented at 1, the "negro" at 5. I locate the extraterrestrial alien's large eyes, small chin, and slender nose in the speculative terrain between the frog and "negro," which is imagined to be more "humanoid" than the bestial frog, but less human than the animalized "negro." I argue that the extraterrestrial serves as a border between the sheer abasement of the purely nonhuman animal and the commencing humanity of Black peoples. Unlike the frog and negro, however, the extraterrestrials in both Dunn's and Hill's drawings have large skulls, an indication in Lavater's physiognomy of suprahumanity, or an embodied form that also points away from the human to speculative celestiality. That the alien hovers specially between the nonhuman animal and the Black(ened) animalized human but is visually linked to the celestial domain is telling—extraterrestrials reinforce constructions of Black subjects as dysgenic beings, as animalized humans, and as galactic nonhuman Others. Physiognomic constructions of extraterrestrial aliens as Black(ened) and animalized beings in their own right are key to making sense of how and why extraterrestrial aliens function in the American popular imaginary, and how they are used to construct Black terrestrial, extraterrestrial, and animal being in kind.

Being, Seeing, and Being Seen: Racialization and the Spectacular Logics of Cartoon Physiognomy

I argued in the previous section that physiognomists hierarchize Black people, extraterrestrial aliens, and nonhuman animals (specifically frogs and monkeys) according to their "visible superficies," constructing them as dysgenic beings whose physical appearance is evidence of their sub- or nonhumanity. Karen E. Fields and Barbara J. Fields describe this process as "racecraft," or a tentacular public/private system of perception—visual, social, cultural, political, scientific, and legal—that "transforms racism into race [by] disguising collective social practice as inborn individual traits."[30] More specifically, Fields and Fields contend that racecraft "*govern[s] what goes with what and whom (sumptuary codes), how different people must deal with each other (rituals of deference and dominance), where human kinship begins and ends (blood), and how Americans look at themselves and each other (the gaze). These ideas do not exist purely in the mind, or only in one mind. They are social facts.*"[31] In other words, racecraft is a function of everyday lived experience, shaping in multiple interlocking ways how we move through the world, interact with one another, and (co)exist.

---

30. Fields and Fields, *Racecraft*, 19. For more information about the science of physiognomic seeing, see Ran Hassin and Yaacov Trope, "Facing Faces: Studies on the Cognitive Aspects of Physiognomy," *Journal of Personal and Social Psychology* 78, no. 5 (2000): 837–52.

31. Fields and Fields, *Racecraft*, 25, emphasis in original.

Of particular interest here is *the gaze,* or what Fields and Fields describe as the process of learning *how to see* other beings as racialized bodies, and, correspondingly, how to turn them into racialized beings *by seeing* them; to that end, the gaze as a physiognomic analytic, predicated on "what another person looks like, at a glance, to a viewer observing quickly and superficially." In the United States, for example, people "observe themselves and each other through their own eyes and those of others, all the while classifying and evaluating. Thus racecraft has an inner horizon that turns out to be densely populated with sometimes peculiarly selected physical traits. A living person, to be met presently, ascribes meaning to the shape of his jawbone." In these "intimate yet public practices that organize individual perception of physical appearance," people are transformed from a "seeing subject" into a "seen object," in which their capacity to look at themselves and/or look back is obliterated by the force of the taxonomic gaze. I argue that seen objects experience themselves as *being seen,* rather than as simply *being,* and that, as a consequence of this physiognomic gaze, subjects can *become* Black. Blackness is understood here not as a biological identity but as a spatiotemporal metamorphosis, a sociolegal event, a racecraftian sightline that takes stock of visible physical features, or attributes "which simply are what they are," and ascribes to them either grotesque or positive qualities, all while expanding, collapsing, and collating intersecting matrices of colonial and imperial fantasies and anxieties about racialized bodies. As "racecraft's inner horizon [. . .] inhabit[s] perception itself," "split-second judgement explosively merge[s] a person with a stereotype," radically altering the seen object's self-perception and ability to move unencumbered through space.[32]

From the first glance to a prolonged gaze, racecraft shapes not only *how* we see what we see and *what* we see when we see, but what *images* we produce of ourselves and others, how we read them, and how they make us feel. According to Alia Al-Saji, "racialization describes the ways in which colonialism and white supremacy divide bodies politically, economically, spatially, and socially in order to dominate them. Racialization comprises [. . .] the historical social, economic, epistemological, and affective processes—the (de)structuring violence and colonizing formations—by which races are constructed, seen, and, when interiorized or 'epidermalized,' lived." Like Fields and Fields, Al-Saji configures racialization as a dermopolitical perceptual system, or an "imaginary constellation [. . .] acquired through childhood education, scholarly manuals, language, media, comic books, stories, films,

---

32. Fields and Fields, *Racecraft,* 70, 70, 70, 70, 72.

and images. As a result, particular ways of imagining, thinking, and seeing become normative." This imaginary constellation has historically codified Blackness as a permanent, heritable marker of dysgenicity, aesthetic inferiority, and moral degeneracy. As the "racialized self is put together by others,"[33] seen objects apprehended as Black are endlessly concretized, (re)circulated, and (re)invented by a violently reductive gaze.

Al-Saji notes that Frantz Fanon's 1952 philosophical treatise *Black Skin, White Masks* [*Peau Noire, Masques Blancs*] examines "how racialization not only structures how bodies are represented and perceived, but also configures our affective, perceptual, and cognitive maps, our imaginary and aesthetic life."[34] Fanon outlines what I describe as a visual theory of *being, seeing,* and *being seen,* in which a white gaze transfigures seeing subjects into seen objects. Fanon's explication of this transfiguration lays bare the ontological, visual phenomenological, and affective dimensions of racecraft, and demonstrates how physiognomy functions as an (at times) inescapable visual system. Fanon's first-person-narrative explications of the precise moments he becomes Black are instructive; he begins with a description of two phrases hurled in his direction by a white child, while riding a train in the imperial metropole one afternoon: "'Dirty n——r!' or simply 'Look! A Negro!'" It happens all at once: the depersonalizing sightline of the child's "white gaze" transforms Fanon into "an object among other objects," or, more precisely, he is remade as a member of "a new species. A Negro, in fact!" As a consequence, Fanon's originary "body schema" was shattered and replaced; or, rather, he experienced the "slow construction of my self as a body in a spatial and temporal world—such seems to be the schema. It is [. . .] a definitive structuring of my self and the world—definitive because it creates a genuine dialectic between my body and the world." Being seen and speciated as a "Negro" by a "solely negating" white gaze arrests Fanon in spacetime by restructuring his "self" as a nonspecific dysgenic Black "body." Under the power of that gaze, Fanon argued that "I am *fixed.*"[35]

The process of being seen and fixed as Black and fungible—an object among other objects, a body belonging to a nonperson—produces in Fanon a "historical-racial schema," in which the white gaze "had woven me out of a thousand details, anecdotes, stories," and an "epidermal racial schema," in which "my body is returned to me spread-eagled, disjointed, redone [. . .] the Negro is an animal, the Negro is bad, the Negro is wicked, the Negro is ugly; look, a Negro." This gaze ascribes definite meaning to Fanon's body.

---

33. Al-Saji, "Glued to the Image," 476, 476, 478.
34. Al-Saji, "Glued to the Image," 476.
35. Fanon, *Black Skin, White Masks,* 89; 89, 95; 91; 90; 95, emphasis in original.

By becoming a Negro, he is also made "animal," "bad," "wicked," "ugly," and entangled in antiaesthetic relation to dysgenic subhumans and nonhuman animals as a new Black non- and subhuman species. As a consequence of "being aware of my body," or transitioning from an orginary state of *being* to *being seen* as Black by way of this depersonalizing, speciating, and (re)(de)corporealizing white gaze, Fanon comes to "exis[t] in triple." Seen objects become simultaneously aware of themselves as themselves, as embodied objects among other objects, and as repositories for speculative imperialist fantasies about Black form. As a consequence of being seen as Black, Fanon becomes "responsible not only for my body but also for my race and ancestors. I cast an objective gaze over myself, discovered my blackness, my ethnic features; deafened by cannibalism, backwardness, fetishism, racial stigmas, slave traders, and above all, yes, above all, the grinning *Ya bon Banania*. [. . .] I transported myself [. . .] very far, from my self, and gave myself up as an object."[36] Fanon's speciation as Negro recasts his "self" as an indistinct Black "body" immediately visible in his "ethnic features," and informed by a welter of mythical-ideological constructions of Black being and doing that circulate in the minds, cultures, and texts of the seeing subject and seen object alike.

For that reason, Fanon insists that "besides phylogeny and ontogeny there stands sociogeny," or his perception that people become subject to sociocultural forces, structures, and systems—their lived experiences—that are as determinative as evolutionary and organismic development. Wynter argues that racialization can therefore be seen as a spatiotemporal event during which time Fanon "begins to experience himself through the mediation of stereotyped concepts *specific to a particular point of view* and *visual phenomenology*; in other words, *not* as he is, but as *he must be for* a particular point of view." In the process of seeing himself in the third person as a self, a disconnected body, and a cache of "stereotyped concepts," Fanon becomes "the negative other to the human" and is assimilated into "a mode of the human so irrational that it constituted the missing link between [. . .] rational human species and [. . .] animal species."[37] I read Fanonian triple consciousness as a form of experience that is visual and dermopolitical, affective and material, and a mode of being seen in which the "Negro" emerges as a hinge species between Western Man and the nonhuman animal, literally and figuratively drawn from immediate perceptions about their bodies.

The image-text that most critically arrests Fanon—"above all, yes, above all"—is that of the *bonhomme Banania*, introduced by the French company

---

36. Fanon, *Black Skin, White Masks*, 92, 93; 92; 92.
37. Fanon, *Black Skin, White Masks*, 15; Wynter, "Towards the Sociogenic Principle," 43, emphasis in original; 44.

FIGURE 6. "Y'a bon Banania." Lithograph of Banania advertisement, 1915, Bibliothèque Nationale de France, Département Estampes et Photographie, ENT DN-1n(CAMIS)-GRAND ROUL.

Banania in 1915 to market its beverage mix (see figure 6). The advertisement featured a lithograph of a *tirailleur sénégalais*, or Senegalese riflemen who fought for the French Colonial Empire during WWI and were stationed at depots throughout colonial Africa.[38] The *tirailleur* is depicted in the traditional colonial horizon blue uniform with red trim, thickly wound blue

---

38. Though the soldiers were amalgamated as Senegalese, the troops were actually composed of a broad mixture of peoples from sub-Saharan Africa. For more information on Senegalese riflemen, see *"Tirailleurs sénégalais*: quelques objets du Musée," *mag'MA: Le Magazine du Musée de l'Armée*, January 16, 2023, https://www.musee-armee.fr/magazine/tirailleurs-senegalais-quelques-objets-du-musee.html.

socks, heavy leather shoes, and a bright red chechia with tassel, a uniform almost exclusively worn by *tirailleurs* in Africa. Africa is more obliquely evoked in the lithograph's near-empty natural background, reinforcing colonial perceptions of the continent's desolateness and lack of civilization. The *tirailleur* rests upon an unopened wooden crate of product, lifting a spoonful of Banania from a metal cup into his wide grinning mouth. His skin is dark brown, with black and blue highlights that accentuate and reinforce its darkness, his teeth large, uneven, and bright white, eyebrows arched in overexaggerated delight. The advertisement's slogan—"Y'a bon," or "It's good"—is a form of pidgin French, an imperial fantasy of a folksy, ignorant African speech. Though the image of *tirailleur* is not precisely a caricature, it is nevertheless grotesque. As Anne Donadey explains, because the beverage was "intended for private consumption, was to be kept in one of the most private spaces of the home (the kitchen, a space earmarked for women as well), and was targeting children as its main market, Banania images could only be the most peaceful, asexual and nonthreatening of representations." These "Banania-type images" circulated representations of "benevolent, domesticated otherness" that rested alongside and in startling intimacy with "images of cannibalism and bloodthirsty, animal-like rebel warriors."[39] Though the *tirailleur* appears to singularly invoke the colonialist fantasy of a happy and docile indigene who joyfully consumes the empire's goods while under occupation, it masks adjacent constructions of Africans as violent and dangerous.

Fantastical Banania-type images of colonial inferiority, the authors of *NégriPub* explain, appeared as image-text in many forms and on a variety of products, including posters, "cardboard, metal, or Bakelite packaging, wooden sculptures, bottles, ceramic or porcelain figurines, pottery, dolls, every day or decorative objects, record sleeves, covers of musical scores, postcards or sales cards, calendars, announcements, etc."[40] By mapping white colonial and imperial perceptions of Blackness onto a range of easily accessible and widely used home goods proliferated in both public and private spheres, these images and the products associated with them worked to interpellate Black terrestrials throughout the diaspora as seen objects. In the US, figures such as Aunt Jemima, Uncle Ben, Cream of Wheat's Rastus, and the Fairbank's Gold Dust Twins were associated with domestic labor and food consumption, and they served as in-home reminders of a mythical

---

39. Donadey, "'Y'a bon Banania,'" 14, 14.
40. Bachollet et al., *NégriPub*, 12. All translations my own. [*emballages en carton, en métal ou en bakélite, sculptures sur bois, bouteilles, figurines en céramique ou porcelaine, poteries, poupées, objets usuels ou décoratifs, envellopes de disques, couvertures de partitions musicales, cartes postales ou commercialies, calendriers, annonces, etc*].

US South replete with submissive, happy slaves eager to continue serving their white masters. *NégriPub* notes that the image of "the Black West Indian appears frequently, and still today, on posters and labels of exotic products, such as cane sugar, rum, or bananas."[41] Rather than feature representations of blissful domestic servitude, advertising images from the Caribbean tended to show Black people laboring in fields in conditions reminiscent of slavery. That said, *NégriPub* argues that it is a mistake to read globalized images of Black people in Africa, the Caribbean, and the US as discrete and unrelated, given that

> these three currents of representation, initially linked to the geographical origin of each subject—the more or less emancipated slave of the West Indies or America, the savage of Africa, and the civilized apprentice of Europe—combine, mix, oppose, and, through their fantastical imbrication in the Western imagination, contribute to removing from the Black subject their own qualities in order to make them an undifferentiated and anonymous being.[42]

As this miasma of antiblack imagery circumambulates the globe, Black seen objects are brought into taxonomic alignment with historical-racial and epidermal-racial constructions of Black dysgenicity.

David Bindman locates the aesthetic systematization of this visual phenomenological process in the art and visual culture of the nineteenth century, during which time "widespread distribution of ideas of race [. . . were found in] popular everyday imagery, mainly advertisements. Such works were enabled by the enormous technological advances in reproductive media like lithography and machine printing, which resulted, through mass-produced images and 'humorous' coloured prints, in the creation of vast numbers of demeaning stereotypes mainly of those of African descent in Europe and the Americas."[43] During this same period, as the Banania ad makes clear, the aestheticization of African peoples resulted in a global visual culture that generated colonial representations of the inherent savagery, physical

---

41. Bachollet et al., *NégriPub*, 15. [*le Noir antillais apparaît fréquemment, et encore de nos jours, dans les affiches et les étiquettes de produits exotiques, comme le sucre de canne, le rhum ou la banane*].

42. Bachollet et al., *NégriPub*, 16. [*ces trois courants de représentation, liés initialement à l'origine géographique des uns et des autres—l'ancien esclave plus ou moins émancipé des Antilles ou d'Amérique, le sauvage d'Afrique et l'apprenti civilisé d'Europe—se conjuguent, se mélangent, s'opposent, se superposent et, par leur imbrication fantaisiste dans l'imaginaire occidental, contribuent à retirer au Noir ses qualités propres pour en faire un être identique et anonyme*].

43. Bindman, *Race Is Everything*, 30.

difference, and lack of civilization of Africans and their descendants. This increasingly technologized visual culture was explicitly grounded in what Bindman terms an "art of physiognomy" that structured and gave meaning to representations of embodied form in all artistic mediums, including painting, lithography, photography, and drawing. As art and visual cultural technologies became more easily and widely circulated, stereotyped representations of dysgenic Black bodies appeared everywhere as image-text in an increasing variety of forms, from postcards to food products to newspaper caricature.

I argue that the most consequential and most frequently overlooked physiognomic art form to appear in the nineteenth century was that of the cartoon. Indeed, Fanon himself asks us to "look at children's comics books: all the Blacks are mouthing the ritual, 'Yes, boss.'" Early cartoons were almost entirely grotesque caricatures of colonial subjects and immigrants, images Rebecca Wanzo describes as "visual imperialism"—caricature is, to that end, "a way of excessively marking difference," "a means of describing how people are seen and the caricatured subjects' relationship to the communities they inhabit." These highly exaggerated renderings of racialized bodies often highlighted the subject's aesthetic and biologic inferiority and sociopolitical incompetence, all while justifying and glorifying the ongoing violence of the state. Cartooning is also an extension and aesthetic systemization of Lavater's physiognomic science. Art Spiegelman has argued that comic art is composed of "charged or loaded image[s]" that "mak[e] use of the discredited pseudoscientific principles of physiognomy to portray character through a few physical attributes and facial expressions."[44] I agree that all cartoons, caricature or otherwise, grapple with and respond to the functionalization of physiognomy as a visual logic, and therefore must also contend with processes of being, seeing, and being seen.

The new media technology of cartooning was invented in the nineteenth century by Swiss artist Rodolphe Töpffer as a way to narrate images across space and time. E. Wiese explains that in his 1845 text "Essay on Physiognomy," Töpffer defined comics as "visual art as a sign-system" with an in-built "physiognomic syntax." Töpffer made the case that cartoonists "do not need to build [. . . cartoon] grammar, [because] a hierarchical ordering of expressive shapes [. . .] exists already in the human face. [. . .] Involuntarily, we scan a set of features to classify correctly, as friend or foe, the stranger bearing them. The job of the physiognomic artist is to discover the

---

44. Fanon, *Black Skin, White Masks*, 17; Wanzo, *Content of Our Caricature*, 4; and Spiegelman, "Drawing Blood," 45.

fundamental rules according to which we instinctively 'read' the character, capabilities, and immediate emotional set of the individual confronting us." In other words, cartoons transform physiognomy into a visual language operating in two-dimensional narrative spacetime. Töpffer's cartoon system of signs was intended to function as "an intelligible grammar of physiognomic expression," in which "human features [do . . .] not merely [. . .] invoke a mood but [. . .] convey precise information to the observer."[45] Cartoon language therefore represents beings according to permanent and non-permanent signs. Non-permanent signs are "fixed and reliable indicators of any given expression—laughter, tears, fright, or whatever," and therefore do not shift face-to-face: a smile is a smile, a frown a frown, no matter who does it. Permanent signs, on the other hand, articulate a range of "positive" expressions of being, including high "intelligence," "strength and delicacy," "energy, power, and tumultuous passion," "nobility," and beauty, in addition to dysgenic "negative" expressions of being, such as "stupidity," "mental weakness," "depravity," and ugliness. Permanent signs are variable and changeable from being to being, but become most apparent in the "shape of the forehead, eyes, or nose [. . .] the mouth, the chin." Depending on their shape, angle, and placement on the face, combination with expressive signs, and the text's narrative action, eyes can be "stupid," noses "melancholy—sly—sad—indignant,"[46] or mouths cruel. Over time, repetition of these permanent and non-permanent signs forms a critical vocabulary that functions as easily deployable markers of embodied form.

Töpffer was opposed to the social instrumentalization of physiognomy and phrenology, believing them to be unreliable predictors for marking character and ability in everyday life; he argued that physiognomic "method[s] [. . .] that tak[e] the slant of the forehead [. . .] from the dog to the monkey, from the monkey to the Negro, and from the Negro to the white" are "general indicators, at best approximate" representations of superior or inferior being, rather than "absolutely sure criterion." In spite of Töpffer's skepticism about the use of physiognomy as a real-world scientific rubric, cartoons have the potential to reinforce the inherent violence of seeing and being seen because, Weise explains, "pictorial signs, directly related to the world of natural appearances, lack the flexibility of verbal symbols."[47] Cartoonists therefore bear a great deal of responsibility, particularly given that images "above all" have the power to fix a subject as an object by interpellating them as dysgenic, antiaesthetic, or sub/nonhuman.

---

45. Wiese, "Language of Physiognomy," xviii, xviii, xviii.
46. Töpffer, *Enter: The Comics*, 11–12, 17, 19.
47. Töpffer, *Enter: The Comics*, 22; and Wiese, "Language of Physiognomy," xxvii.

The earliest cartoon representations of Black being, Charles Johnson explains, were "generic, dancing silhouettes: savage, cannibalistic Africans; language-mangling Bosco's; and bubble-lipped, buffoonish sidekicks." Johnson makes clear, however, that "the creators of this inhuman iconography [. . .] did not envision [. . .] Black Americans as their audience. We were not part of the artist/audience equation. These were the products [. . .] that included supposedly Black characters but were composed *by* and *for* whites." I understand Johnson to be making the case that if cartoonists can deploy an inhuman iconography in the service of white supremacist and antiblack logics, they can also make other grammars possible, ones that push back against hierarchized and violent representations of racialized others. To that end, I follow Wanzo's suggestion that "placing a possible black perspective at the center of our reading practice" can demonstrate how Black comics creators make possible what she terms a "visual grammar about identity."[48] Given that cartoons are paradoxically a flexible and fixed visual medium, I argue that Black creators and readers can manipulate and ultimately reject eugenic physiognomic visual logics that insist on narrating embodied form for an exclusively white gaze.

As I have argued here and elsewhere, ways of seeing are shaped by myriad internal and external factors, such as race, class, sexuality, ability, and gender identity.[49] Black gazing, in particular, has always been fraught and political. As bell hooks notes, "white slave owners (men, women, and children) punished black people for looking" because direct and sustained Black "looks [. . .] were seen as confrontational, as gestures of resistance, challenges to authority." As a consequence, what hooks describes as a "black peoples' right to gaze" has historically been denied to Black spectators. Yet hooks argues that "spaces of agency exist for black people, wherein we can both interrogate the gaze of the Other but also look back, and at one another, naming what we see. The 'gaze' has been and is a site of resistance for colonized black people globally." hooks describes this resistant act as an "oppositional gaze," "a critical gaze" that can be seen as a deliberate technique of "contestation and confrontation" to confront white supremacy and "engage its negation of black representation," a method that responds

---

48. Johnson, "Foreword," 4, 8; and Wanzo, *Content of Our Caricature*, 4–5.

49. See Joanna Davis-McElligatt, "Black Looking and Looking Black: African American Cartoon Aesthetics," in *The Cambridge Companion to the American Graphic Novel*, eds. Jan Baetans, Hugo Frey, and Fabrice Leroy (Cambridge: Cambridge University Press, 2023), 193–209; and Joanna Davis-McElligatt, "White Black Men and Black White Men: Reading Race as Violence in Mat Johnson and Warren Pleece's *Incognegro: A Graphic Mystery*," in *BOOM! SPLAT! Comics and Violence*, eds. Jim Coby and Joanna Davis-McElligatt (Jackson: University Press of Mississippi, 2024), 83–99.

to the violence of looking relations in the global white supremacist racial imaginary through the development of new art forms, modes of discourse, and critique.[50] A Black gaze therefore also actively pushes back against physiognomic logics that categorize Black being as dysgenic, antiesthetic, and irrational sub- or nonhuman Others. We might then see the Black gaze in this context as a critical response to the visual phenomenological problem of Fanonian triple consciousness. Rather than represent Black being as constellated embodiments of white colonial fantasies, cartoon image-text can foment a Black gaze and an image of differentiated Black life that functions, as Fanon argues, as "an *affirmation*" which demonstrates that Black (extra) terrestrials are "not this grinning *Y a bon Banania* figure he [the bearer of the white gaze] persists in imagining I am."[51]

I suggest that an oppositional Black gaze is concerned with the manufacture of artistic and cultural productions that privilege Black looking as fundamental to their aesthetic function, in opposition to systems of seeing and being seen. Indeed, as Tina Campt argues, "rather than looking *at* Black people, rather than simply multiplying the representation of Black folks," a Black visual aesthetic engendered by an oppositional gaze encourages "*see[ing] oneself through* the complex positionality that is blackness—and work[ing] through its implications on and for oneself." This distinctly Black gaze, Campt claims, "shifts the optics of 'looking at' to a politics of *looking with, through, and alongside another.*"[52] Campt's analysis highlights the importance of thinking critically and intentionally about the function of art produced by Black creators for a specifically Black gaze. In the next section, I demonstrate how the formation of a Black cartoon counterpublic that foments an oppositional Black gaze is catalyzed in the comics form as a narrative and spatiotemporal network that can highlight visual slippages between extraterrestrial and terrestrial form, while challenging visual phenomenological constructions of Black embodiment as dysgenic.

Black Skin, Human Masks, Alien Form: Constructing Black (Extra)terrestrial Cartoon Counterpublics in Milestone's *Icon* (1993–1997)

In this section I offer a critical reading of Dwayne McDuffie and M. D. Bright's *Icon* (1993–97), a series that traces visual slippages between nonhuman

50. hooks, *Black Looks*, 115, 116; 115; 116; 117, 116.
51. Fanon, *Black Skin, White Masks*, 197, 203, emphasis in original.
52. Campt, *Black Gaze*, 7, 8.

animals, extraterrestrial alien forms, and Black terrestrial embodiment, all while refusing to reduplicate the logics of white physiognomic optic politics. *Icon* was the signature release of the all-Black Milestone Media, an imprint of DC, founded by Derek Dingle, Dwayne McDuffie, Denys Cowan, Michael Davis, and Christopher Priest in 1993; the series ran for forty-two issues, alongside others located in the fictional Dakotaverse—*Static*, *Hardware*, and *Blood Syndicate*.[53] *Icon* follows Arnus of Terminus, a citizen of a socially advanced intergalactic constellation of planetary communities known as the Cooperative, comprising "10,000 civilized planets, with almost as many member races."[54] The Cooperative is, "by human standards [. . .] utopian," as they are able to "creat[e] unlimited matter generation," freeing them from the labor of energy harvesting, food production, and the powering of material and social infrastructures, and enabling them to clone, recombinate, and shapeshift with ease; as a consequence, its interplanetary citizens are predominantly philosophers, envoys, and mediators (*Icon* 8, 21). Arnus, who works as a conflict mediator, is traveling on an interstellar pleasure cruise to a resort planet when his spacecraft is attacked. After fleeing the ship in an escape pod, Arnus is directed toward Earth, the closest planet with sentient life, and crash-lands in 1839 on a cotton plantation in the US South. In anticipation of "the xenophobia of primitive peoples" (25, 9), the spacecraft's escape pod is designed to protect its occupant by recombining their physical and genetic structure to take on the appearance of an infant child of the first intelligent lifeform to discover the vessel. Upon landing on Earth, Arnus is discovered by Miriam, an enslaved woman of African descent, who names him Augustus, and raises him as her own kin. In his recombinated state, Arnus looks like other Black terrestrials but retains all of his alien abilities: decelerated aging; superhuman strength, speed, agility, reflexes and stamina; flight; enhanced vision, hearing, smell, taste, and touch; invulnerability to impact force, including bullets and bombs; accelerated healing; self-sustenance, or the ability to go for long periods of time without oxygen, food, or water; and the ability to manipulate and project energy in the form of force and stun bolts through his palms to engage in energy-enhanced hand-to-hand combat or to generate a force field. Perhaps most importantly, Arnus retains all of his memories of his former world and self; to that end, his Black terrestrial form

---

53. Milestone Media operated from 1993 to 2008, when it became defunct. In 2020 DC launched *Milestone Returns*, or *Earth-M*, with Derek Dingle and Denys Cowan, the two surviving founders. The relaunch features reconceptualizations of the origin texts, including *Icon*, *Static*, *Hardware*, and *Blood Syndicate*.

54. McDuffie and Bright, *Icon* 8, 21. Further citations to this series (issue, page number) appear in the text.

is an elaborate raciospecial epidermis, a fleshy mask intended to "arouse feelings of protectiveness among those who encountered me" (25, 14, 10). Though Arnus bonds with and is cared for faithfully by Miriam, who teaches him that "humans did, in theory if not in practice, share many of the values of civilized species through the galaxy," the effectiveness of his human mask is hampered by global systems of white supremacy which "involve[e] an intricate caste system based on [...] skin color" (25, 11). As a consequence of being seen as Black, Arnus is transformed from a Terminian into a fungible object, forced into chattel slavery, and denied the benefits of humanity.

In the comic's present moment of 1993, after, in his words, "having been stranded here" (*Icon* 19, 20) on Earth for several generations and repeatedly (re)appearing as his own descendant in order to avoid detection, Arnus has been alive for 154 years, and is known publicly as Augustus Freeman IV, a wealthy lawyer working in Dakota City, the central metropolis in the Milestone universe. Despite living for more than a century in the US masked as a Black terrestrial, surviving slavery and the Civil War, and operating as a second-class citizen throughout the *longue durée* of the Civil Rights era, Arnus finds it difficult to identify with the struggle for Black liberation. As a political conservative, Arnus believes that Black terrestrials should be responsible for their own social, economic, and political progress, and, as an extraterrestrial alien desperate to return home, is dismissive of the permutations of earthly sociopolitics and its "primitive culture" (25, 30). Arnus's perspective begins to shift when he meets Raquel Ervin, a young Black woman from Paris Island, the poorest and most vulnerable section of Dakota City. After discovering his powers, Raquel convinces him to become a superhero named Icon, and instantiate her as his sidekick, Rocket, in order to advance racial uplift and protective justice for Black terrestrials. Because Arnus has maintained possession of his escape pod, though damaged and running low on power, he is able to put to use many of its advanced technologies, including constructing an inertia belt for Raquel that generates a protective field, and enables the harnessing of kinetic energy to punch, blast, throw, and fly. Over the course of the series, readers are asked to consider how visual slippages between Arnus's animalized extraterrestrial alien and Black terrestrial forms challenge physiognomic hierarchization, and make possible radical new sociopolitical intimacies.

I turn to *Icon* here for two reasons. First, the creators of the series reimagine the visual phenomenological relation between extraterrestrial aliens and Black terrestrials by entangling their experiences of being and being seen, narrating multiple positions in spacetime all at once on the same page by literally and figuratively drawing the ways and means by which Black (extra) terrestrials are transfigured and resist transfiguration as seen objects, and therefore exist in embodied relations beyond the purview of the white gaze. Arnus becomes Black in two ways: through interactions with and resistance to the antiblack carceral state and its systems and agents of control (signified by terrestrial and galactic police forces, government entities, and individual white supremacist villains), and through a radical enjoinment and entanglement of self with Black terrestrial collectivities and communities in the pursuit of liberation and justice. Given that Arnus appears as a Black man, I pay close attention to the way *Icon* frames triple consciousness in response to varying dynamics of class, ability, gender, and sexuality, and how racecraft shapes his experience of extraterrestriality, Blackness, and humanness. Second, *Icon* revises the standard superhero narrative by creating an explicitly Black alien cartoon hermeneutic and critical counterpublic that center an oppositional Black gaze as a radical analytic. As Arnus makes the transition from private citizen to public superhero, he becomes subject to the violence of being seen as alien *and* Black, as paradoxically dysgenic and celestial, as a threat and potential savior. As such, *Icon* serves as a critical visual and narrative antithesis to traditional hierarchical and often eugenic constructions of white superheroic bodies and being.

As I discussed in the previous section, Black folks' "right to gaze," as hooks frames it, has historically been hampered by white supremacist systems of control that overdetermine the politics of looking while Black. And yet, in spite of this repression, Black people have consistently generated alternative counterpublics, discourses, and modes of representation. Margo Natalie Crawford has observed that scholars and artists in the Black Arts movement intentionally developed a "type of counterpublic [. . .] that aimed to offer privacy for ideal black readers" who could imagine "that they were looking into a countermirror, a mirror that countered a dominant, hegemonic lens—the white gaze." I argue that Black comics creators have likewise developed a cartoon counterpublic, culminating in what Wanzo has described as an "identity hermeneutic"[55] that centers and embraces the radical representational and political potential of Black ways of reading. I adhere to I. Bennett Capers's description of "reading Black" as a system of meaning-making focused on reading against the grain of Manichean formations that situate Blackness as the foil in binary power relationships, such as Black/human, human/alien, "master/slave, civilized/primitive, enlightened/backward, good/evil [that] have been embodied in the American

---

55. Crawford, "Black Aesthetics Unbound," 10, 11; and Wanzo, *Content of Our Caricature*, 4.

consciousness." Reading Black is an intersectional framework, attentive not only to race but also to "class, gender, sexuality, and other hierarchical structures. As a reading strategy, it seeks to decode the coded, to say the unsaid, and to render visible the gaps, the fissures, and the solecisms. Reading black is a reading against—a reading that it is counter-discursive and counter-hegemonic."[56] In the remainder of this chapter, I examine how techniques of reading Black countermand constructions of Black (extra)terrestrial embodiment as dysgenic, creating new strategies for making sense of Black being and community.

Icon centralizes reading Black as a critical hermeneutic by formally representing networks that frame visual processes of seeing and being seen as distinct-yet-interrelated narrative sites. Following Thierry Groensteen, I approach comics here as an "oriented network" that operates according to a "dechronologized mode."[57] Groensteen argues that cartoons work as a "series," or a "succession of continuous or discontinuous images linked by a system of iconic, plastic or semantic correspondences." Within this serialized network, "each panel is equipped with spatio-topical coordinates by the page layout that constitutes a *site*," or "chrono-topical coordinates" that situate the panel as its own temporal location. When we treat cartoons as a network, we can understand "the strip, the page, the double page, and the album [. . .] as nested multiframes, systems of increasingly inclusive proliferation," or, in other words, as endlessly open networks that encourage multiple and unpredictable modes of engagement. As readers move through any given cartoon text, the panels, frames, and gutters dictate how the narrative can be (or should be) read. And yet this is not necessarily always or exclusively a sequential process for readers. Cartoon narratives rely, for example, on an accumulation of images deployed in repetition over a number of sites, pages, or issues. These "iconic resonances," as Hannah Modriag describes them, "bridge dispersed panels and draw them into correspondence," a narratological process that "can override linear narrative progression, and [. . .] challeng[e] [. . .] preoccupation[s] with sequentiality."[58] Readers of comics can choose to approach cartoons in sequence or read the text out of joint by lingering on some images and glancing at others, moving forward or backward in a single text or across issues. Cartoon readers must therefore

---

56. Capers, "Reading Back, Reading Black," 12, 12–13.

57. Groensteen, *System of Comics*, 146–47. For more on cartoon sequentiality, see Will Eisner, *Comics and Sequential Art: Principles and Practices from the Legendary Cartoonist* (New York: W. W. Norton & Company, 2008); and Scott McCloud, *Understanding Comics: The Invisible Art* (New York: William Morrow, 1994).

58. Groensteen, *System of Comics*, 122, 124; and Modriag, *Comics as Language*, 110.

also rely on their visual memory, recalling or anticipating symbols, colors, or motifs, or making connections between sites on the page, text, or series.

Neil Cohn and Hannah Campbell argue that even though reading written language is typically understood to be a straightforward process, "the reading order for comics is more complex because panels can be arranged in numerous ways across the 'canvas' of the page." Though scholars have long assumed comics readers follow the "Z-path" by deploying a "left to right and down order [. . .] to read text," Cohn and Campbell contend that readers instead confront "various manipulations to the arrangement of panels," which can require them "to navigate panels in alternate routes." For that reason, comics make possible—and might even be said to reward—what Charles Hatfield has described as "self-paced reading, slow or fast according to the reader's desires, even recursive if need be."[59] Cartoon meaning-making can generally be understood as a process of relation between the creators who devise and organize chronotopical sites and the readers who make sense of them in whatever ways they wish. Comics is, in other words, a co-constructive medium, simultaneously predetermined and open-ended, structured and flexible. *Icon* frames multiple sites, as present-time grids, juxtapositions, series, cliff-hangers, flashbacks, recollections, and memories, where Arnus must navigate the physiognomic politics of being seen as Black, and either capitulates to, resists, or malforms the white gaze. In this way, reading Black operates as diegesis and exegesis, as a spatiotemporal narrative logic embedded in the text itself, and as a way of reading and seeing guided by and yet external to it.

Beginning immediately in issue 1, "She's Got Your Hero Right Here," *Icon* deconstructs for readers the visual logics of being seen as Black and (extra)terrestrial, while highlighting and undermining physiognomic optic logics. The first several pages of the issue feature Arnus's origin story as he flees a damaged starliner, crash-lands in an escape pod on a plantation in the US South, and is discovered by his surrogate mother in a series of images that initially introduce him in his Terminian form. The main action begins in 1839 in a galaxy utterly unlike the Milky Way, given the strange planets and unfamiliar gas formations clustered in the sky—the date orients readers toward Earth time, not Terminian time. The central figure in each site, or panel, is Arnus in his Terminian form. Though his skin is a bright cerulean and his jaw is wide set, his body is in many ways reminiscent of the stereotypical Gray: he is bipedal, his hands have only three digits, and his feet

---

59. Cohn and Campbell, "Navigating Comics II," 193, 193; and Hatfield, *Alternative Comics*, 74.

are webbed with two toes on each end. Arnus's face is also a physiognomic echo of Barney Hill's drawing of an extraterrestrial; he has no visible nose, his lips are rendered as a straight line, and his large, bulbous eyes are set on the far side of his head, which, according to Lavater, indicate bestiality and nonhumanity. Arnus might therefore be said to fit into the speculative celestial-animal category of being in Lavater's taxonomy of embodied form, occupying a middle place between frog and "negro."

This visual intimacy is confirmed by Arnus himself later in the series, in issue 8, "The Brother from Another Planet," when he explains to Raquel that before his recombination he resembled "Kermit the Frog. With a better profile" (*Icon* 8, 20). I read this as an intentionally physiognomic response, insofar as Arnus contends that unlike the line of animality of the frog, his "profile," or his prominent forehead and large jawbone, both signs of special superiority and celestiality, elevates him into a higher category of aesthetic (and intellectual) being than a nonhuman animal. And yet, when Raquel laughs at the comparison, Arnus insists that he is "serious. In any case, in my culture physical appearance is not an issue. Your world is very immature in this regard" (8, 20). Arnus's simultaneous deployment and rejection of the physiognomic logics that treat his visual intimacy with nonhuman animals as a sign of dysgenicity can be read as an implicit critique of human logic, an attempt to establish critical distance between himself and other Earthlings. According to Arnus, the human tendency to instrumentalize physiognomy is in and of itself confirmation of their barbarity and lack of sophistication.

Given that he is nude from the waist up, we are implicitly asked to read Arnus as a kind of man, much like Dunn's shirtless aliens (female aliens must be fully covered up in order to comply with the strictures of the Comics Code Authority). That said, there is no sense in the comic that Terminians share Earthlings' conceptions of sexuality and gender presentation. Arnus is as tall as an average human, but he is stronger and more powerful, represented by his bulging muscles and lithe movement; the text reinforces his Terminian physical prowess by featuring his entire body in motion as he jumps, runs, navigates the pod, and escapes into interstellar space across several panels that highlight his superior ability. These early representations of Arnus's Terminian physicality frame the stakes of his transfiguration into human form. The narrative juxtaposes Arnus's recombination—and, in many ways, cosmic regression—in two panels that feature Arnus as a Terminian and as a Black terrestrial infant (see figure 7). According to Cohn and Campbell's taxonomy of cartoon form, the page employs the panel structure of *blockage,* when a long vertical panel "'blocks' the Z-path and pushes readers to move vertically instead of horizontally," and *staggering,* when

FIGURE 7. Arnus is recombinated into a human and taken in by his surrogate mother, Miriam. *Icon* 1, "She's Got Your Hero Right Here," Milestone Media, 1993.

different panel sizes prevent the interframe space "from extending contiguously between adjacent panels."[60] As a consequence, readers are asked to draw Arnus-as-Terminian and Arnus-as-Black-terrestrial into direct visual alignment, reading the blocked and staggered panels vertically and immediately closing the gaps in his transition that are more fully narrativized on the right side of the page. This visual slippage reinforces the vulnerability of Arnus's human mask. As an infant, Arnus is entirely reliant upon the care of Miriam for all of his needs and is also imperiled by the system of chattel slavery that interpellates his body not as human but as property. Though the bottom two panels on the page demonstrate the promise and potential of Miriam's care—she reaches into the pod to pick him up, and cradles him close—his fleshy mask diminishes his physical, communicative, and intellectual agency.

Arnus nevertheless bears the trace of his alien embodied form as an iconic resonance in the narrative, represented diegetically by his retention of his Terminian powers and his strong desire to return to his home planet. In *Icon* 25, an anniversary issue in which Arnus has, at long last, returned to his home planet and recounted his Earth adventures to a Cooperative council on Justice Moon, the collective's arbitration planet, Arnus explains that on Earth he "quickly learned not to reveal them [my enhanced abilities]. Some humans who discovered my abilities, considered them to be magical in nature. Others considered them demonic" (*Icon* 25, 14). Though Arnus secretly uses his powers to assist in the Underground Railroad, he fights in the Civil War and World War II with only a gun, refusing to lend his energy fields to battle. It is during the Civil War, however, that Arnus "realized the extent of my human body's full potential" (25, 20), when he heals from a direct cannonball blast. As a consequence of Arnus's Terminian longevity in terrestrial form, he must recursively stage his death and return as his own son in order to escape detection. At the same time, his longevity also enhances his ability to negotiate life in the afterlife of slavery, not only because he is physically resilient and powerful but because he can accumulate vast amounts of wealth by growing and then repeatedly inheriting his own estate. Arnus attends Fisk University law school during Reconstruction, and begins a practice which, when the narrative begins, has been in operation for more than a hundred years. During the Harlem Renaissance, he marries a wealthy Black industrial heiress named Estelle Jackson, and the two of them move into a brownstone on Harlem's Striver's Row, which grants them access to "many important and influential figures of

---

60. Cohn and Campbell, "Navigating Comics II," 193.

this period" (25, 23). Given his Black terrestrial embodiment, Arnus's alien abilities and immense wealth cannot wholly eradicate the effects of white supremacy, so he and Estelle expatriate to France, seeking an environment unrestricted by Jim Crow; when they return to the US after the end of World War II, they discover that in the postwar era, systems of white supremacy "reemerged, with renewed vigor" (25, 23). Arnus eventually lends his legal talents to the Civil Rights movement, but, after its end in 1965, removes himself from the struggle and settles into a comfortable life with Estelle in New York City. Upon learning of his origin late in her life, however, Estelle encourages Arnus to use his powers to become a "symbol for an oppressed people"—though he refuses to become wholly visible, his "'heroic' feats did increase in scope and frequency" in secret (25, 30).

After Estelle's death in 1977, Arnus decides to entirely withdraw his support and protection of the oppressed, in particular for other Black terrestrials, and to "never allow myself to know love . . . to be touched by the very humanity I'd sworn to serve. [. . .] I chose to redouble my efforts to find a way to return home" (*Icon* 25, 31). In service of this goal, Arnus moves to Dakota's "ultra-exclusive" Prospect Hills neighborhood close to Alva Industries, an advanced technologies company he hopes will soon develop the machinery he needs to repair his escape pod. While he waits, Arnus works as a personal lawyer to politicians and corporate hegemons, executor for dozens of multimillionaires, and board member for billionaire companies. As a result, Arnus secures for himself "rarefied air" for a Black terrestrial, and before long "dozens of 'years' had passed since I was personally confronted by racism of any consequence, even longer since I had mingled with black people of any kind" (25, 33). Arnus sees himself as, and, in his capacity as Augustus Freeman IV, is seen as, the promise of American exceptionalism and the culmination and realization of the struggle for Black terrestrial freedom: "I truly believed in America as the land of opportunity. I truly believed that the long fight for equality was won in 1964 with the signing of the Civil Rights Act" (25, 33).

Arnus's belief in a postracial future manifests as a refusal to commit to Black political struggle—a rejection, in other words, of the potential of a cosmic diaspora—is, in part, a function of his wealth and accumulated social power. Arnus-as-Augustus effectively purchases peace for himself by manipulating capitalist and social power structures—but even then, he can only shield himself from the impacts of "racism of [. . .] consequence," not eradicate or avoid it altogether. Arnus's rejection of Black political life is also, however, a function of his extraterrestriality. As an alien enfleshed in and masked by a Black terrestrial form, Arnus considers himself to be

Terminian, not Black or human; indeed, as andré m. carrington argues, for Arnus "humanity and Blackness alike are constructed, technologically mediated experiences."[61] Arnus himself explains that while masked as Augustus he became

> a staunch "Republican," a by-your-own-bootstraps Booker T. Washington conservative. I had little patience or understanding for apologists for black people's "condition." Nor did I wish to hear any arguments about racism or oppression. Had I been frank with those who would put forth such arguments, I would have said, "I was born a *slave* and I made it. What's your excuse?" I had forgotten, if not where I came from, at least what I had been through. (*Icon* 25, 34, emphasis in original)

But, of course, Arnus cannot be frank without revealing his extraterrestriality given that no terrestrial, Black or otherwise, could have survived as long as Arnus has. Though it might be true that Augustus was "born a slave," Earth is not where *Arnus* "came from." For that reason, Arnus describes his Blackness as phenomenological and experiential rather than biological or endemic: Blackness is an experience made evident in "what I had been through," rather than an extension of "where I came from." Even so, Arnus's rejection of Black political struggle can be seen as a function of his identification with Black subjectivity; though he thinks of himself as superior to Black terrestrials and cannot relate to their "condition," he also believes himself to be intimately related to them because of his decades of experience living as and among them.

This is where readers find Arnus when the series begins—immediately after Miriam carries him away, the narrative jumps forward 154 years to Arnus at work in his law office in downtown Dakota, gazing at a pair of heavy iron shackles (see figure 8). In an example of narrative prolepsis, the now-adult Arnus-as-Augustus is pictured "daydreaming" (*Icon* 1, 7) a specter of Miriam carrying his infant self, an iconic resonance that reminds readers that his human form is an embodied mask. As visual symbols, shackles in African diasporic symbology signify the bondage and constraint of slavery and its afterlife, serving as acute reminders of his former enslavement; to that end, one might read Miriam's superimposition as a sign that Arnus continues to live in the wake of slavery, both as a memory and lived experience, and as a gesture toward the possibilities of a cosmic diaspora inclusive of extraterrestrial aliens and Black folk. The four panels on the right side of the

---

61. carrington, *Speculative Blackness*, 128.

FIGURE 8. In his law office in Dakota City, Arnus contemplates his former life as an enslaved person. *Icon* 1, "She's Got Your Hero Right Here," Milestone Media, 1993.

page that show Arnus's interaction with Saul overlap the long, single panel of Miriam on the left, formally driving home the intrusion of the past in the future—as Cohn and Campbell explain, overlapping panels interrupt the traditional Z-path because they "brin[g] panels closer together rather than moving them further part." Though readers familiar with the Z-path might initially be drawn to Miriam, the elongated and overlapping spacetime of the single leftward panel forms a "contiguous vertical grouping that can progress as a whole to the rightward stack."[62] As Arnus's reverie intrudes into the now, and as the boundaries between distinct spatiotemporal cosmoi are blurred, readers must consider how his enslaved past and extraterrestrial origin continue to matter for Arnus-as-Augustus (and, therefore, for other Black terrestrials).

Arnus explains to Saul that his reverie was prompted by a recent meeting with Raquel Ervin. In an example of narrative analepsis, the story moves backward in time, shifting perspective from Arnus to Raquel, who dominates the majority of narrative threads in the series. Raquel and Arnus meet during an attempted burglary of his property; though initially reluctant, she agrees to join her friends with the aim of finding a word processor so that she can realize her dream of becoming a novelist like Toni Morrison, her favorite writer. A voracious reader and burgeoning intellectual in her own right, Raquel is immediately drawn to Arnus's book-lined study, correctly identifying that "whoever lived here had more than money. They had *knowledge*. They had *history*. And I *wanted* it. More than I had ever wanted anything in my life" (*Icon* 1, 10). Arnus's study evidences the scale of his socioeconomic privilege, historically denied to Black terrestrials like Raquel, who comes from Paris Island, a housing project in Dakota populated almost entirely by poor Black terrestrials.

At the moment Raquel reaches for Arnus's computer, he appears in the doorway. When Raquel's friends first see Arnus they take him to be the household butler because he is also Black; their initial perception is a testament to the social position of ordinary Black subjects in Dakota. When Arnus clarifies that he owns the home and intends to defend it, one of her friends shoots Arnus repeatedly, which ultimately has no effect on him; terrified, they flee on foot. In a full display of his extraterrestrial power, Arnus flies in pursuit of Raquel and her friends, grabbing them, lifting them into the air, zipping around and between them. When Arnus finally corners Raquel and her friends, he aligns himself with them by arguing that their "behavior reflects poorly on our people and on yourselves" (*Icon* 1,

---

62. Cohn and Campbell, "Navigating Comics II," 194, 198.

18). There is a tremendous visual gap, however, in Arnus's appearance, or, more specifically, his dark skin, tightly coiled hair, and human form, and his wealth, invulnerability, and ability to fly. Of particular note to Raquel is Arnus's power of flight, which becomes for her a radical symbol of escape, transformation, and deliverance—indeed, she explains that "just *seeing* him opened up a whole new world of possibilities for me . . . how I thought he could help lots of people, if only they could see what he can do" (1, 20). Arnus functions for Raquel as one possible material realization of Black terrestrial metaphors for freedom. In other words, he is metaphor made flesh, the embodiment of Morrison's 1977 novel *Song of Solomon,* which utilizes the trope of flight as a literal and metaphorical means of escape: "I read this book called 'Song of Solomon' where this man wanted to fly. Not like in an airplane, but for *real*. In the book, though, flying didn't mean flying. It meant something else. Flying was like freedom. I thought I understand the book, but I didn't. Not really. Not until I saw it . . . When you can fly, there's no burden you can't bear. When you can fly, gravity can't touch you. When you can fly . . . you can do anything" (1, 16–17). The promise and potential of Arnus's flight is more than symbolic for Raquel; rather, it is a sign of collective liberation, a way of reading beyond the boundary of dysgenic constructions of Black terrestrial limitations, a material manifestation of cosmic diasporic potentiality.

After the attempted robbery Raquel returns to Arnus, hoping to convince him that he has a responsibility to Black terrestrials not only because he looks like one, and is therefore at the very least visually aligned with their plight, but because the force of his being seen as Black and a superhero in public could offer vital protection to oppressed Black people, serving as a critical promise of social uplift. Raquel recommends that Arnus assume a public-facing identity as Icon, which, she explains, refers to "an example or an ideal," and become "like a super-hero. And set an example for people, like you did for me and my friends" (*Icon* 1, 21). Raquel also recommends that she work as his sidekick, Rocket, to help him navigate Black life in Dakota, and to help her escape and expand the confines of her life in the Paris Island projects. Because working together will necessarily draw them into visual similitude, Raquel is, in essence, asking Arnus to become Black, to allow himself to be publicly seen as Black, as working with and for Black communities. In doing so, Arnus must simultaneously remask and unmask himself, keep his identity as Augustus Freeman IV separate from his superheroics, and make known his secret extraterrestrial Terminian abilities as Icon. Arnus initially refuses, returning to the familiar self-improvement logics that had long guided his perception of Black Dakotan life: "People don't need any example, child. If you aren't doing well, you haven't tried hard enough. If you want a better life, don't look for examples. Do what I did: pull yourself up by your own bootstraps!" (1, 21). Raquel immediately reminds him, however, that "it's a lot easier to pull yourself by your bootstraps, Mr. Man—if you already know how to fly!" (1, 21).

After turning Raquel away, for the first time in many years Arnus flies to Paris Island, an urban deindustrialized area of Dakota across the bridge from his gated community. While there he finds crumbling concrete buildings, piles of garbage, and dirty streets, alongside laughing Black children who are playing tag and splashing in puddles. Arnus's perception that individuals are singularly responsible for themselves comes to a head as he observes the innocent children at play, prompting him to acknowledge that he "pretended that those who suffer under such conditions must have brought them upon themselves. And while they have lived without hope [. . .] I have lived a lie" (*Icon* 1, 23). Arnus agrees to join Raquel but does not wholly shift his perspective—he still wants to return home, and, to the extent that he sees himself as Black, continues to struggle to acknowledge the power of social systems to destroy and control Black terrestrial life.

This is particularly evident when Arnus and Raquel head out for their first heroic endeavor to save the mayor of Dakota, Thomasina Jefferson, from angry citizens who want her to be held accountable for unleashing a "Big Bang" neurotoxic event in Paris Island that resulted in the mutation of several inhabitants, wreaking increased havoc in an already vulnerable community. Raquel understands that because she and Arnus are Black, in addition to dealing with the hostage crisis they will also have to confront the state-funded S.H.R.E.D. police force who will code them as threats, rather than partners or colleagues. When they arrive at City Hall, Arnus confirms that, in Raquel's words, he plans to "land in the middle of eighty bazillion cops and ask them if they need a hand," a plan she believes is at best "naïve," at worst dangerous: "You think the cops are sitting around waiting for a flying n———r to drop out of the sky and do their job for them?" (*Icon* 1, 26). Raquel knows that Icon's extraterrestrial ability—his flight, strength, and energy manipulation—will be overshadowed by his Blackness, subsuming his ability and intent to the process of being seen as Black, and therefore violent, by the state; Arnus, however, admonishes her not to "assume everything's racial. If you want to do this you'll have to show respect for authorities" (1, 26).

Raquel's insistence that they will be met with derision, suspicion, and racist violence by the state is accurate—*immediately* after Arnus introduces himself to a police officer as Icon, he is threatened with violence and illegally detained. Indeed, the first issue ends with Arnus and Raquel surrounded by a dozen faceless and heavily armored cops, each of whom has drawn and readied their guns, made evident by the chorus of K-CHAK, KLIKT, KLIK, and KLAK sounds (see figure 9); as Raquel predicted, by being seen as Black they become subject to forms of violence most familiar to Black folks living in the afterlife of slavery. As they stand before the flank of armed police soldiers, Raquel quips sarcastically: "Don't assume everything is racial, huh? I'll try—but I bet this never happens to Superman" (*Icon* 1, 27). By drawing a distinction between Superman and Icon at the level of their interactions with the state, Raquel reframes the optic logics of the scene by asking Arnus (and therefore the readers) to look at it from her perspective, rather than from the vantage point of the police. The structure of the splash page reinforces this perspective. Raquel and Arnus are the primary figures, and the only two in shades of red, blue, and green. Arnus occupies the largest and most prominent place in the image, one hand balled into a fist, the other splayed out in a defensive gesture; his body language is protective of Raquel, and simultaneously poised and ready to move should there be further violence.

Taken as a whole, the action in this page can be read as a simultaneity of sound, sight, and movement that reinforces the way Arnus and Raquel are seen as Black dysgenic subjects by the police state, drawing them into visual intimacy in spite of the very real differences between them. On the one hand, the perspective of this splash page aligns the reader with the gun barrel and police officer at the bottom, inviting readers to see Arnus and Raquel from the position of the cops, and therefore as threats or potential menaces. Yet the central placement of Arnus, combined with Raquel's statement that this form of violence is exclusively reserved for Black bodies, directs readers to return the gaze, and in the process read against the grain of the cop's sightline, instead seeing the police as Arnus and Raquel see them. I argue that this double visual identification enables readers to see the simultaneous processes of seeing and being seen, and to make sense of the complex ways comics creators navigate the superhero genre when constructing Black aliens.

In the second issue, "Stop! Do Not Hop on Cop!," the interaction between Arnus, Raquel, and the police turns violent quickly when one of them attempts to backhand her, only to be rebuffed by her protective energy shield. Though Arnus warns her not to resort to violence in return, while punching the police officer back she draws a critical distinction between her resistive Black politics and his assimilationist stance: "I'm *definitely* gonna hurt him. I ain't Martin Luther King, all right?—And I ain't Rodney King either!" (*Icon* 2, 7). Arnus remains out of the fray for some time in a purely

FIGURE 9. Arnus and Raquel are surrounded by S.H.R.E.D. police officers. *Icon* 1, "She's Got Your Hero Right Here," Milestone Media, 1993.

defensive mode; it is only after a police officer smashes his head and face with a rifle butt so hard it shatters against his nose that he begins to physically defend himself. Eventually, Arnus demands that Raquel return home and he turns himself in, believing that it is better to allow the cops to perform their duties than to intervene. As Arnus is handcuffed by the shackles—an iconic resonance from his reverie of Miriam—he notes that it has "been over one hundred years since I allowed myself to be shackled. [. . .] It hasn't become any easier with time" (2, 20). Readers are asked to consider how the violence of his detainment is a function of the cop's racism but also the result of his ongoing refusal to use his extraterrestrial superpowers to resist the racist cops, or protect himself, Raquel, and, by extension, other Black folks in Dakota. Arnus's Blackness, in other words, troubles his alienness, making it difficult for him to perform the necessary functions of the superhero—to protect vulnerable and innocent people with the aid of his special skills and abilities.

This is in large part why the creators of *Icon* pushed back against fan interpretations of the series that read Icon as a Black(ened) version of a white superhero, as they did in the letters column in the second issue: "You know, we've heard this 'Black Superman' thing several times in the past few months. While there ARE parallels, I think the resemblance doesn't go much beyond Augustus being a 'strange visitor from another planet.' [. . .] ONCE AGAIN: He's NOT a 'BLACK SUPERMAN!'" (*Icon* 2, 28). The creators codify this response later in the series during a "World's Collide" crossover run featuring Superman and Superboy alongside Icon and Rocket, and other superheroes in the Dakotaverse, including the Blood Syndicate, Static, and Hardware. In the run, a supervillain named The Rift collapses spacetime between Metropolis and Dakota, and, after insisting that there is now only room for one superhero, pits Superman and Icon against one another in a fight to the death. The storyline highlights important differences between Kal-El's and Arnus's experiences of extraterritoriality, demonstrating how axes of race, gender, and citizenship overdetermine and shape the way they are seen as superheroes, their ability to use their superpowers publicly (even if masked), and their capacity to inhabit the body politic as protectors. As The Rift explains, Kal-El is adopted by white human parents and assimilated into their communities without complication or distress, so much so that, by adulthood, in his role as Superman he is "the ultimate immigrant," "the personification of the American dream" (16, 4). Kal-El's physiognomy—light skin, straight dark hair, and blue eyes—are as (if not more) protective on Earth as his heat vision, flight capabilities, or longevity; as a result, Superman's visual and enculturated whiteness effectively mask his extraterrestriality as humanity, making it possible for him to be interpellated as a kind of intergalactic celestial European who experiences very few social barriers in becoming the "greatest hero this planet has ever seen" (16, 4).

Though Arnus is "yet another castaway from space," The Rift contends that Icon must confront the reality that on Earth "by the virtue of the color of your skin you were a slave. You were not permitted to bring your knowledge, skills, and culture to the mainstream. Only your labor was considered to be of value. So, instead of bequeathing your great gifts to the benefit of your new world, you turned them to the daily struggle for survival" (*Icon* 16, 9–10). Unlike Kal-El, who becomes a model for American assimilation and white eugenic superiority, Arnus is denied full participation in the body politic, configured by The Rift as an excision from "the loving arms of an adopted family" (16, 10), and forced to occupy the subject position of slave, a genealogical isolate who experiences social death. Arnus's experience of Black terrestrial embodiment both during enslavement and in its aftermath impacts the way he is seen as a superhero, the way he is able to perform and protect, and the way his superpowers can be made publicly known. In Fanonian terms, beginning from the moment he arrives on Earth, Arnus becomes subject to the effects of a historical-racial schema and an epidermal-racial schema, and to the physiognomic logics of a white gaze that overdetermine his ability to move freely in public space, or join the body politic as a citizen, let alone serve as a hero-protector. I read this run as a reflection on the limitations and possibilities inherent in the construction of Black superhero narratives, and a simultaneous attempt to construct a Black superhero counterpublic that accounts for the ways Black embodiment is experienced, visualized, and imagined.

Arnus must negotiate how his role as Black superhero is seen by both the state-funded police and by Black terrestrials, who are most likely to be at the receiving end of his correction, because the lack of resources in the Paris Island community has driven its inhabitants to forms of petty crime in order to meet their immediate needs. Shortly after defeating The Rift and preserving Dakota, Arnus more fully inhabits his role as a superhero, working with Raquel in increasingly public ways in the wealthy majority-white downtown, where he focuses his efforts on preventing accidents and saving lives, and in Paris Island, where he primarily works to stop crime from taking place, using his superheroics as an intercessor for the state authorities. Arnus-as-Icon is particularly brutal when accosting Black subjects, even for people engaged in nonviolent crime, freely using physical violence to detain them, even though terrestrials are far less powerful. As a consequence, Kelsohn Styvens, a Black community leader, begins to lead a community resistance effort to Icon, arguing on the evening news and in the daily newspaper that he is "BIASED AGAINST ETHNIC CRIMINALS" (*Icon* 17, 10). Arnus's use of violence against Black subjects in the service of the police state is read as a deep betrayal of the Black community and treated as further evidence of his outsiderness, extraterrestriality, and nonhumanness. Indeed, Styvens argues that Arnus's inability (or unwillingness) to protect Black life and treat it as sacred, to identify the state as the primary agent of harm, to combat white supremacy, and foment Black survival is evidence that he is not Black, and also not a "man" (17, 18). In a tense standoff between Arnus, Styvens, and a large group of Black protestors, the crowd explicitly rejects Arnus's claims to Blackness, referring to him as a "self-hatin' chump," "white boy," "wanna-be," and "Tom!" (17, 18). This rejection comes from the community's suspicion that, though he may be seen as Black, he is something else altogether—an agent for the white state or an imposter in blackface.

After the public confrontation with Styvens, Raquel draws Arnus's attention to the gaps between his appearance and his actions, between his public function as a superhero and his refusal to protect Black life. The most specific complaints Raquel levies concern Arnus's performance of Blackness and his connections to the broader community of Black Dakotans, or his refusal to embrace the community with whom he is visually, politically, and historically aligned: "You don't talk like a Black man or live with Black people . . . or even live like a Black person and . . . you do mostly arrest people of color. When we patrol nightly, what neighborhoods do we patrol . . . what people do we protect? But at your job you protect rich white—" (*Icon* 17, 19–20). Raquel identifies a gap in Arnus's self-presentation as a Black terrestrial and his function as a public Black alien superhero; she believes that he should unequivocally defend his fellow Black folks from the quotidian violence of the white state. And yet Arnus defends his remove from the conditions of Black terrestriality by framing it as a function of his individual success, or as evidence that he has become "everything I can be" (17, 20). Arnus does not acknowledge systems that have benefited him—his longevity, imperviousness to harm, self-investments and self-inheritances—preferring to see himself instead as having risen to his position on his own without the aid of his Terminian abilities. Raquel insists that "you can't understand because you're not really Black! You're an alien! You can fly!" (17, 20). Arnus retorts, however, that he has "been a Black man for longer than anyone alive on this planet. [. . .] Yes, my special abilities protected me from more physical harm that others endured, but my mind, my heart, and my ego had no such protection" (17, 20).

Given that Blackness is a visual phenomenological experience, Arnus has experienced the consequences of being seen as Black by the state in ways that no living Black terrestrial can claim—he is a survivor of the slave trade, a once-object become subject. And yet, as Raquel notes, his extraterrestrial origin is a distinction worth making between them. Having lost their history and memory of home, Black terrestrials can make no claims to another planet, and must therefore navigate the complex ways their existence has been compromised in the wake of enslavement, a mode of being from which there is no escape. During this confrontation, Arnus and Raquel, both masked as Rocket and Icon, are represented as mirror images, facing and turning away from one another; in the top long panel, Arnus is turned away from Raquel, floating in the air as he is wont to do, a distance that is echoed in every panel on the page. And yet readers are asked to confront the ways Arnus and Raquel are visually aligned in the bottom two panels, through close-ups that eclipse the physical distance between them by highlighting the ways in which they are alike: their dark skin, broad noses, thick lips, and elaborate masks. In this instance, Black phenotype is represented not as a dysgenic quality but as a form of intimacy between Arnus and Raquel that entangles them as Black subjects in the world of the comic and for readers in the world beyond it. Though this page benefits from being read along the Z-path, given the way the dialogue is designed to move the reader through time, readers are also asked to confront how Arnus and Raquel are subject to the logics of racecraft that interpellate them as dysgenic objects, and to the ways they experience their Blackness in different and often contradictory ways.

Following this confrontation, Arnus finds a way to return to his home planet when a member of the Blood Syndicate, a group of mutated Dakotans from Paris Island, informs him that he is also an extraterrestrial and arranges for Arnus to leave Earth. Once he arrives at the Cooperative's Justice Moon, Arnus's re-entry is facilitated by Arnus II, a clone created after his disappearance to fulfill his duties. As I discussed earlier in this section, Arnus is asked to describe his Earth experiences to the council; after sharing that he was brutalized as a Black man because Earth operates according to a physiognomic system that violently hierarchizes embodied form, the members of the Cooperative, headed by Arnus II, explain to Arnus (now Arnus Prime) that Earth is too dangerous to be allowed to exist. Over time, Arnus and Raquel convince the Cooperative that Earthlings, though unable to join the interplanetary collective because of their interspecial immaturity and predisposition toward violence, must be given time and space to develop, change, and grow with the understanding that they will either meet the challenge or destroy themselves in the process.

In the end, Arnus decides to return to Earth in order to continue his work as Icon alongside Raquel. Central to Icon's defense of Earth is that its people are not inherently bad; Arnus was cared for faithfully, enabled to survive, and given opportunity because of the broad networks of Black community. He acknowledges that he would never have survived without the care of Miriam, or Estelle's love and affection—or without Raquel's urging him to participate in public life as a superhero. In other words, Black life becomes for Arnus a radical model of special maturity, the finest example of what humanity has to offer the universe, and in turn he becomes determined to push all Earthlings to meet their example. Raquel serves as an ally, a partner, and an important link connecting Arnus to experiences of Blackness he had previously refused to understand; in other words, together they represent the fullest potential of the cosmic diaspora. Rather than continue to resist visual and sociopolitical alignment with Black subjects, Arnus determines that he will return to Earth in the embodied form of a Black man, even though the Cooperative offers to transform him back into his originary Terminian form. Arnus explains to Raquel that though he had "long had an idea of myself as Arnus of Terminus,"[63] his experiences on Earth had fundamentally shifted not only how he came to be seen by others but how he sees himself. Arnus observes that whereas Arnus II inhabits comfortably his blue, three-fingered, frog-eyed form, he no longer needs to claim it as his own: "You could say that Augustus Freeman is my idea of myself, and Arnus II is his."[64] Without access to the Cooperative's technology, Arnus argues that his embodied Black form "made me more self-reliant,"[65] and therefore more himself.

Arnus determines that his Blackness will no longer function as a mask but as a mode of intentional being, an expression of his truest sense of self. In other words, Arnus's Blackness becomes a cosmic performance aligned with, evolving from, and fully expressing his extraterrestriality. At the end of the series, there is no longer any tension between his Black embodiment and his alien consciousness. Arnus decides to risk being seen as Black alongside Raquel and other Black terrestrials in order to work to defeat the Earth systems—racism, capitalism, sexism, ableism, and ecocide—that imperil Black life, and therefore also jeopardize Earth's participation in the Cooperative. Arnus's revelation is framed as a dechronologized network structured by jagged and uneven gutters which draw close-ups of Arnus, Arnus II, and Raquel into visual and physiognomic alignment (see figure 10). Arnus's face in the top and bottom left of the page, are balanced against Raquel's and

---

63. Ching and Birch, *Icon* 37, 4.
64. Ching and Birch, *Icon* 37, 4.
65. Ching and Birch, *Icon* 37, 4.

FIGURE 10. Raquel and Arnus discuss Arnus's future superhero practices. *Icon* 37, "Icon in the 20's," Milestone Media, 1996.

Arnus II's in the top right and middle right sites. Readers are encouraged to see the ways Arnus and Arnus II are aligned visually. Though Arnus II is blue, his jawline, head shape, and facial expression with the slightly parted mouth are echoes of Arnus-as-Augustus's face; though Arnus determines that he will retain his Black embodied form, he is still intimately related to his former self, and to Arnus II by extension. Readers are asked to consider how Raquel is also visually and sociopolitically aligned with Arnus-as-Augustus and Arnus II in her own way. In the bottom left panel, as Arnus and Raquel face one another, their intimate profiles and loving eye contact can be read as a sign of their complicity, intimacy, and commitment not only to one another but to advancing justice for all Earthlings. Indeed, Arnus plans to remain on Earth for as long as it takes "to make my adopted home a better place to live. Until all of humanity is ready to take their place as a mature species, Icon is here to stay" (*Icon* 36, 17).

Shortly after Arnus returns to Earth to work as a Black alien superhero, Milestone Comics shuttered and the series ended. Though the creators did not have an opportunity to elaborate how Arnus's decision to embrace the cosmic diaspora by *being Black* and join terrestrials by *being seen as Black* impacted his superheroics, the series nevertheless asks us to consider how the processes of *reading Black* engender an expansive superhero counterpolitics that configures Blackness as a differentiated, visual phenomenological experience, and a sociopolitical and collective commitment. As Arnus comes to know and work with Raquel over the course of the series, readers must consider how Black alien superheroes necessarily demand resistance to physiognomic logics that spectacularize and taxonomize embodied form along scales of superiority and dysgenicity. As Arnus comes to embrace his Blackness and, by extension, his involvement in and intimacy with Black terrestrial community, the series foments a Black cartoon counterpublic that encourages a radical embrace of Black looks, Black being, and Black community, gesturing toward a cosmic Black diaspora that extends far beyond the boundaries of Earth into new alien worlds.

CHAPTER 3

Black Alien M/other

Correcting the Intergalactic Archive

In a 1996 interview with *Science Fiction Studies,* Octavia Butler was asked whether it was intentional that so much of her work to date—*Wild Seed, Mind of My Mind,* "Bloodchild," and her *Xenogenesis* trilogy (renamed *Lilith's Brood* in 2000)—explored "the exploitation of reproduction and, by extension, of family." Butler's response is instructive. She explained that, as a Black woman living in the late twentieth century, she could not "help dwelling on the importance of family and reproduction. [. . .] Even though I don't have a husband or children, I have other family, and it seems to me our most important set of relationships. It is so much of what we are." Butler drew an important distinction between "reproduction," on the one hand, and "family," on the other, implying that they are not necessarily related—being childfree and single did not preclude her from belonging to family systems. She insisted that "family does not have to mean purely biological relationships either. I know families that have adopted outside individuals; I don't mean legally adopted children but other adults, friends, people who simply came into the household and stayed. Family bonds can even survive really terrible abuse."[1] Though reproduction is, of course, required for the propagation of the species, Butler believed that family bonds were equally

---

1. Butler and Potts, "We Keep Playing," 333, 333, 333.

essential to our survival, because they form the basis for "what we are" as people, fundamentally shaping how we live, interact, survive. Family is more comprehensive than "biological" relation, and must be understood as complex structures of fictive kinship, chosen family, and interdependent community, such as friend-kin, othermothers, play cousins, foster parents, and babysitters or minders, in addition to complex relations of (non)biological, common-law, or legally recognized spouses, parents, siblings, cousins, aunts and uncles, and grandparents—as well as connections to all other living organisms, including nonhuman animals, nonsentient organic matter, and the land itself.

I have so far in this book explored genealogical relations between Black terrestrial aliens and extraterrestrial aliens—in the form of time-traveling spacetime-bending descendants from other historical planets, and as visual and political intimacies between terrestrials and extraterrestrial aliens in Black cartoon counterpublics. In this chapter, I extend these conversations by examining how Butler's *Xenogenesis* trilogy imagines kinship futures between Black terrestrial aliens, extraterrestrial aliens, nonhuman animals, and organic matter at the axis of what Alexis Pauline Gumbs, China Martens, and Mai'a Williams have described as "revolutionary mothering." As I will explain in greater depth in the first section of this chapter, revolutionary mothering must be understood "not as a biological function, but as a *social practice*,"[2] or as networks of interrelation, social and political organization, and community-based care that require interdependence, mutual regard, healing and harm mitigation, and a holistic respect for all living beings and their material worlds. I argue that *Xenogenesis* constructs a queer human-alien horizon that centers revolutionary mothering—and, more specifically, Black mothering praxes—as essential to human well-being, and therefore critical to our collective survival in the future. As the series moves forward in space and time, each text builds toward an increasingly complex kinship network comprising humans, extraterrestrials known as the Oankali, and their offspring, known as constructs, in addition to cells, seeds, and microorganisms.

Butler's *Xenogenesis* is composed of three novels: *Dawn* (1987), *Adulthood Rites* (1988), and *Imago* (1989). In the opening sentences of *Dawn*, the trilogy's central protagonist, Lilith Iyapo, discovers herself "alive . . . again"[3] on what she will eventually learn is Chkahichdahk, a living female bioship

---

2. Oka, "Mothering as Revolutionary Praxis," 51.
3. Butler, *Lilith's Brood*, 5. Further citations to this work appear in the text.

orbiting space just beyond Earth's moon, piloted by a peripatetic extraterrestrial alien species, the Oankali, who explain to Lilith that they are gene traders, driven by "a tiny organelle within every cell of our bodies" to "acquire new life—seek it, investigate it, manipulate it, sort it, use it" (41). Lilith is informed that she will eventually have children with the Oankali, but that, in the process, her genes, body, and future will be irrevocably altered; as she learns to mother aliens in an increasingly queer assemblage of animals, plants, land, Oankali, humans, and constructs, Lilith ushers in new kinship structures, systems of belonging, and networks of care and community. *Xenogenesis* too imagines a world in which humans and aliens are partners in a reproductive future that is predicated on genetic manipulation. In the years Butler planned and wrote the trilogy, scientific communities made significant advances in genetic engineering—the first successful "test tube" baby was born in 1978, paving the way for IVF and prenatal genetic testing, and the first genetically modified (GM) foods were entered into the environment, though the ability to manipulate DNA and edit genes with the use of CRISPR would not take place until long after her death. Butler maintained an interest in genetic engineering in much of her work—for example, in her Patternist series, which is motivated by the godlike entity Doro's obsessive drive to create a family system of telepathic Africans—but I argue that *Xenogenesis* is her most sustained study of a potential reproductive, genetic, and kinship relation between true aliens and human aliens. Unlike human beings, whose genetic diversity is the result of sexual reproduction, the Oankali manipulate life in their cells, transforming themselves and other organisms in the process, a biological imperative that "enables us to survive as an evolving species instead of specializing ourselves into extinction or stagnation" (45). As I make clear in this chapter, *Xenogenesis* follows Lilith Iyapo for more than five hundred years, tracing her development and function as a Black Alien M/other to a progressively queer and strange community of construct children, Oankali-human mated partnerships, violent human resisters, the living land, and all of its organisms.

In the first section of this chapter, "From the Golden Record to Xenogenesis: Meditations on the Monophobic Response," I argue that *Xenogenesis* offers a narrative correction to the Golden Record, Carl Sagan's archive of Earth sounds and images appended to the Voyager spacecrafts and launched into outer space in the late 1970s. I offer a brief explication of the record's contents, which intentionally occluded representations of violence, politics, identity, ideology, religion, spirituality, and aesthetics, at the same time that it sought to speculatively represent the planet to extraterrestrial aliens as a global community that was on its way to becoming a peaceful US-led civilization. I explore how Octavia Butler's contribution to Connie Samaras's 1996 visual art exhibit *A Partial Correction to the Representations of Earth Culture Sent Out to Extraterrestrials on the United States 1977 Voyager Interstellar Space Probes*, an essay entitled "The Monophobic Response," challenges the record's representations of extraterrestriality and humanity by asking us to imagine ourselves as always-already intergalactic kin. I make the case that Butler's central correction to the archive in *Xenogenesis* is her construction of Lilith as a Black Alien M/other, a figure who represents mothering and networks of care as essential to human development; Lilith's mothering praxes function as a model of radical struggle against and in spite of oppressive regimes, and are therefore uniquely designed to make collective survival possible. In the second section, "Living with Aliens: Sociobiology, the Monophobic Response, and Praxes of Revolutionary Black Mothering," I argue that *Xenogenesis* rejects a biological or genetic basis for the Monophobic Response, or the irrational human fear of difference and willingness to make aliens of one another. I examine how Lilith's mothering practices challenge claims that human beings are unable to move beyond their initial prejudicial or fear-based responses to the world around them, and demonstrate how Lilith's Black Alien M/othering strategies create the necessary possibilities for Oankali-human survival by centering ways of being in and knowing the world that emerge from the undercommons. Finally, in the last section, "An Illegible Thing, a Queer Thing: Making Construct Kin in the Chthulucene," I read Lilith's Black ancestral othermothering praxis alongside the Oankali ability to perceive the potential and possibility for interconnections, entanglements, mutabilities, and hybridization on scales ranging from microscopic to the galactic. I argue that the world of *Xenogenesis* can be read as an example of what Donna Haraway defines as "sympoiesis," or the making of kin in complex networks of aliens and special strangers. I contend that *Xenogenesis* propels itself toward a queer horizon; as humans, Oankali, and their construct children attend to the local and emergent crises of everyday survival, they begin to live radically differently, bonding with and creating family in new systems of community, care, and kin-making. As the novels move into increasingly queer and deliberately entangled cosmic family systems that include an ever-widening circle of kin, including cells, inorganic compounds, plants and nonhuman animals, humans, aliens, land, domiciles, and the cosmos itself, Butler pushes us further and further away from heterosexual sexual relationships as the rubric for human reproduction toward "sibships," friendships, and interspecial community.

From the Golden Record to Xenogenesis: Meditations on the Monophobic Response

In June 1977, President Jimmy Carter wrote a statement of greeting to extraterrestrial aliens in anticipation that, among "the 200 billion stars in the Milky Way galaxy, some—perhaps many—may have inhabited planets and spacefaring civilizations."[4] The message was encoded on two gold-plated copper LPs, known as the Golden Records, secured to the outer frames of Voyagers 1 and 2, and launched into the cosmos from Cape Canaveral—Voyager 1 is now adrift in interstellar space approximately 165 astronomical units from the sun and 15 billion miles from Earth, making it the first human-made machine to travel beyond our solar system. Carter's statement rightly anticipates a vast expanse of time between the spacecraft's launch and its eventual discovery, noting that "it is likely to survive a billion years into our future, when our civilization is profoundly altered and the surface of the Earth may be vastly changed." Despite the certainty of disjunctions in spacetime between late twentieth-century Earth cultures and whichever cultures a spacefaring civilization might find here at some point in the next billion years, the Voyagers were designed with two purposes in mind: to continuously transmit data about the universe to NASA scientists on Earth, and to serve as US-global interstellar emissaries in the event of contact with aliens. Carter works toward this second purpose by nationalizing and globalizing the Voyager mission, beginning first at the point of state ownership of the vessel itself: "This Voyager spacecraft was constructed by the United States of America, a community of 240 million human beings among the more than 4 billion who inhabit the planet Earth." How to explain planetary politics to an extraterrestrial alien without also acknowledging the systems

---

   4. Carter was no stranger to alien encounters. In 1973, while serving as governor of Georgia, Carter filed a statement with the International UFO Bureau in Oklahoma City that provided details regarding his sighting of a UFO in 1963 in Leary, Georgia. Carter explained that around seven o'clock in the evening, following a speech at a Lions Club meeting, Carter and other guests witnessed an unusual bright white object in the sky, as bright as the moon, move toward them before hovering in the pine trees. The object changed colors from white, to blue, to red, and then back to white, before disappearing. As Carter explained in his statement, "A kind of green light appeared in the western sky. This was right after sundown. It got brighter and brighter. And then it eventually disappeared. It didn't have any solid substance to it, it was just a very peculiar-looking light. None of us could understand what it was" (Sheaffer, 20–21). For more on Carter's UFO sighting, see International UFO Bureau, "Report to the International UFO Bureau," by Jimmy Carter, 1973; and Robert Sheaffer, *UFO Sightings: The Evidence* (Buffalo: Prometheus Books, 1998).

of power that have apportioned to such a small fragment of the world's population the resources for an intergalactic mission on its own? Carter defaults to the imaginary. Though at the end of the twentieth century "we human beings are still divided into nation states," he insists that Earthlings are "rapidly becoming a single global civilization."[5] Made manifest in his signature as "President of the United States of America" in "THE WHITE HOUSE," Carter's enmeshment of US nationalism with the broader planetary community in his interstellar communication is an attempt to colonize the future. The Voyager spacecrafts themselves are products of an imagined US national community and lodestars for a future US-led global borderless society that is "rapidly becoming" on Earth; seen this way, the Voyagers and Carter's missive are works of speculative fiction writ in outer space.

The Golden Record localizes and regionalizes the globe in a manner compatible with Carter's imperialist discourse. The record's collection of sound, audio, and writing—selected during a four-month period by the Golden Record Committee under the leadership of Carl Sagan, including Linda Salzman Sagan, Ann Druyan, F. D. Drake, Timothy Ferris, and Jon Lomberg—ostensibly represents life on Earth in the late twentieth century. Sagan and NASA were keen, however, that Earthlings appear nonviolent to extraterrestrials. Jon Lomberg explains that the Golden Record Committee prohibited any representation of war; death; pain; crime; poverty; ethnic, racial, tribal, or national identity; sexuality; disability; religion; and politics in the archive:

> It would be naïve to deny the importance of these phenomena in human culture and history [. . .] yet we felt that we were making something that would survive us and our time—something that might be the only token of Earth the universe would have. We decided that the worst in us needn't be sent across the galaxy. Also, we wanted to avoid any political statement in this message, and a picture of Hiroshima or My Lai—or of a noble and heroic warrior, for that matter—seemed more an ideological statement than an integral part of an image of Earth. Nor did we want to any part of the message to seem threatening or hostile to recipients ("Look how tough *we* are"), which is why we didn't send a picture of nuclear explosion.[6]

Carter's speculative construction of the Voyager as a beacon made by the US on behalf of a future US-globalized Earth civilization reinforces the

---

5. Carter, Voyager Spacecraft Statement.
6. Lomberg, "Pictures of Earth," 76, emphasis in original.

committee's erasure of structural violence from the Golden Record. Though Carter refers elliptically to "the problems we face," he assures any aliens who "can understand these recorded messages" that by the time the spacecraft is intercepted, Earthlings will "hav[e] solved" them, and will be ready "to join a community of galactic civilizations."[7] In addition to planetarizing the US nation-state in the Voyager mission, the Golden Record archive also argues for the total globalization of US power, even a billion years into the future, while invisibilizing the atrocities that must continue in order to maintain and expand that power.

The Golden Record is thus framed by Carter as a gift, "a present from a small distant world, a token of our sounds, our science, our images, our music, our thoughts and our feelings."[8] The record's aluminum cover, electroplated with an ultra-pure sample of uranium-238, features several etchings that explain the spacecraft's origin and how to recover information from the LP: a pulsar map, indicating the precise location of our solar system; a drawing of the transition between the two lowest states of the hydrogen atom, or the fundamental time scale; diagrams of waves and binary code that demonstrate how to access the images and video signals on the recording; and instructions for using the stylus and cartridge to play the record's sound. The center label on the A-side of the LP reads "The Sounds of Earth, NASA, United States of America, Planet Earth," configuring the US as synecdoche for the planet in a manner compatible with Carter's statement. Intending to highlight linguistic and cultural diversity, the record begins with fifty-five traditional greetings in languages representing more than half the world's speakers; arranged in no particular order, they are simultaneously deterritorialized and hyperlocalized, gesturing toward a complexity of human social organization on Earth that is never fully elaborated on the record. Following immediately after is a twelve-minute acoustic essay of nonspeech and nonmusical Earth sounds—animal, human, and environmental—which likewise specify no particular location, including whale sounds, dogs barking, thunder, a human heartbeat, a mother stilling her infant's cries, an EKG monitor, brainwaves, laughter, fire, stone on stone, car horns, and the Saturn V lift-off, among many others. Ann Druyan explains that these sounds were "conceived for two audiences: the human and the extraterrestrial. In the former, we hoped to evoke smiles of recognition, and in the latter, a sense of the variety of auditory experiences that are part of life on Earth."[9] Though the archive provides no information for

---

7. Carter, Voyager Spacecraft Statement.
8. Carter, Voyager Spacecraft Statement.
9. Druyan, "Sounds of Earth," 150.

listeners about *where* on Earth the sounds were recorded, Druyan and the Sagans created the list of sounds themselves while in upstate New York. Despite Druyan's hope that the sounds would evoke universal nostalgia in human listeners, the acoustic essay is more properly reflective of the committee's white upper-class engagements with their own local and regional environments.

The audio section concludes with a ninety-minute selection of twenty-seven classical and folk songs from locations around the planet. The committee's ability to compile music was hampered by NASA's requirement that they secure copyright permissions—as Sagan explains, "the International Copyright Convention restricts the use reproduction of a piece of music 'for any purposes whatever,' presumably including even extraterrestrial purposes."[10] This section contains the record's only evidence that human beings are aesthetic and emotional beings who create art for pleasure. As with all other sounds and images on the record, Timothy Ferris explains that their choice of music selections was limited by their "own cultural biases. [. . .] We had to contend with a sharp drop in information that imposes itself when one looks beyond one's own culture."[11] Indeed, the record contains no music from the Caribbean, Central America, or the Middle East—and only two from the continent of Africa—but a preponderance from Western Europe, including three pieces *each* by Johann Sebastian Bach and Ludwig von Beethoven. The record includes no information about the artists and their music, though the consequences of this erasure are most serious for songs created under highly specific local linguistic and regional sonic traditions—for example, Mangunegara IV's Indonesian gamelan "Ketawang: Puspåwarnå," the Mbuti of Zaire's folk song "Alima Song," and the Azerbaijani ballad "Muğam (Çahargah ahəngi)" are stripped of political and historical significance. In the same vein, Sagan represents US musical traditions with exclusively Southern and Southwestern Black and Indigenous artists—Louis Armstrong's jazz, Blind Willie Johnson's blues, Chuck Berry's rock and roll, and a Navajo Night Chant performed by Ambrose Roan Horse—yet fails to mention the precarity of Black, Brown, and Indigenous human life on Earth at the hands of the US empire that led to the formation of blues and jazz in the first place.

The record contains 118 numbered photographs and other images that represent a diverse ecology of life on Earth. Though many of these images testify to the prevalence of special, ecological, and geographic difference on

---

10. Sagan, "For Future Times," 23.
11. Ferris, "Voyager's Music," 162.

Earth, the photographs representing human-animal interactions—Jane Goodall studying chimpanzees, San peoples hunting deer with a spear, and a Thai construction worker riding a domesticated elephant—represent nonhuman life on Earth as subservient to, existing to provide sustenance for, and as profoundly Other than humans, erasing the extent to which people exist in intimate and interpersonal relation with nonhuman beings. The remainder of the images depict human bodily functions, human-human and human-technology interactions, and the built environment, including dwellings (a round thatched-roof mud hut somewhere in Africa, an old New England–style house); urban skylines in Boston and Oxford, UK; the Great Wall of China and the Taj Mahal; crowded highways in India, Pakistan, and New York; and the interior of a factory. These images offer some sense of how human beings manipulate and traverse the land, use plant life to construct their homes, aestheticize the planet by region, and live and work collectively, but provide no broader explanation for the diversity of human experience. This missing context is key to the record's rhetorical functioning—any explanation the committee could offer for the built environment would necessitate addressing war, disease, religion, politics, and poverty, at the very least. What Lomberg describes as "different human gene pool[s] and culture[s]"[12] are localized by title, including "Man from Guatemala," "Dancer from Bali," "Andean Girls," "Thai Craftsman," "Chinese Dinner Party," "Old Man from Turkey," and "Japanese schoolroom." But what could "Andean," "Chinese," "Turkey," "Thai," "Japanese," "Bali," or "THE WHITE HOUSE" possibly signify to an alien without a map of nation-states, or a description of terrestrial cultures, genetics, and environmental diversity? These place-based national markers connote racial difference without violating the committee's prohibition on representations of politics or ideology, but more importantly draw the extraterrestrial's attention to Earthlings who are not (yet) included under the banner of "The United States of America."

Finally, the record includes several pictures of the human body: transparent overlays of human anatomy; a diagram of human sex organs; a photograph of conception and a corresponding silhouette; a fertilized ovum; a fetus and corresponding silhouette; and a silhouette of a man and pregnant woman. The original portfolio submitted to NASA also included a photograph of a naked man and pregnant woman, Lomberg notes, in order to "show recipients how our bodies look. We wanted to be neither sexist, pornographic, nor clinical. [. . .] NASA refused to include it" because it was deemed *potentially* pornographic; the image was included in silhouette in

---

12. Lomberg, "Pictures of Earth," 102.

order to complete the "continuity of the human reproduction sequence."[13] Other photographs show humans eating, breastfeeding, shopping, cooking, walking, diving, working, climbing, and performing gymnastics, highlighting how the body moves, how nourishment is taken in, and how people interact. However, there are almost no representations of human bonding—a father holding his child and a mother nursing her infant are the sole representations of family intimacy. Appearing singly, in pairs, or small groups, human beings seem isolated from one another on the record; there are no photographs of mass gatherings, such as church services, festivals, or crowded parks, no evidence of the extent to which human beings depend upon one another and their ecosystems for survival. The archive almost entirely eclipses the gamut of human feeling—though occasionally people smile, they never weep or shout. As a consequence of the committee's exclusion of ideology, politics, religion, and visual and narrative art, the record completely ignores human imagination, desire, abstract thinking, and spirituality.

In the nearly fifty years since the Voyagers launched, it has become clear that the Golden Record is less a sophisticated representation of Earth cultures than a speculative archive of US imperial hubris. Connie Samaras's 1996 visual art exhibit *A Partial Correction to the Representations of Earth Culture Sent Out to Extraterrestrials on the United States 1977 Voyager Interstellar Space Probes* rejects the committee's erasure of negative affect, identity, sexuality, war, poverty, oppression, and violence. In her artist statement, Samaras claims that her installation of photographs, diagrams, text, and video "is a progressive feminist and lesbian correction to the representations of earth culture sent into space by NASA in 1977 on the two Voyager spacecrafts." *A Partial Correction* is sharply critical of the committee's refusal to acknowledge "any vestiges of, at that time, recent U.S. social change movements (civil rights, anti-war, feminist, gay & lesbian liberation, global disarmament) resulting in a predictable privileging of elite white male Eurocentric culture where women's bodies are depicted as reproductive vessels, non-western communities are timelessly portrayed as outside technology, and where 'whiteness' goes unremarked." I turn to Samaras here because she amends the archive to include, among many other things, INS regulations for extraterrestrial aliens, and discussions of dreams, incest, racism, policing, queerness, gestation, autism, abuse, abduction, disability, intimacy, extinction, physical beauty, relationships, surveillance, and sex work. Given that the Voyagers are billions of light years from Earth, Samaras's "corrections"

---

13. Lomberg, "Pictures of Earth," 74, 74.

refer instead to revision, an opening up to "inevitability of change,"[14] and the possibility for radical human adaptation and resistance to stasis.

Samaras's most pointed corrections converge at the axes of alienation and alienness, reproductive futurity, state power, and mothering. For example, in "Correction to Voyager Image #32: 'Silhouette of Man and Woman,'" Samaras and visual artist Marilyn Zimmerman offer a multitext revision to the record's representations of human anatomy and reproduction, specifically targeting the censored silhouette of the naked man and pregnant woman. Zimmerman and Samaras correct the archive in three ways: with a photograph of Zimmerman as a naked pregnant white single mother; a test photograph of Zimmerman posing in parental embrace with her naked four-year-old daughter, Roxanne; and a report submitted to the Detroit police department by one of Zimmerman's colleagues at Wayne State University, who suspected her of trafficking in child pornography after finding a discarded proof of the test photograph in a wastebasket. This correction introduces into the archive several key concepts: pregnancy and mothering can be and often are done without partners; the bonds between mothers and their children are intimate and private; human beings wear clothing out of a sense of modesty and are punished for failing to do so in specific contexts; children can be and often are harmed by their parents; there can be a power imbalance between children and their parents, one that is unevenly policed by the state; and there is a power imbalance between humans and their institutions. These corrections also draw our attention to the committee's sublimation of the possibilities of queer kinship to cisheterosexual systems of relation by framing women's reproductive capabilities exclusively within patriarchal power structures. For example, Samaras introduces "Mother/Daughter Relationships" as a new category, including an extended meditation on why, as a lesbian, she "would not presently date her [mother]."[15] Samaras reads her mother's aloofness and drive against her own brashness and anxiety, her lesbianism in contrast to her mother's heterosexuality, their shared determination but varied access to opportunity. The piece introduces into the archive conceptions of sexual desire (and sexual repulsion); fear and anxiety; memory, history, and forgetting (or never knowing); emotional need and deprivation; intergenerational discord and conflict; and feminism as a political response to gendered oppression.

Octavia Butler's contribution to *A Partial Correction*, a short essay entitled "The Monophobic Response," serves as a narrative hinge between

---

14. Samaras, *Partial Correction*, 2, 2, 2.
15. Samaras, *Partial Correction*, 3.

the new categories of "Mother/Daughter Relationships" and "Abduction Experiences," which also features an essay on the planetary history of alien abductions. Butler's essay serves as a correction to the record's construction of extraterrestriality, its exclusion of xenophobia and intraspecies conflict, and its erasure of the centrality of family systems, siblings, and kinship to human social relations. Butler first considers what it means that in our current moment extraterrestrial aliens are speculative entities functioning exclusively at the level of a metaphor or possibility: "At the moment, there are no true aliens in our lives. No Martians or Tau Cetians, to swoop down in advanced space ships." Rather than maintain the record's fantasy of an ideal extraterrestrial audience—figments of the committee's collective imagining of what difference is or should be—Butler instead draws a clear distinction between "true aliens," beings we have not (yet) encountered, and "the human alien from another country, culture, race, ethnicity, religion, class . . . This is the tangible alien whom we can hurt or kill. This is the one we can blame for all manner of wickedness. This is the one we can feel superior to, the one we can feel certain isn't quite as human as we are. This is 'they,' 'them' 'those people!'" Because human beings "project alienness onto another," there is "a vast, terrible sibling rivalry going on within the human family as we satisfy our desire for territory, dominance, and exclusivity." Butler argues that human beings are nevertheless cosmic kin, children of an indifferent universe "that cares no more for us than it does for stones, for suns, for any fragments of itself." Humanity, overdetermined by an innate fear of difference, exists in a fraught kinship relation with itself—in our "ongoing eagerness to create aliens, we express our need for them. [. . .] And yet we are unable to get along with those aliens closest to us, those aliens who are, of course, ourselves."[16] Butler's construction of humans as siblings is not intended to frame humanity as essentially the same, but to demonstrate that we are bound to one another as Earthlings, and members of a special family system.

Butler's metaphorization of siblings is critical because, as Shawn D. Whiteman, Susan M. McHale, and Anna Soli explain, not only are "sibling relationships the longest-lasting relationship that most individuals have," these bonds are "multidimensional, and [. . .] vary across time and place. [. . .] The processes that affect sibling relationships operate at a variety of levels, ranging from intrapsychic processes, such as attachment and social comparison, to relational dynamics, such as social learning and more distal forces beyond the family, such as sociocultural influences." Imagining

---

16. Butler, "Monophobic Response," 5, 5, 5, 5, 5.

human beings as planetary and special siblings directs our attention to the ways family groups operate as "open systems—subject to external influences" which require families to "strike a balance between stability and change."[17] Siblings can be biogenetic, but also social and cultural—adopted and stepchildren, for example, influence the family dynamic in equally complex ways. Butler's construction of humanity as siblings requires thinking beyond the family as a genetic structure, and considering how siblings participate in, deviate from, and radically alter individual family systems.

Butler concludes by asking whether true aliens might catalyze human togetherness by providing us with "new siblings to rival."[18] In her imaginary, the confirmation that the "universe has other children"—our "distant siblings"—may serve to "bring us together, all human, and much more alike than different [. . .] Humanity. 'E pluribus unum,' at last, a oneness focused on, and in a sense, fertilized by the certain knowledge of alien others. What will be born, then, of such a strange and ironic union?"[19] Butler's construction of humans and extraterrestrials as cosmic siblings, and her reliance on the language of reproduction and kinship—fertilized, born, union—imagines humans and extraterrestrial aliens as intergalactic kin and transspecial family. Would "the certain knowledge of alien others" push humanity to realize Carter's vision of a "single global civilization"? In the face of true special difference, would human beings come to understand their constructions of alienness to be mere projections, fantasies, or exaggerations? What unions and connections—sexual, reproductive, fraternal, social, cultural—might emerge from human alien and true alien contact?

Butler's most expansive thinking on these matters, and her most elaborate correction to the Golden Record's archive, can be found in her *Xenogenesis* trilogy: *Dawn* (1987), *Adulthood Rites* (1988), and *Imago* (1989). In notes for a 1998 lecture, Butler explained that she developed her conception of the Monophobic Response while writing *Xenogenesis,* texts she described as meditations on "memories of my own aliens," and the human susceptibility to "irrational fears" of other beings—in her case, a

> phobic terror of wormy-things—slimy things that make do without bones and look as though they also make do without skin. Slugs, night crawlers, maggots . . . leeches. So naturally I decided to go to the Amazon jungle to research my *Xenogenesis* novels. In reading [. . . I] discovered [the] botfly's nasty habits. How to live with the real possibility of my worst fear growing

17. Whiteman, McHale, and Soli, "Sibling Relationships," 134–35, 135.
18. Whiteman, McHale, and Soli, "Sibling Relationships," 135.
19. Butler, "Monophobic Response," 5.

under my skin, eating me? I wrote a story about human beings used by centipede-like nonhumans in this way—and had it all done in fear, but also in love & caring.[20]

In *Xenogenesis*, Butler's irrational fear of wriggling invertebrates is represented by the Oankali, an intelligent extraterrestrial species who communicate using clusters of writhing wormlike tentacles. The Oankali are a polytypic species—in other words, they comprise several distinct but reproductively compatible subspecies. Self-described "gene traders" compelled by adaptation, alteration, and change, the Oankali are driven by a xenophilic imperative to genetically engineer and reproduce with dissimilar species. After coming across an Earth ravaged by nuclear war, the Oankali bring the remaining human and animal survivors onboard their moon-orbiting spaceship. Enthralled and repulsed by humanity in equal measure, the Oankali become convinced that the human tendency toward xenophobia is in fact a genetic expression of a destructive hierarchicalism combined with intelligence, and they decide to give humankind two choices: reproduce with us and be forever changed, or lose your ability to make generations entirely. The first human being the Oankali select for reproductive and genetic trade is Lilith Iyapo, a Black woman tasked with convincing a preselected cohort of human beings to join their Oankali mates in a new reproductive future on a terraformed, but vastly different, planet Earth. Over the course of the trilogy—more than five hundred years of Earth time—Lilith joins her human and Oankali mates and their children, known as constructs, in a multispecies procreative future.

In the remainder of this chapter, I make the case that Butler's *Xenogenesis* operates as a radical multitext correction to the Golden Record at three critical axes: the importance of Black revolutionary mothering praxis to our collective survival; the interdependence and entanglement of everything in the universe, from cancer cells to galactic ecosystems; and the importance of making queer kin and queering kinship both in the present and for the future. As an exploration of the Monophobic Response, and a careful imagining of the potential for "love & caring" that can be found collective multispecies kinship, *Xenogenesis* is an extended correction to the Golden Record's vision of Earth futures—in fact, the earliest mention of the Oankali in Butler's archive appears on August 18, 1977, two days before the launch of Voyager 2. On that day, as Butler meditated on the direction *Clay's Ark* (1984) might take, and the way human in/tolerance for special difference

---

20. Butler, Living with Aliens: speech, ca. 1998, box 154, OEB 3037, Octavia E. Butler Papers (hereafter Butler, Living with Aliens: speech, OEB 3037, OEB Papers).

would impact the novel's alien-human hybrid clayarks, she observed that "this could become a super involved story requiring a lot of research. I do have a planet to build, after all. The Oankali are the people I want, with all three of their sexes and their complicated reproductive system."[21] Butler's thinking about the meaning of alienness and humanness—her extensive vision of extraterrestrial-human futures borne of repulsion, desire, love, and fear—must be read in light of the US nation-state's representations of extraterrestriality. As I make clear in the following section, the *Xenogenesis* trilogy is a narrative exploration of the problems posed by "The Monophobic Response," or the human predisposition toward xenophobia, and the genealogical, biological, and familial tensions that would inevitably arise from new true alien and human-alien entanglements. For that reason, *Xenogenesis* is a meditation on the ways humanity constructs the alien; the visual, social, and political forces that organize human perceptions of self and other; and the possibilities for radical change in our collective genealogical futures.

Living with Aliens: Sociobiology, the Monophobic Response, and Praxes of Revolutionary Black Mothering

In notes taken during the writing of *Dawn*, Butler described *Xenogenesis* as a meditation on sociobiology and adaptation: "Precieving [sic] *Xenogenesis* as my Sociobiological [Sb] novel—as *Dune* was Herbert's ecological novel. Precieving [sic] Sb as a kind of enternal [sic] ecology—I suspect that people are both freer of 'instinct' and more trapped by it than we know or wish to know."[22] E. O. Wilson, in his controversial 1978 study *Sociobiology: The New Synthesis*, defined the term as "the extension of population biology and evolutionary theory to social organization."[23] Sociobiologists maintain that at least some human behavior is determined by genetics (nature) rather than environment (nurture). Critics of the field, most notably Stephen Jay Gould, deny that genes and evolution are the primary determinants for human behavior, arguing instead that traits such as aggression or violence are more readily explained by social environment.[24] Butler was clear that her interest in sociobiology was not a unilateral endorsement of it: "Some readers

---

21. Butler, journal, 1977, box 57, OEB 1004, Octavia E. Butler Papers.
22. Butler, *Dawn*: novel: notes and fragments, ca. 1985, box 27, OEB 396, Octavia E. Butler Papers (hereafter Butler, *Dawn*: novel: notes and fragments, OEB Papers).
23. Wilson, *Sociobiology*, x.
24. For more on the limitations of sociobiology, see Stephen Jay Gould, *The Mismeasure of Man* (New York: W. W. Norton & Company, 1981).

see me as totally sociobiological, but that is not true. I do think we need to accept that our behavior is controlled to some extent by biological forces. Sometimes a small change in the brain, for instance—just a few cells—can completely alter the way a person behaves." Butler pointed to cross-species examples in "the fungus that causes tropical ants to climb trees to spread its spores, or the disease that makes a wildebeest spend its last days spinning in circles. But I don't accept what I would call classic sociobiology. Sometimes we can work around our programming if we understand it."[25] Scholars have taken a range of approaches to Butler's interest in sociobiology and its expression in *Xenogenesis*, often conflating her ideas with those of the Oankali, who argue repeatedly in the trilogy that human (male) aggression, xenophobia, and hierarchical social organization are a genetic maladaptation that led humanity to destroy itself in nuclear war.[26]

Butler's meditations on sociobiology have a corollary in the "Monophobic Response," or, as I discussed in the previous section, an irrational human fear of difference and willingness to make aliens of one another. In notes for a talk entitled "Living with Aliens," Butler explained that her thinking on sociobiology began during the Reagan-era Cold War nuclear arms race amid the threat of mutual assured destruction:

> My XG novels tell the story of humanity forced to undergo such a radical change through the Genetic Engineering efforts of aliens who are natural genetic engineers. XG was inspired by Ronald Reagan—by early Reagan Era talk about Winnable Nuclear War, Limited N-War, More Nukes = safety. Something, I decided, not for the first time, must be intrinsically wrong with humanity. Basic bio-flaw—built in self-destruct. My Aliens say: Intelligence v. Hierarchical behavior.[27]

---

25. Butler and Potts, "We Keep Playing," 332–33, 333.

26. For more on Butler and sociobiology, see Nancy Jesser, "Blood, Genes, and Gender in Octavia Butler's *Kindred* and *Dawn*," *Extrapolation* 43, no. 1 (2002): 36–61; J. Adam Johns, "Becoming Medusa: Octavia Butler's *Lilith's Brood* and Sociobiology," *Science Fiction Studies* 37, no. 3 (2010): 382–400; Jim Miller, "Post-Apocalyptic Hoping: Octavia Butler's Dystopian/Utopian Vision," *Science Fiction Studies* 25, no. 2 (1998): 336–60; Cathy Peppers, "Dialogic Origins and Alien Identities in Butler's *Xenogenesis*," *Science Fiction Studies* 22, no. 1 (1995): 47–62; and Hoda M. Zaki, "Utopia, Dystopia, and Ideology in the Science Fiction of Octavia Butler," *Science Fiction Studies* 17, no. 2 (1990): 239–51.

27. Butler, Living with Aliens: speech, OEB 3037, OEB Papers. For further discussion of *Xenogenesis* and the Cold War, see Butler's interview with Joshunda Sanders, "I've Always Been an Outsider," in *Octavia E. Butler: The Last Interview and Other Conversations* (Brooklyn: Melville House, 2023), 133–47.

Butler's thinking through the implications of a "basic bio-flaw" in humanity led to the creation of what the Oankali ("My Aliens") describe as "The Human Contradiction [. . .] The Contradiction, it was more often called among Oankali. Intelligence and hierarchical behavior. It was fascinating, seductive, and lethal. It had brought Humans to their final war" (*LB* 442). The Oankali are motivated to trade genes with human beings because of their highly adaptive cancer cells, an organic technology the Oankali are able to put to positive nonlethal use for the purposes of limb regeneration and shape-shifting. This desire for trade is complicated, however, by what they perceive as a fatal human inability to control their special dispensation toward violence.

In the earliest moments of *Dawn*, Lilith learns from Jdahya, the first Oankali she meets while still in captivity, that The Contradiction will drive their treatment of her and all other humans:

> You have a mismatched pair of genetic characteristics. Either alone would have been useful, would have aided the survival of your species. But the two together are lethal. It was only a matter of time before they destroyed you. [. . .] You are intelligent. [. . .] That's the newer of the two characteristics, and the one you might have put to work to save yourselves. [. . .] You are hierarchical. That's the older and more entrenched characteristic. We saw it in your closest animal relatives and in your most distant ones. It's a terrestrial characteristic. When human intelligence served it instead of guiding it, when human intelligence did not even acknowledge it as a problem, but took pride in it or did not notice it at all. [. . .] That was like ignoring cancer. (39)

The Oankali believe human hierarchicalism is "entrenched," its expression as violence unavoidable. In their view, nuclear apocalypse resulted from biological human behavior, as endemic and destructive as uncontrolled cancer, proof of a human special failure to control their dangerous genetic impulses. In their trade with humans, the Oankali initially determine to breed out these "terrestrial characteristic[s]" by restricting human reproduction and preventing male and ooloi constructs from being conceived.

There is ample scientific evidence, however, that hierarchicalism is a socially adaptive behavior. As Jessica Koski, Hongling Xie, and Ingrid R. Olson explain, many Earth species organize themselves according to social hierarchies in order to apportion resources, establish community norms, maximize individual functioning, and increase group success, even though in these social systems "some individuals within the hierarchy—those at the top—will be afforded more resources and benefits than others, thus affecting morbidity and mortality. Despite the fact that there are always losers in this scenario, social hierarchies are highly pervasive across human cultures and they appear to emerge naturally in social groups [. . .] suggest[ing] an innate preference, or utility, in the differentiation of power and a possible evolutionary origin." Though stratified social groupings appear to be "important and unavoidable," they are not required to be asymmetrical, coercive, or predicated on abuses of power. Koski, Xie, and Olson helpfully draw a distinction between "hierarchy," or a "ranking of members in social groups based on the power, influence, or dominance they exhibit," and "status," which "can be measured through social opinion and reputation and is generally associated with admiration and respect." Though dominance and competitive hierarchicalism are pervasive, human beings "undoubtedly vary in the skills and traits we possess,"[28] and therefore also in our vision for how society should be structured. Instead of apportioning power and resources to a few people at the top of a vertical chain of being, for example, social hierarchies may instead select leaders based on their reputations for wisdom and kindness, their ability to take on a particular task in a given moment, or their willingness to work collectively with and for members of their community. For that reason, Koski, Xie, and Olson reject the bioessentialist claim held by the Oankali that human social organization will inevitably self-destruct.

Lilith also rejects the Oankali claim that nuclear apocalypse resulted from a "genetic problem. [. . .] I just don't believe it's that simple. Just a bad gene or two" (39). Though Jdahya clarifies that "it's many [genes]—the result of a tangled combination of factors that only begins with genes" (39), he offers no further explanation. Implicit in Lilith's rejection of The Contradiction, however, is her awareness that nongenetic social and historical factors led to nuclear war, chief among them imperialism, nationalism, capitalism, colonization, patriarchy, religious and political ideology, and the desire for global power. Unlike Ronald Reagan or Mikhail Gorbachev—men with sufficient power to destroy the world—Lilith occupied what Butler described in a 1976 journal entry as "the bottom": "Where is the bottom? The bottom is where the black women are. They're at the bottom economically, socially . . . We. And I could say much worse than that if I was talking about myself alone."[29] I read Butler's "bottom" as a correlate to Fred Moten and Stefano Harvey's "undercommons," or "the underground, the downlow lowdown maroon

---

28. Koski, Xie, and Olson, "Understanding Social Hierarchies," 528, 528, 528, 528.
29. Butler, journal, 1976, box 57, OEB 1002, Octavia E. Butler Papers.

community [...] where the work gets done, where the work gets subverted, where the revolution is still black, still strong."³⁰ As a Black woman at the bottom, Lilith worked in contradistinction to the state before becoming an unwitting victim of its capriciousness. The ultimate violent actor at the end of the world was therefore not a human "genetic problem" but powers aggregated in specific spacetime by systems far beyond Lilith's knowledge or control. In Lilith's view, the Oankali deliberately ignore the historical dynamics of power on Earth; like Sagan and Carter, their essentialist vision of humanity evinces no awareness of the political, ideological, and cultural distinctions in the late twentieth century. The Oankali never acknowledge at any point in the trilogy that human systems on Earth produced deadly inequity by transforming some (nonwhite/Black, queer, disabled, migrant, poor) subjects into aliens, nonhumans, or chattel—but neither do they acknowledge that many human beings also resisted and worked to destroy structures of domination and oppression and create new, more equitable systems.

Jack Halberstam explains that one of the most important realizations to arise from the undercommons / the bottom is that power-based hierarchical "structures ... are not only bad for some of us, they are bad for all of us. Gender hierarchies are bad for men as well as women and they are really bad for the rest of us. Racial hierarchies are not rational and ordered, they are chaotic and nonsensical and must be opposed by precisely all those who benefit in any way from them."³¹ Halberstam rejects the notion that gender and racial hierarchies are genetic or biological—they are "chaotic," "nonsensical," imagined, fantasies. In a lecture at the 1985 Clarion Science Fiction Writer's Workshop, Butler made it clear that she too rejected the argument that power-based human social systems are genetic: "It would be deadly for us to fall back on the excuse of biology. The danger of sociobiology is not only that it can be used to oppress people and blame their own genetic endowment for their oppression, but that it can be used also to excuse infantile, uncivilized behavior on the part of the oppressor—who can be said, after all, to be acting in accordance with his genetic programing (i.e. he can't help it)."³² Though Butler rejected sociobiological (and Oankali) explanations for human behavior, she was driven to understand how and why oppressive racial, sexual, and gender hierarchies cohere. In that same lecture, Butler argued that humanity's oldest impulse is "the creation of outcasts: more bluntly put, the creation of n——s. [...] The need for n——s—'low' people

---

30. Harvey and Moten, *Undercommons*, 26.
31. Halberstam, "Wild Beyond," 10.
32. Butler, Untitled essay, ca. 1985, box 143, OEB 2789, Octavia E. Butler Papers (hereafter Butler, Untitled essay, OEB Papers).

whom others can feel superior to—has been strong down thru history."[33] For Butler, the dawning of antiblack racial capitalism—the "creation of n———s" and "human aliens" for the sake of global profit—was the root of Earth's violent systems. Inequitable systems of difference-making are constructed, historical, and malleable; to Butler, the "creation" of racial capitalism, the fungibilization and enslavement of Black people, and the transformation of bodies into flesh are *not* biological mechanisms but motivated by desire for power and resources.

Even if humans have an inborn capacity to irrationally fear difference—for example, Butler's fear of slimy invertebrates, or Lilith's initial panic upon meeting Jdahya—they can adapt, change, and grow; after all, Butler confronted her phobia and traveled to the Amazon to research *Xenogenesis*, and Lilith becomes reproductive kin with other Oankali. In other words, Butler did not believe that the Monophobic Response was an entrenched terrestrial characteristic that could not be controlled:

> Is it biological? Something we do in response to genetic programming? It may be. That gets into sociobiology—a dangerous topic—and science fiction, less dangerous. If the making of n———s in all its ugly forms—racism, sexism, colorism, classism, religious intolerance, etc.—if all of these have some genetic base—a kind of inborn xenophilia—then like other inborn impulses—fight or flight, for instance, it must be controlled. We don't—most of us don't—attack or flee when we are startled or angry, in spite of the adrenaline suddenly released into our blood, urging us on. We're taught as children that running away or lashing out on a small provocation is unacceptable.[34]

Butler acknowledged that the human fear of difference may at some point have served an evolutionary function. In a draft of an unpublished 1993 essay, she argued that humans are "all prejudiced. We've all experienced racism, sexism, classism, ethnocentrism, religious enmity (both as victim and as victimizer). It is forever easier to suspect the worst of the different ones."[35] However, Butler was clear that she believed human beings can be taught to manage their perceptions of difference:

> Kill the different ones. Avoid the different one. At least, suspect and fear the different one. You can't trust them. They're probably up to no good. They're

---

33. Butler, Untitled essay, OEB Papers.
34. Butler, Untitled essay, OEB Papers.
35. Butler, Untitled essay on prejudice, 1993, box 143, OEB 2791, Octavia E. Butler Papers (hereafter Butler, Untitled essay on prejudice, OEB Papers).

not like us anyway. The way they act, sometimes I wonder if they're even human. When some version of the above thinking pops into your mind—and it will—as you go about your dealing with people who belong to groups other than the one you call your own, it is prejudice. When you feel this prejudice toward whole other races, religions, ethnicities, etc., and you will, it is racism. If you act on your racist feelings—and here's where choice comes into the picture—you have committed a racist act. [. . .] It isn't very nice somehow to admit that we, like every other animal species on earth, have built in tentancies [sic] that may be triggered without our conscious awareness or desire. Or course, after such tendencies have been triggered a few times, something other than biology kicks in. Habit kicks in, and we come to *know* that there's something wrong with *those people*.[36]

Butler was willing to entertain the notion that human beings may not *initially* be able to control their "prejudice," describing those fears as tendencies that arrive "without our conscious awareness or desire." However, Butler believed humans can overcome these instincts by refusing to let them become "habit" and develop into "racism." The Monophobic Response may be rooted in a biological response to difference, but its expression as systems of inequitable, asymmetrical relation are manifestations of human "choice." Butler was clear that "we can nudge people—intellectually, emotionally, creatively. We can make people do what they're so reluctant to do. We can seduce people into changing behaviors. [. . .] We can disturb their prejudices."[37]

Xenogenesis is an exploration of humans who repeatedly "disturb their prejudices" and do what "they're so reluctant to do" in order to survive, people who make the choice to push beyond their initial prejudicial fears of difference, and make kin with extraterrestrials in an increasingly queer holobiont, which I discuss in great depth in the next section of this chapter. Butler's refusal to imagine a world where human beings dominate extraterrestrials is one of her primary corrections to the intergalactic archive: "So often you read novels about humans colonizing other planets and you see the story taking one of two courses. Either the aliens resist and we have to conquer them violently, or they submit and become good servants. [. . .] I don't like either of those alternatives, and I wanted to create a new one. I mean, science fiction is supposed to be about exploring new ideas and possibilities." *Xenogenesis* instead reimagines humans and Oankali as loving community members, co-parents, and lovers, relations that come to fruition

---

36. Butler, Untitled essay on prejudice, OEB Papers, emphasis in original.

37. Butler, Notes for speeches, ca. 1998–2000, box 154, OEB 3046, Octavia E. Butler Papers.

through Lilith's Black revolutionary mothering praxis, or what Cynthia Dewi Oka describes as a "revolutionary struggle against a colonial, racist, heteropatriarchal capitalism which has for centuries separated us; arranged us in structured oppositions to each other; reduced our bodies to raw resources for abuse, exploitation and manipulation; and [. . .] occupied our breathing. [. . . Revolutionary mothering] is today the struggle for a world—no, many worlds—where we might exist and thrive as each other's beloved." If we understand that Black mothers have always struggled for their own liberation and that of their children, rather than working as passive participants in systems that devalue their lives, we see that "mothering is a primary front in this struggle, not as a biological function, but as a *social practice.*"[38] *Xenogenesis* is best understood as a speculative disquisition on mothering and an antidote to our "enternal ecology," or Butler's belief that human beings are bound by their instincts but able to control them, molded by their environments, shaped by their communities, and simultaneously driven by individual unconscious (or, as the case may be, biological) desires and fears. Butler's humans are adaptive, capable of change, and, most importantly, able to forge intimate interspecial mothering bonds and kinship networks that offer support, protection, and love—even (or especially) for subjects at the bottom.

Because the Oankali believe human beings are driven by hierarchical relations, their selection of Lilith as the first human being for trade is perhaps confounding. What would motivate them to choose a Black woman who did not influence cultures of power on Earth? The Oankali refuse to discuss Earth history with Lilith, but they are well aware of it. In addition to possessing genetic maps for every single surviving human, plant, and animal from Earth, they can produce facsimiles of any Earth text—as Jdahya explains to Lilith, "we have studied your bodies, your thinking, your literature, your historical records, your many cultures" (32). When they finally provide Lilith with reading materials, pens, and writing paper, their selection belies a deep understanding of her potential interest in US global-*cum*-racial politics and its constructions of biopower: "a spy novel, a Civil War novel, an ethnology textbook, a study of religion, a book about cancer and one about human genetics, a book about an ape being taught sign language and one about the space race of the 1960s" (108). Lilith accepts the texts without comment, and no Oankali offers to discuss them with her. Given the way they highlight Earth cultures of white supremacy, nationalism, scientific racism, and racial capitalism, however, I read them as evidence that the

---

38. Butler and Potts, "We Keep Playing," 332; and Oka, "Mothering as Revolutionary Praxis," 51, 53.

Oankali understand the histories of enslavement, antiblackness, misogyny, and state violence and are therefore also aware of Lilith's place at the bottom of Earth's former hierarchy.

If the Oankali are cognizant of Earth cultures of violence and oppression, and structures of resistance to those cultures, I argue that the Oankali paradoxically select Lilith *because* of her position on the bottom—or, more specifically, because of her Black ancestral and embodied approaches to mothering. In an early draft of *Dawn*, Lilith expresses confusion about why she was "chosen": "I wasn't anybody back on Earth. I wasn't important. [. . .] I mean, nobody you awaken is going to pay any attention to me or anything I say. Whatever you want me to do with them, forget it. It won't work no matter how willing I am."[39] The Oankali explain that her lack of status and power on Earth "recommends you—considering," and confirm that, having tested her repeatedly, she remains "the appropriate choice."[40] Though this exchange is missing from the published version of the novel, Lilith is still repeatedly tested "physical[ly] and mental[ly]" (8) by the Oankali, beginning during her initial period of captivity. Lilith's testing coheres at the axis of her ability to create intimate bonds with other humans and Oankali. For the first 250 years following nuclear war, Lilith is alternatively kept in a state of unconscious suspended animation inside of a genetically engineered plant pod, and awake in a small, two-room enclosure, frequently naked and alone. For much of that time, the Oankali communicate with her as disembodied voices that appear to come from the shelter's ceiling. During Lilith's first Awakening, as she describes them, the Oankali ask her to detail her age (twenty-six), former work status, and former kinship relations, including marriages, former children, and extended family. Lilith explains that her son and husband died in a car accident before the war began, and that she can only assume that the remainder of her family—"two brothers and a sister [. . .] a mother, a father [. . .] various aunts, uncles, cousins, nieces, and nephews" (8)—perished in nuclear winter. Lilith quickly grows frustrated that the Oankali refuse to reveal themselves or answer direct questions; in an act of incredible will, Lilith gradually refuses to respond to questions or follow directions until, after months of isolation, she begins to exhibit signs of psychosis. The Oankali learn from this exchange that Lilith is capable of resisting outside pressures (even to the point of mental debility) and that she is further able to turn her refusal into action; they eventually drug Lilith and return her to suspended animation rather than continue to try (and fail) to coerce her into participation.

---

39. Butler, *Dawn*: novel: notes and fragments, OEB Papers.
40. Butler, *Dawn*: novel: notes and fragments, OEB Papers.

When she is Awakened for the second time (and for every time thereafter), Lilith is more willing to participate in the testing; in return, the disembodied voice engages her in increasingly complex conversation. At one point, Lilith Awakens to discover that she has been given a five-year-old boy to care for, approximately the same age her son was when he died; the Oankali provide neither with information about the other's name or origin. Lilith is attentive to the child's emotional needs; she gives him both space and time to see that she will not harm him. Over time, Lilith learns his name—Sharad—and the pair begin to communicate, exchanging words, songs, cuddles, and games. Lilith quickly bonds with Sharad, and before long begins to "worr[y] about him and wonde[r] how to protect him" (10). Lilith chooses to feed, nurture, touch, and love Sharad, even in spite of her certainty that "she had no more power than he did" (11). Sharad is removed just as suddenly following her next Awakening, and the Oankali refuse to answer her questions about him. When Lilith first meets Jdahya, however, she immediately asks after Sharad, who explains that he was returned to suspended animation with his parents and siblings; unlike adults, children were not kept in prolonged isolation but left in semipermanent states of unconsciousness or raised with Oankali families. Jdahya explains that many adults killed themselves while in isolation, or, when placed with other people, harmed or killed one another; in light of this, Lilith's choice to care for Sharad is regarded as exceptional and unusual. Lilith admonishes him, however, that the Oankali "shouldn't have isolated any of us unless your purpose was to drive us insane. You almost succeeded with me more than once. Humans need one another" (19).

Lilith's insistence that human beings *must be* in community with one another—and the Oankali's inability to understand this need—is reinforced when she gains permission to meet another adult human being, a Black man named Paul Titus who was Awakened at age fourteen and spent more than half his life with an Oankali family. The Oankali expect that Lilith and Titus will have sex, a fundamental misapprehension of human attachment, sexual desire, and intimacy. Lilith believes that Titus, prevented from growing up in human community, is in a state of arrested development—when he makes a move to touch her shoulders, she recoils and finds herself looking at him the way "her mother had looked at her. [. . .] She had caught herself giving her son the same look when she thought he was doing something he knew was wrong. How much of Titus was still fourteen?" (93). Permanently cut off from his former life on Earth and prevented from forging new human bonds, Titus failed to develop intimate, protective bonds with his Oankali family, and maintain a meaningful connection to his humanity. In a violent explosion of grief, rage, and confusion at her rejection of him, Titus attempts to rape Lilith, in the process beating her unconscious. Upon coming-to after the assault, Lilith is furious with the Oankali, who insist they "didn't know how the male would behave" (98). It is at this moment that Lilith feels a gap of "unbridgeable alienness" (97) between herself and the Oankali—not because of their physical appearance or strange ecology but because of their inability to understand how essential it is for human beings to be nurtured, supported, and nourished in communities of care.

These ethics of connection and care drive Lilith's final test, which is to form a meaningful bond with an ooloi, the Oankali third sex responsible for reproduction and adaptation, and help it move through its period of sexual maturation; this process is required of Lilith before she can Awaken other humans and join the Oankali on Earth. Lilith is terrified when she first encounters Jdahya in her shelter; she is repulsed by "his alienness, his difference, his literal unearthliness" (13), represented by the multiple, quivering sensory organs that cover his face and body: "The tentacles were elastic. At her shout, some of them lengthened, stretching toward her. She imagined big, slowly writhing, dying night crawlers stretched along the sidewalk after a rain. She imagined small, tentacled sea slugs—nudibranchs—grown impossibly to human size and shape, and, obscenely, sounding more like a human being than some human. [. . .] Silent, he was utterly alien" (14). Modeled on Butler's "phobic terror of wormy-things," Lilith experiences what she describes as a "true xenophobia" (21), an irrational terror at his visible difference. Unlike other humans, whom Jdahya explains tried to kill him, Lilith resolves to push beyond the Monophobic Response and get "rid of [the phobia] as quickly as possible" (23). She is eventually successful; as she comes to know Jdahya, the two develop a close friendship, and he takes her to his home to live with his family. It is there that she meets her future partner, Nikanj, Jdahya's ooloi child, and her Oankali mates, Ahajas and Dichaan, with whom she develops a lifelong partnership.

As Lilith bonds with Nikanj, before long "only Nikanj gave her any pleasure, any forgetfulness" (59). Nikanj gives Lilith her first kinship name—Dhokaaltediinjdahyalilith eka Kahguyaht aj Dinso[41]—which she accepts, in addition to the responsibility to teach and learn from it, and help it grow.

---

41. An Oankali kinship name represents a cluster of relations:

> The *Dho* used as a prefix indicated an adopted non-Oankali. *Kaal* was a kinship group name. Then Tediin and Jdahya's names with Jdahya's last because he had brought her into the family. *Eka* meant child. A child so young it literally had no sex—as very young Oankali did not. [. . .] Then there was Kahguyaht's name. It was her third "parent," after all. Finally, there was the trade status name. The Dinso group was staying on Earth, changing itself by taking part of humanity's genetic heritage. (64)

When Nikanj explains to Lilith that, because its sexual maturation is arriving more quickly than anticipated, it will need to alter her brain chemistry to improve her memory and cognitive speed so she can better assist it, she initially refuses, terrified that it might accidentally damage her brain. Lilith eventually comes to accept this trade from Nikanj, allowing herself to be permanently changed by it—as Kahguyaht, Jdahya's ooloi mate, explains to Lilith, it could not have healed her or improved her memory without "leaving its mark" (110). Lilith assists Nikanj in its final transformation into adulthood, during which time it is immobilized as it grows sensory arms, or trunklike appendages that resemble a "blunt, closed elephant's trunk" emerging from its armpit, and ending in "eight fingers—or rather, eight slender tentacles arranged around a circular palm that looked wet and deeply lined. It was like a starfish—one of the brittle stars with long, slender, snakelike arms" (111). In addition to its sensory arms, ooloi also develop a *yashi*, an organelle that it uses to "perceive DNA and manipulate it precisely" (41).

After Lilith successfully helps Nikanj transition into adulthood, Kahguyaht explains to her that it "didn't want to accept you, Lilith. Not for Nikanj or for the work you'll do. I believed that because of the way human genetics were expressed in culture, a human male should be chosen to parent the first group. I think now that I was wrong" (111). When Lilith asks if the Oankali intend for her to be "their *mother*" (111, emphasis in original), Kahguyaht's response is, essentially, yes—she will be expected "to teach, to give comfort, to feed and clothe, to guide them through and interpret what will be, for them, a new and frightening world" (111). Its response directly undermines the Human Contradiction; Kahguyaht acknowledges that according to the narrow Oankali interpretation of the way "human genetics" were expressed on Earth, a Black woman might be seen as a poor choice if the accumulation of power is the goal. However, as Lilith demonstrates in her care for Sharad, Paul Titus, and Nikanj, she excels at the work the Oankali need a *mother* to do—to provide care, guidance, love, community, and protection for a new human alien/true alien community.

Butler's construction of human-alien kinship in *Xenogenesis* and her representation of narrative spacetime imagines the future as a making of queer intergalactic kin fomented and sustained by Black alien m/others—bloodmothers, othermothers, sibmothers, and self-mothers—and is a core correction to the Golden Record Committee's repressive representations of mothering, family, and kinship. I argue that mothering in the trilogy can be seen as both a form of essential communal labor that actively resists the violence of the Human Contradiction and Monophobic Response, and a speculative extension of ways of being and doing in the world enacted by Black women for centuries. Lilith's mothering praxis is a perpetuation of what Patricia Hill Collins has described as "organized, resilient [. . .] networks of bloodmothers and othermothers," systems that have remained "central to the institution of Black motherhood." Hill Collins defines "bloodmothers" as "biological mothers," who are often assumed to take primary responsibility for their children. In the event that a bloodmother is either temporarily or permanently unable or unwilling to provide care for her child, "African and African-American communities have also recognized [. . .] othermothers—women who assist bloodmothers by sharing their mothering responsibilities." Hill Collins reminds us that during slavery, older women were called upon to serve as nurses and midwives for white and Black folk alike, in addition to "caring for the children of parents who worked. Informal adoption of orphaned children reinforces the importance of social motherhood in African American communities. The relationship between bloodmothers and othermothers also survived the transition from a slave economy to post-emancipation Southern rural agriculture. Children in Southern rural communities were not solely the responsibility of their biological mothers. Aunts, grandmothers, and others who had time to supervise children served as othermothers." These networks of "fictive kin"[42] were essential to enslaved Black people on plantations; not only were children frequently raised by othermothers while their parents labored, children whose parents had been sold or killed were informally adopted and cared for by others in the community. In other words, structures of othermothering and collective childcare are fundamental to Black diasporic communities. I argue that Butler imagines these networks of care as equally essential to life in the cosmic diaspora.

Black mothering praxes emerged as explicitly political ways to ensure collective survival; indeed, "experiences both of being nurtured as children and being held responsible for siblings and fictive kin within kin networks can stimulate a more generalized ethic of caring and personal accountability." Revolutionary Black mothering praxes are therefore life-sustaining, inherently activist systems. While living on the ship, Lilith serves as othermother to Sharad, Nikanj, Paul Titus, and, over the course of her life, as we will see in the following section, to dozens of construct children, human neighbors, and Oankali mates. Over time, Lilith's mothering praxis becomes a generative and vitally important way of living in community. Because of their ability to create the conditions for collective survival, Black mothers have enjoyed high status and community authority; in early enslaved

---

42. Hill Collins, *Black Feminist Thought*, 193, 192; 192; 195; 195; 205.

communities, relationships between bloodmothers and othermothers and the broader community ensured that children were given love, affection, and care amid the chaos of family separations. Black mothering can therefore also be seen as an expressive medium, a way for Black caretakers to create meaningful change in the world: "Motherhood can serve as a site where Black women express and learn the power of self-definition, the importance of valuing and respecting ourselves, the necessity of self-reliance and independence, and a belief in Black women's empowerment. [. . .] Motherhood [. . .] provid[es] a base for self-actualization, status in the Black community, and a catalyst for social action."[43] In other words, Lilith's role as mother becomes a way for her to ensure the survival of her kin group but is also a way of being and doing in the world.

That said, Black mothers and mothering praxes have often been impugned by the state, their labors misrepresented by "the controlling images of the mammy, the matriarch, and the welfare mother . . . [that are] designed to oppress." If *Xenogenesis* offers a dual correction to Carter's attempt to planetarize the US and Cold War nuclear weapons strategy, it is also a revision of Reagan's weaponization of Black mothers as "welfare queens," or his perception that Black motherful people were lazy social parasites whose many illegitimate children were destined to become a permanent financial burden to the state. In defiance of this antagonistic vision of revolutionary mothering, Butler configures Lilith as a Black Alien M/other, or a counterfigure who corrects controlling images of Black mothers as deficient, neglectful, and unsafe. Represented by Lilith's repeated efforts to reject hierarchicalism in order to offer humans and true aliens access to structures of motherlove, the Black Alien M/other builds interconnected networks of caregiving; protects and builds community; pushes for reproductive autonomy and control; cares for children and people in relations of biological and fictive kinship; and develops mothering praxes and structures of social care, community work, and holistic communitarian approaches to childbirth and childcare. Lilith's revolutionary mothering praxis imagines systems of care from the bottom, sustained in the undercommons. To that end, I take seriously here Alexis Pauline Gumbs's argument that "the radical potential of the word 'mother' comes after the 'm.' It is the space that 'other' takes in our mouths after we say it. We are something else. We know it from how fearfully institutions wield social norms and try to shut us down. We know it from how we are transforming the planet with our every messy step toward making life possible."[44] By mothering *as an alien other,* and by mothering

---

43. Hill Collins, *Black Feminist Thought,* 205, 191.
44. Hill Collins, *Black Feminist Thought,* 191; and Gumbs, "m/other ourselves," 21.

true aliens *who are inherently other,* Lilith's function as Black Alien M/other is Butler's firmest repudiation of sociobiology, a rejection of claims that human beings are singularly overdetermined by a violent and fearful "enternal ecology" and a deliberate move toward the potential inherent in "something else." As we will see in the remainder of this chapter, Lilith's Black Alien M/othering praxis forms the foundation for Oankali-human community for hundreds of years. By refusing to surrender to the Monophobic Response and learning to live with, love, and mother aliens, Lilith becomes Butler's model for understanding how we can survive together now and after the end of the world.

An Illegible Thing, a Queer Thing: Making Construct Kin in the Chthulucene

In notes on the major themes of *Xenogenesis,* Butler explained that the trilogy would tell

> the story of two peoples, one human, one very definitely nonhuman who biologically meld into each other in only a few dozen generations. The following are factors and/or innovations of XG.
>
> - Honest, sustained, nonpolemic matriarchy in a human group.
> - Cancer as a biological tool of human evolution and development.
> - Birth defects as a way of human life.
> - Metamorphosis as a necessity of human life.
> - Human-nonhuman matings that in roundabout fashion become ordinary, then essential.
> - Three-person marriages—two humans and an ooloi—as the best possible arrangement. [. . .] A couple is simply not enough.[45]

Given Lilith's function as a Black Alien M/other, it makes sense that Butler would center matriarchy and mothering as "honest, sustained" systems of community organization. In many ways, *Xenogenesis* is a complex fantasy of Oankali-human reproductive kin-making in the cosmic diaspora, an intergalactic family system unfolding in trilogic narrative spacetime. Lilith learns early on in her captivity that she will be one of the first humans to engage in reproductive trade with the Oankali by giving birth to generations

---

45. Butler, *Xenogenesis*: notes, ca. 1985, box 151, OEB 2993, Octavia E. Butler Papers (hereafter Butler, *Xenogenesis*: notes, box 151, OEB Papers).

of human-Oankali children who will be known in their community as "constructs." Each of Lilith's children has four additional parents: a human male, Oankali male, Oankali female, and ooloi, the Oankali third sex responsible for genetically engineering all life. As Butler explained in her notes, after contact "the ooloi now play the same reproductive role among humans as they do among their own people. Human sperm and egg will not unite outside the body of an ooloi. And within the ooloi, changes are made. Defective Human genes are recognized and replaced. Some genes, neither defective nor essential, are replaced with Oankali genes. Thus, Human young are reprogrammed to be free of hereditary disorders and to become, from their generation on, part Oankali."[46] This is not, however, a eugenic future; as we will see, the Oankali manipulate and incorporate disease and disability rather than destroy it. Lilith and her female Oankali mate gestate (eleven months for humans, fifteen for Oankali) and give birth to constructs designed and implanted by their ooloi mate; construct siblings share a special and intimate bond with one another that is distinct from the bonds they share with their many parents. All children are *eka*, or sexless, until they go through their sexual metamorphosis, during which time they become male, female, or ooloi, often matching the parent or sibling they are closest to; ooloi go through two distinct metamorphoses and are far more rare. Lilith learns that her future will be reproductive, but without sexual intercourse—after mating with an ooloi, humans will find it deeply unpleasant to touch another human's skin, making physical sexual contact impossible. All Oankali mates are siblings or cousins who partner with an ooloi from outside their immediate family system; for this reason, reproduction is viewed by the Oankali as cooperative partnerships with their closest and most compatible family members, creating structures of care that emphasize collectivity, friendship, and love rather than sexual or romantic attraction. In order to convince the first humans to participate in their reproductive scheme, the Oankali pair genetically diverse heterosexual couples together—ooloi can induce chemical relaxation, and simulate sensations of sexual pleasure for human partners with their sensory arms, dense clusters of tentacles that they use to see, hear, smell, taste, and touch, synthesize organic matter, heal wounds, and genetically alter organic matter. Unlike humans, who cannot communicate by touch, Oankali transmit information directly to one another via clusters of tentacles spread out over their bodies, an ability construct children also share. By the trilogy's end, however, human-Oankali mating

---

46. Butler, *Dawn*: novel: outline—draft, ca. 1985, box 29, OEB 427, Octavia E. Butler Papers (hereafter Butler, *Dawn*: novel: outline, OEB Papers).

systems are rapidly moving away from sexual attraction as a determinant for reproductive compatibility to procreative sibling structures that mimic Oankali understandings of family intimacy.

As I explained in the previous section, Lilith is selected as the first mother because of her knowledge of revolutionary Black mothering praxes—but the Oankali also select her because of her "talent for cancer" (22). While still on the ship, Lilith learns that the Oankali performed surgery on her immediately after the war, removing tumors from her uterus and ovaries before inducing her body to absorb the remaining cancerous cells, and turning off the gene responsible for their uncontrolled growth. Her reproductive cancer was hereditary, binding Lilith to the other women in her family: "Her mother had died of cancer. Two of her aunts had had it and her grandmother had been operated on three times for it. They were all dead now, killed by someone else's insanity. But the family 'tradition' was apparently continuing" (21). Though a tragedy for her family, the Oankali insist that her ability to grow cancer is "a gift": "You can't control it . . . but we can. Your body knows how to cause some of its cells to revert to an embryonic stage. It can awaken genes that most humans never use after birth" (237). The Oankali and her construct children repeatedly use Lilith's hereditary genetic ability to regenerate limbs, shape-shift, and heal genetic birth defects, often with her direct participation. Lilith's cancer genes can be read as a kinship relation that binds her in community to her ancestors. In her new Oankali family system, however, cancer is transformed from a marker of disease and early death into a regenerative, holistic program of communal healing. Lilith is therefore hailed as a mother on two significant fronts: as the first human mother to Oankali-human constructs, and as a genetic mother whose cancer cells paradoxically lead to multispecies survival and the creation of new life.

I have argued so far that *Xenogenesis* is a multipart correction to the Golden Record Committee's occlusion of life at the bottom from their archive. By configuring Lilith as a Black Alien M/other who builds structures of multispecies community and offers protection for the people in her community, Butler focuses our attention on what Hill Collins describes as the "fluid and changing boundaries . . . central to the institution of Black motherhood."[47] These boundaries shape the contours of Lilith's revolutionary mothering praxis for true aliens, including for her biological children who are profoundly other than her. This is, in fact, how Butler defines the term in her early notes: "XENOGENESIS—production of offspring wholly & permanently unlike the parent. [. . .] Xenogenesis the living world,

---

47. Hill Collins, *Black Feminist Thought*, 192.

life-loving, life-incorporating, carboniferous, utterly capable of defending itself, ordering its environment, and seeing to its future."[48] Lilith mothers her construct children in an intergalactic community radically different from the one she lived in before the war. At the beginning of *Adulthood Rites*, the second book in the trilogy, we learn that Lilith has been living for more than fifty years in the Amazon basin with her Oankali family—Ahajas and Dichaan, her female and male mates, respectively, and Nikanj, her ooloi mate, along with several of her female construct children, and her new infant son, Akin, the first male construct born on Earth. Lilith also lives with several other Oankali-human families, each sharing responsibility for structural improvements and design, child care, hunting and farming, and community learning. As she prepares to care for her new son, Nikanj reminds her to be flexible in her approach to mothering as he grows older: "Families will change, Lilith—are changing. [. . .] Trade means change. Bodies change. Ways of living change. Did you think your children would only *look* different?" (260). And, indeed, this is true—Akin will eventually convince the Oankali to give humans back their reproductive destiny, and the option to live free from Oankali constraints on Mars; at trilogy's end, Akin has been helping a community of humans terraform Mars and regrow their population for more than one hundred years with no intention of ever returning to Earth. Over time, Lilith learns to mother in the midst of these changes: planetary change, as the Earth, continuously altered by the Oankali, no longer resembles the place she left behind; interpersonal change, as she works to create new social systems with humans and Oankali, stepping into her role as mother to her community and children; and personal change, as she reckons with the way the Oankali have altered her body and its DNA, including giving her extended life, imperviousness of physical injury, incredible strength, and resistance to cancer mutation. At its most fundamental, then, I argue that *Xenogenesis* is a meditation on what it means to survive amid cataclysm.

Scholars have paid closest attention to the first book in the trilogy, *Dawn*, as I did in the previous section, because of the many ways Butler innovates on the human-alien encounter in the novel, offering us a speculative future that reconstructs boundaries between Blackness, humanness, and alienness. *Dawn* provides an early glimpse of what, following Edward Soja, I describe in chapter 1 as a Black alien Thirdspace, or a space of openness, resistance, and renewal that encourages us to think beyond the borders of oppositional binaries—Black/Human or Human/Alien—and embrace new systems of belonging. In the remainder of this chapter, however, I focus my attention on

---

48. Butler, *Xenogenesis*: notes, ca. 1985, box 150, OEB 2981, Octavia E. Butler Papers.

Imago, the final novel in the trilogy, because it offers the most fully realized vision of the Black alien Thirdspace as a cosmic diaspora, future spacetime, and expression of narrative possibility. At the time *Imago* begins, Lilith is still partnered with her Oankali mates, Ahajas, Dichaan, and Nikanj, and has been living on planet Earth in a community of Oankali and humans for more than two hundred years. The novel is narrated from the first-person perspective of Jodahs, Lilith's birth child, and the first ooloi construct to be born on the planet—importantly, this is the only novel in the trilogy to adopt this point of view (*Dawn* and *Adulthood Rites* are both written in third person), which highlights the uniqueness of Jodahs and its Oankali-born sibling Aaor, who is also ooloi. Because ooloi directly manipulate life, the Oankali issue a prohibition on the creation of ooloi constructs, believing that they would find the imperative to trade too difficult to control. Lilith's family break Oankali protocol and keep Jodahs and Aaor with them on the planet, choosing not to send them back to the spaceship where they would be raised in a controlled environment. Though Lilith is a committed bloodmother and community othermother to her children, she was given no opportunity to consent to reproductive mothering, a trauma that surfaces again and again in *Xenogenesis*. While still on the spaceship, Lilith's first human mate, Joseph, was murdered by other humans suspicious of his relationship to her and her closeness to the Oankali; immediately after his death, before transporting her to Earth, Nikanj impregnates Lilith without her knowledge or consent. Lilith repeatedly expresses anger and resentment that she was denied the choice to determine when and how to create a family. This is not to say that Lilith regrets her pregnancies, is not connected to her Oankali family, or remains entirely resentful of her new community life; Lilith eventually finds another human mate on Earth, Tino, with whom she has several more children. Rather, Lilith mourns what never was and can never be again—her life with her human husband and child on pre-apocalyptic Earth, a world without fear that she has betrayed the human species by giving into reproductive trade, and her total reproductive autonomy. That said, her willingness to defy the Oankali and her refusal to part with Jodahs and Aaor is evidence of her role as Black Alien M/other who creates the conditions of survival for her children and broader community.

Though Lilith influences many aspects of human-Oankali social life through her revolutionary mothering praxis, Butler explained elsewhere in her notes that the Oankali control all aspects of reproduction and environmental change:

> The Oankali are all artists. Some reproduce meaningful (focused intense bits of a thing that highlight, distort, intensify, blur, symbolize . . .) representations

> in life—in living flesh. The highest art is flesh. This group produces shapes meaningful to them and their people. Some shape plant life, some shape animal life. Only the very best shape intelligent life. Only the ooloi shape intelligent life. Actually, only the ooloi shape any animal life. Males and females design, support, and make geographic changes. Generally the three decide what they will create. Then they set up everything—prepare climate, geography, plant life, atmosphere. In this, the ooloi merely helps, suggests, directs when it seems something has gone wrong. Later all is the ooloi, observing, understanding, then slowly, deliberately changing them, either by forced matings (unconscious victim, no memory) or by seduction.[49]

The Oankali perceive that their imperative to "shape life"—land, climate, atmosphere, flesh, flora, fauna—is a biological or genetic requirement, and therefore morally neutral, even in spite of their total control over life, and their inability to ensure that nothing will "go wrong." The central conflict in *Xenogenesis* rests in the tension between the Oankali's total control over "intelligent life" in their trade—their stated imperative to "highlight, distort, intensify, blur, symbolize" all aspects of life—and the human desire to retain their special distinctiveness. Again, in her notes Butler makes it clear that "to the Oankali gene trading is as essential as our humanity is to us. Our shapes, appearance, beliefs, cultures—we need these things. They sustain us. The Oankali would distroy [sic] or change all. They would, most obviously, change our shape. And in that change lies the seeds of many others."[50] In some ways, the Oankali imperative to trade is an eerie echo of Lilith's former experiences at the bottom of the pre-apocalyptic Earth, where Black people were subject to nonconsensual experimentation, forced sterilization, and the violent usurpation of their bodies, organs, or cells (as was the case for Henrietta Lacks); denied access to collective forms of history and memory; and prevented by the state from joining the systems of related living. That said, though the Oankali do intentionally control and delimit freedom of movement, genetic futures, and individually directed opportunity for humans, in the process of "chang[ing] all" aspects of life, the Oankali *themselves* are also irrevocably changed in unpredictable ways, producing a true xenogenesis in which the children are permanently different from *every* parent. The Oankali intend for their trade to create something new, to produce both synthesis and unforeseen innovation or error.

---

49. Butler, *Xenogenesis*: notes, box 151, OEB Papers.
50. Butler, *Dawn*: novel: notes and fragments OEB Papers.

In *Imago*, construct children are, indeed, radically different from their parents. Constructs retain the Oankali ability to manipulate their environment, communicate with one another through the use of tentacles, and trade genes, but they also retain the human need to bond with others in social and emotional care networks of kin and community. Unlike the Oankali, who do not show emotions on the surface of their bodies and transmit all feelings directly through their tentacles, constructs are emotive, physically communicative, and deeply in tune with all aspects of the world around them, from cells and seeds to people and animals to the land. For that reason, I read the world of Oankali, humans, and constructs in *Imago* as an example of what Donna Haraway has described as "sympoiesis": "Sympoiesis is a simple word; it means 'making-with.' Nothing makes itself; nothing is really autopoetic or self-organizing. [. . .] Earthlings are *never* alone. That is the radical implication of sympoiesis. *Sympoiesis* is a word proper to complex, dynamic, responsive, situated, historical systems. It is a word for worlding with, in company."[51] Butler argued as much in her notes on *Imago*, observing that the novel rejected terrestrial constructions of "exclusive" "animal life on Earth [. . .] each breeding within its own species."[52] Rather, the novel was intended to embrace the Oankali perspective that life was "inclusive, incorporating (through the activities of their third sex, the ooloi) useful characteristics of almost any intelligent carbon based species they come upon, thus fitting themselves into new ecological niches, new worlds that might otherwise be deadly to them. [. . .] Instead of killing, they absorb."[53] By "absorb[ing]" life rather than "killing" it, the Oankali are driven by their trade to perform sympoiesis by "worlding with" other beings.

Following Haraway, I describe this inclusive and incorporated Oankali-human world, in which all carbon-based species ("intelligent" and otherwise) can be potential mates or interspecial kin, as a *holobiont*, or what she describes as

> symbiotic assemblages, at whatever scale of space or time, which are more like knots of diverse intra-active relatings in dynamic complex systems, than like entities of a biology made up of pre-existing bounded units (genes, cells, organisms, etc.) in interactions that can only be conceived as competitive or cooperative. [. . .] My use of *holobiont* does not designate host + symbionts because all of the players are symbionts to each other,

---

51. Haraway, *Staying with the Trouble*, 58.
52. Butler, *Dawn*: novel: outline, OEB Papers.
53. Butler, *Dawn*: novel: outline, OEB Papers.

in diverse kinds of relationalities and with varying degrees of openness to attachments and assemblages with other holobionts.[54]

In other words, the symbiosis represented by the Oankali-human world and its construct children is not a relation between "host"—or the Oankali—invading a cluster of symbionts—or humans and the natural world—who in the process remain unchanged, but should rather be understood as a entangled network of "heterogeneous webbed patterns and processes of situated and dynamic dilemmas and advantages." In other words, in the radical holobiont of *Xenogenesis* *everything* and *everyone* is changed, altered, and made new in a radical alternative worlding that "entangles myriad temporalities and spatialities and myriad intra-active entities-in-assemblages—including the more-than-human, other-than-human, inhuman, and human-as-humus."[55] In a journal entry written the same year *Imago* was published, Butler described symbiotic assemblages that emerge on Earth as "true colony organisms," such as slime molds or Portuguese Man o' War:

> Not everything is as fully differentiated (plant or animal) as we would expect. Most slime molds are made of amoeba (like?) parts that feed separately, then, when food supply is exhausted, they come together, crawl to a suitable place as a multicellular "slug." There it builds a "tower" of its own cells—of itselves and a few at the top produce spores which scatter on the wind from the fruiting body (tower). Is it an individual with parts mobile? Is it an agragate [sic]—many individuals? Is it a 'mating group'? A Portuguese Man-o-War is a colony acting as a single animal. [. . .] Consider: Agragate [sic] multi-dividuals are intelligent or can develop intelligence as units. Never as individuals.[56]

Butler's "multi-dividuals," or aggregates of individual organisms that work together collectively, offer a way to understand the holobiont of *Imago*, in which plants, animals, people, and aliens are not "fully differentiated" but interconnected and interdependent—and at times indistinguishable. In the process of xenogenesis and the making of an Oankali-human-construct holobiont, individual organisms come together to operate as "units," losing aspects of their distinctiveness and individual will in order to become "intra-active entities-as-assemblages" that work together. In Butler's view,

---

54. Haraway, *Staying with the Trouble*, 60.
55. Haraway, *Staying with the Trouble*, 60, 101.
56. Butler, Notes on organisms, 1988, box 83, OEB 1625, Octavia E. Butler Papers.

as she noted in a journal entry, "there is nothing alien about nature,"[57] and therefore no reason why very different sorts of beings and entities could not be induced to sympoiesis. In other words, Butler's vision of multi-dividuals as communities of mutually cooperative intelligence blurs the boundaries of speciality, dissolving differences between plants and animals, animals and humans, humans and aliens, aliens and the world.

Among the clearest examples of a holobiont in *Xenogenesis* are human and Oankali organisms themselves. The Oankali, for example, are multi-organisms that operate as one; as I mentioned earlier, the Oankali communicate with one another directly using their tentacles, conveying information, emotions, and ideas to one another instantaneously, collapsing psychic boundaries and fostering a closeness between them that borders on telepathy. Each Oankali also carries an organelle called a *yashi* in each cell. As Oankali interact with the world around them using their tentacles, they extract data from organisms and store them in a *yashi* until they are able to transfer the data to an ooloi, drawing from "bits of fur, flesh, pollen, leaves, seeds, spores, or other living or dead cells from plants or animals that we had questions about or that were new to us" (532). An ooloi's *yashi* is larger and more complex than other Oankali's—in addition to storing genetic material, its *yashi* analyzes and manipulates genetic material, creates life, heals and regenerates, and produces consumable matter, including *qashi*, a consumable cheeselike protein substance everyone relies on when traveling in shuttles to outer space. As Nikanj explains to Lilith, the *yashi* was, like the human mitochondria, at one point an entirely different organism:

> Anything to do with Humans always seems to involve contradictions. [. . .] Examine Tino. Inside him, so many very different things are working together to keep him alive. Inside his cells, mitochondria, a previously independent form of life, have found a haven and trade their ability to synthesize proteins and metabolize fats for room to live and reproduce. We're in his cells too now, and the cells have accepted us. One Oankali organism within each cell, dividing with each cell, extending life, and resisting disease. Even before we arrived, they had bacteria living in their intestines and protecting them from other bacteria that would hurt or kill them. They could not exist without symbiotic relationships with other creatures. [. . .] I think we're as much symbionts as their mitochondria were originally. They could not have evolved into what they are without mitochondria. (124)

---

57. Butler, Notes for speeches, ca. 1998, box 82, OEB 1581, Octavia E. Butler Papers.

According to Nikanj, humans and Oankali live together in and as a holobiont, an accretion of multispecial living; in other words, both are multi-dividual species capable of radical adaptation and symbiosis. Among the strongest Oankali criticisms of human beings is their ignorance and fear of multi-dividual living, even within themselves; just as the mitochondria altered the human capacity to "live and reproduce," the Oankali also change and alter human cells—again, Lilith is stronger, resistant to disease, and long-lived—in order to become one with humans. Jodahs explains that the introduction of the *yashi* utterly changed the orientation of Oankali life, just as the mitochondria made possible human evolution: "We were what we were because of that organelle. It made us collectors and traders of life, always learning, always changing in every way but one—that one organelle. Ooloi said that we *were* that organelle—that the original Oankali had evolved through that organelle's invasion, acquisition, duplication, and symbiosis" (544). Jodahs and Nikanj blur the boundaries between themselves as individual organisms, their collective and special relation to the Oankali as ooloi, and their evolutionary relationship with the *yashi*—they function together, driving the species to learn and change as one.

What does it mean to *make kin* in symbiotic assemblages with humans and Oankali? I read *Imago* as a study of what Haraway describes as the Chthulucene, or "an intense commitment and collaborative work and play with other terrans, flourishing for rich multispecies assemblages that include people. [. . .] I am calling all this the Chthulucene—past, present, and future." The Chthulucene in speculative imaginaries can be read as the age of "abyssal and elemental entities, called chthonic," or what she terms "tentacular ones": "The tentacular ones make attachments and detachments; they make cuts and knots; they make a difference; they weave paths and consequences but not determinisms; they are both open and knotted in some ways and not others. SF is storytelling and fact-telling: it is the patterning of possible worlds and possible times, material-semiotic worlds, gone, here, and yet to come." I find the Chthulucene to be an effective way of thinking about the world of *Imago*, which is overrun with tentacular ones—humans with their wiggling fingers and toes, the Oankali's squirming tentacles that discover the world, the construct's strange and unpredictable flesh, the changing shape of the land, the advent of living ships and transplanted organelles. Haraway explains that making kin in the Chthulucene must "mean something other/more than entitles tied by ancestry or genealogy. [. . .] Kin making is making persons, not necessarily as individuals or as humans. [. . .] It is past time to practice better care of kinds-as-assemblages (not species one at a time). Kin is an assembling sort of word. All critters share a common 'flesh,' laterally, semiotically, and genealogically. Ancestors turn out to be very interesting strangers; kin are unfamiliar (outside what we thought was family or gens), uncanny, haunting, active."[58] In other words, making kin in the Chthulucene requires us to move away from traditional Western constructions of the family as linear genealogies that stress individual bloodlines as the apex of belonging in exchange for kinship structures that imagine "kinds-as-assemblages," as rhizomatic forms of relation that do not produce the same, but are instead made up of groups of "strangers" who are "unfamiliar."

It is clear from the first Oankali words Butler recorded in her notes, taken from a mixture of English, Swahili, and Japanese, that she was thinking early on in the writing process of the ways *Xenogenesis* could construct alternative visions of kinship and community: "Kin/jamaa/miyori—nijaa (ooloi word corresponding to brotherhood/sisterhood)"; "Companion/Mwenzi/Nakama—Nwati (casual friend)"; and "Companion/Rafiki/Aite (partner)—Naurasti (sibling partner)."[59] Other words, including "Companionship," "Trade," "Hybrid," "Mix," "Mixture," and "Life," demonstrate the importance of networks of belonging in the trilogy. Indeed, there are many distinct and overlapping kinship structures in *Imago*. For example, the Oankali kinship system is interconnected and yet distinct, a kind-as-assemblage that shares a "common flesh." Once the Oankali select a species worthy of trade, as they do with humans, they split into three groups: *Akjai*, who keep their original Oankali forms, do not participate in trade, and remain on the ship, named Chkahichdahk, which circles the Earth just beyond the moon; *Toaht*, who take part in human-Oankali trade, do not settle on planet Earth, but keep their constructs on Chkahichdahk until they find another species to trade with at a later date; and *Dinso*, Lilith's kinship group, who settle on Earth, transforming the planet into a new ship that will eventually take flight, leaving behind a barren lifeless husk behind. In order to better facilitate trade with humans, all Dinso and Toaht Oankali were physically modified and given cosmetic limbs, ears, and vocal chords to more closely resemble human form. The Akjai, no more or less Oankali than Dinso or Toaht, maintain their original special form as elephant-sized caterpillars without ears or mouths who communicate exclusively via direct tentacular neural connections. Dinso and Toaht Oankali will cease to exist in their present form, though as the generations give way to construct-only communities and become estranged from one another in spacetime, they will remain intergalactic kin.

---

58. Haraway, *Staying with the Trouble*, 101, 31, 102–3.
59. Butler, *Xenogenesis*: notes, box 151, OEB Papers.

The Oankali also live in kinship with the very land itself, mothering it and allowing it to mother in return; as Jdahya explains, Chkahichdahk is both "plant and animal" and "more," a living being with the capacity for intelligent independent action: "That part of it is dormant now. But even so, the ship can be chemically induced to perform more functions than you would have the patience to listen to. It does a great deal on its own without monitoring. And [. . .] the human doctor [Awakened on the ship] used to say it loved us. There is an affinity, but it's biological—a strong, symbiotic relationship. We serve the ship's needs and it serves ours. It would die without us and we would be planetbound without it. For us, that would eventually mean death" (35). Just as humans and the Oankali operate as symbiotic assemblages, so too does Chkahichdahk—a sentient plant-animal hybrid with the capacity to communicate, make decisions, and evolve. In order to transform the planet into a ship of their own, Dinso ooloi plant on Earth Chkahichdahk's "seeds," carried within their *yashi*, which over time bloom into ever-expanding tentacular ones, or rhizomatic organisms that cover the ground, searching out nutrients and water, and synthesizing food for its hosts; Lilith's Earthseed is named Lo, but each Oankali-human community plants and grows their own Earthseeds. Within one thousand years, each individual Earthseed will meld into a single planet-sized ship that will travel space looking for further opportunities for trade; at that time, anyone not living in communion with the land will be left behind, unable to survive in the remaining wasteland. The Oankali communicate directly with Lo using their tentacles, instructing it to build shelters and objects, produce food, grow plants, or craft space shuttles for travel to Chkahichdahk. The Oankali also use Lo to contact Oankali on Chkahichdahk or communicate with one another across distance—using their tentacles, one Oankali can leave a message that will move across the ground alerting everyone in its path.

For Lilith, life on Lo is communal and collective. All Oankali-human families raise one another's children, share food, living space, community governance, and responsibilities for cooperative care; as Jodahs explains, "Lo was more than a town. It was a family group. All the Oankali males and females were related in some way. All constructs were related except the few males who had drifted in from other towns. All the ooloi had become part of Lo when they mated here. And any Human who stayed long in a relationship with an Oankali family was related more closely than most Humans realized" (557). The Lo community also offers protection from resisters, the human-only communities who are hostile to human-alien collectives. After Akin arranges to transport human beings who are unwilling to enter into construct kinship to Mars, the Oankali reverse their prohibition on human infertility, making human-to-human reproduction possible once more. Though humans are warned that the transformation of the planet is irreversible, resister bands continue to attack Oankali-human communities, at times injuring or killing people and constructs, even though any human being who kills another being (human or Oankali) is removed from Earth and placed in permanent hypersleep on Chkahichdahk or harvested for genetic materials. This is far from a utopia; though an ooloi can heal diseases and extend life, it cannot heal catastrophic injury or prevent death, and though human beings are welcome to their own reproductive futures on Mars, they must also give up any claims to the Earth. In spite of their unpredictable violence, Lilith continues to mother the resisters by maintaining a large garden plot on Earth soil some distance from Lo, hoping to maintain a nourishing kinship connection with them in spite of their refusal to accept the terms of the holobiont.

Xenogenesis concludes with its most radical vision of kinship in the Chthulucene, one inaugurated by Jodahs and Aaor. As I mentioned earlier, these ooloi constructs are the first of their kind; Jodahs observes about itself that it "would be the most extreme version of a construct—not just a mix of Human and Oankali characteristics, but able to use my body in ways that neither Human nor Oankali could. Synergy" (549). Unlike other Oankali, Jodahs and Aaor are as driven to bond with people as they are driven to manipulate genes and trade; for that reason, they are able to shape-shift, changing their physical bodies in order to become one with whomever or whatever they encounter. Jodahs, for example, cannot help but bond with, manipulate, and alter Lo's genetic expression, even when it does not mean to or want to. After Jodahs's first metamorphosis, it begins to accidentally harm Lo as it bonds with the organism: "Lo's natural color was gray-brown. Beneath me, it turned yellow. It developed swellings. Rough, diseased patches appeared on it. Its odor changed, became foul. Parts of it sloughed off. Sometimes it developed deep, open sores. And all that I did to Lo, I also did to myself. But it was Lo I felt guilty about. Lo was parent, sibling, home" (554). In addition to harming Lo and itself, Jodahs also causes injuries to other Oankali through Lo, or during its casual tentacled interactions with others. Jodahs not only causes harm more quickly than it can repair it, but it also cannot comprehend *why* it is causes mutations and disease, limiting its ability to self-correct. Rather than ostracize Jodahs or send it back to Chkahichdahk, Lilith, Ahajas, Dichaan, Tino, and Nikanj decide to temporarily leave their community behind, moving their youngest children, Jodahs, and Aaor to the edge of Lo until their children can learn to trade without causing irreparable communal harm. This is, of course, a sacrifice for everyone, given that, as Jodahs notes, Lo is a member of its family, an extension of itself. Lilith and Nikanj, however, follow Jodahs's lead, who insists that it is meant to be on the planet.

Unlike humans, Oankali, and other constructs, Jodahs and Aaor *must* bond with other beings or risk losing their bodily integrity. Nikanj explains to them that without mates, they will lose ability to manipulate the world around them without causing harm: "With a potential mate—even a very unsuitable one—your control is flawless. Without a potential mate, you have no control. You were surprised when I told you you were losing your hair. You've been surprised by your body again and again. Yet nothing it does should surprise you. Nothing it does should be beyond your control" (554). Indeed, after the family moves to their new location off-Lo away from human or Oankali contact, Jodahs begins to take on the shape of the world around it: "My fingers and toes became webbed on the third day, and I didn't bother to correct them. [. . .] My hair fell out and I developed a few more sensory tentacles. I stopped wearing clothing, and my coloring changed to gray-green" (591). Jodahs and Aaor move in and out of various forms during their metamorphosis, shedding their physical attachments to their Oankali and human family members in exchange for bodies more in tune with the world around them. For example, when Jodahs enters into a period of wandering in the weeks before its second metamorphosis is complete, its body grows scales and it begins to walk on all fours. Much later, in the absence of any mate, Aaor almost disintegrates in a pool of water:

> It kept slipping away from me—simplifying its body. It had no control of itself, but like a rock rolling downhill, it had inertia. Its body "wanted" to be less and less complex. If it had stayed in the water for much longer, it would have begun to break down completely—individual cells each with its own seed of life, its own Oankali organelle. These might live for a while as individual organisms or invade the bodies of larger creatures at once, but Aaor as an individual would be gone. (682)

Jodahs and Aaor's ability to change their bodies and meld with the world around them, taking on the shape and form of whatever carbon-based organism they meet, or dissolving into the natural world their absence, is a way for them to seduce or manipulate potential partners, and usher in new forms of relation in the world. As Nikanj explains to Jodahs, "You're a new kind of being. There's never been anyone like you before" (571).

Imago concludes with the promise of an increasingly queer holobiont, a system of social organization that has never been before. This new symbiotic assemblage is formed between Jodahs and two human siblings, Tomás and Jesusa, who live in a fertile resister colony untouched by Oankali intervention. By shape-shifting into an androgynous form that both siblings find attractive, familiar, and comforting, Jodahs convinces them to join him as mates by promising the pair a reproductive future together. Tomás and Jesusa are at first confused and disgusted by what they expect will have to be heterosexual human reproductive relation. Jodahs, however, explains that the siblings will never touch one another again, instead raising children together as what Butler described elsewhere as "sibmothers."[60] By breaking apart sexual attraction from the reproductive act, and shattering the expectation that human mates be genetic strangers by ensuring them that their child will be free from genetic anomalies, Jodahs, Tomás, and Jesusa structure a new system of kinship that emphasizes emotional compatibility, interpersonal familiarity, and sibling-love as the most important factors for healthy reproductive communities. This new queer horizon—Oankali siblings and human siblings and their construct children—offers an alternative to the patriarchal logics of heterosexual reproduction that dictate who can belong to whom, what families can look like, and who can give birth to whom and in what arrangements. Lizzie Reed and Milou Stella remind us that queer kinship "is not a straightforward reversal of what has come before but [. . .] a *reworking* of ties to generation, and critical evaluation of inheritances through creativity and reflection."[61] As sibmothers, Jodahs and Aaor *rework* the foundations of reproduction and mothering, community and care. After introducing Aaor to other humans in Tomás and Jesusa's community, many of whom agree to join them in the making of a new community, Jodahs generates from its *yashi* a seed that will one day become its own Earthseed community, a new symbiotic assemblage for itself and its sibling-mates: "a single cell within that great store—a cell that could be 'awakened' from its stasis within the yashi and stimulated to divide and grow into a kind of seed. [. . .] My seed would begin as a town and eventually leave Earth in a great ship" (745). This promise of another world is exceeded by the novel's limited vision of the future; at the trilogy's end, we do not know when or where these new Oankali-human construct families will go, but we know that they will find a way to survive far into the future.

---

60. Butler, *Dawn*: novel: outline, OEB Papers.
61. Reed and Stella, "'To Raise a Village,'" 3.

We cannot understand the Black Alien M/other in *Xenogenesis* separate from Jodahs's and Aaor's innovation on the family structure; their care is an extension of hers. Lilith's revolutionary mothering praxis in the Chthulucene—the ways of living well and in kinds-of-assemblages that she brings to her community, and the way those practices yield more expansive and complex structures of belonging and being—must also be understood as a future-praxis, a way of ensuring tomorrow's survival today. This praxis is embedded in the trilogy's expansive approach to narrative spacetime; as each text moves forward in the future, from the spaceship of *Dawn* 250 years post-apocalypse to the postsexual, posthuman, and post-terrestrial landscape of the *Imago* 500 years after the war, we see that the cosmic diaspora Lilith creates and nurtures will stay in motion for thousands of years, becoming a permanent part of the way constructs understand themselves and one another. As is the case for Lilith's alien children, Alexis Pauline Gumbs reminds us that "the queer thing is that we *were* born; our young and/or deviant and/or brown and/or broke and/or single mamas did the wrong thing. Therefore we exist: a population out of control, a story interrupted. [. . .] To answer death with utopian futurity [. . .] is a queer thing to do. A strange thing to do. A thing that changes the family and the future forever. To name oneself 'mother' [. . .] to insist on Black motherhood [. . .] is an almost illegible thing, an outlawed practice, a queer thing."[62] As a correction to the intergalactic archive, readers of *Xenogenesis* bear witness to how Lilith reconciles her initial feelings of fear about mothering aliens to the powerful ways she creates systems of support for her Oankali-human-construct community, an endlessly regenerative and open-ended holobiont that must learn to navigate life together on a planet that is bending and shaping and changing the world with its every collective step forward. Shaped by Lilith's role as Black Alien M/other, in the end the trilogy asks that we imagine how the incomprehensible newness of this construct assemblage in the Chthulucene is an illegible thing, a queer thing that nevertheless *becomes*.

---

62. Gumbs, "m/other ourselves," 21.

CHAPTER 4

"I Am Not of This Planet"

The Making of Le Sony'r Ra's Cosmic Diaspora

In an unpublished essay entitled "I am not of this planet," Sun Ra explained that he was a Black alien from another galaxy, a nonhuman entity who was on Earth at the behest of the Creator of the universe: "I am not of the planet. I am another order of being. I can tell you things you won't believe. [. . .] Because of segregation, I have only a vague knowledge of the white world and that knowledge is superficial. Because I know more about the black than I do the white, I know my needs and naturalness, I know my intuition to be what it is natural for me to be."[1] Sun Ra claimed to have arrived at Birmingham, Alabama, in his early infancy from another planet he could only vaguely recall. Although he was "another order of being," because Ra physically and biologically resembled other Black humans, he was placed by the universe in a loving Black home with a broad kinship network of immediate adopted family, Baptist church community, and musicians. Ra argued that during his childhood, the forces of Jim Crow segregation had paradoxically shielded him from violence by limiting his exposure to the "white world." As a consequence, it was "natural" for Ra to be Black; in other words, Blackness and structures of Black kinship offered him a way of knowing and being in the world that was innately compatible with his extraterrestrial alienness.

---

1. Ra, *Immeasurable Equation*, 460.

And yet, because he was not a human or an Earthling, Ra struggled with intense feelings of loneliness and a deep longing for his other world. These feelings were exacerbated when, at the age of twenty-two, Ra was invited to Saturn by a group of green tentacled aliens, who showed him his future and took him to their planet in a beam of light, changing his body into something else altogether in a process he described as *transmolecularization*. After his visit to Saturn, Ra was forced to more directly confront the ways that white supremacy malformed Black life in America. Over time, he would become increasingly convinced that his "alter-destiny," as he would come to describe it, was to find a way to help Black folk leave the planet. As he argued in the essay, "the only reason I'm here is that the Creator got me here against my will," stuck on a planet that "has never done anything for me but try to stop me, try to make my so-called Life ugly like it did the rest of black people. [. . .] We need to get off this planet as fast as possible."[2] Ra would devote his life to convincing Black people of their alter-destiny, searching for ways to extend the Black diaspora into the cosmos.

In this book, I have so far examined Black aliens as metaphors for enslaved Black linealogies, slippages between visual, political, and narrative constructions of Black extraterrestrial and terrestrial being, and radical Black alien reproductive m/othering practices—but in this chapter I explore constructions of the Black alien as *self*. In other words, I take seriously Sun Ra's claims to a Black extraterrestrial alien identity and attend to how his self-fashioning, self-understanding, and self-perception as a cosmic diasporic subject challenges fixed boundaries between race, species, kinship, and place of origin. Though scholars rarely neglect to mention that Ra insisted upon an off-Earth origin, they are just as likely to describe it as an elaborate performance, a cultish grift, or sign of mental illness. And yet, as John Corbett insists, Sun Ra "presents himself as being extraterrestrial; Ra [. . .] *live*[s] as [a] 'brother from another planet,'" a self-positioning that was "meant literally [. . .] in the case of Sun Ra, who, before he died in 1993, insisted that he was actually, physically born on the planet of Saturn. [. . .] Any serious consideration of [his] music and myth-making has to do with the acceptance of this impossible suggestion of outer-space origins, with believing, for a start, that Sun Ra was not of this world."[3] I agree: in order to understand Sun Ra's art and music, one must accept his claim that he was from outer space. Of course, Ra never needed our belief in his claims to an extraterrestrial Black alienness for it to have been true for him. That said, in this chapter *I do believe him*.

---

2. Ra, *Immeasurable Equation*, 460–61.
3. Corbett, *Extended Play*, 8.

I make the case here that Sun Ra's Black alien myth-making must be understood as a cosmic textual tradition. Over the course of his life, Ra wrote hundreds of poems and dozens of radical broadsides, liner notes, and letters; he was a voracious reader and grassroots intellectual who took seriously the life of the mind. Ra believed that language and sound were vibrationally interchangeable—according to his philosophy, poems were music, and music was words. For that reason, I construct Sun Ra's cosmic diaspora as a spacetime-bending, do-it-yourself politics, a fantasy of intergalactic space travel, and a driving force toward a Black Cosmic Age in which Black terrestrials and Black aliens are liberated from the constraints of the antiblack Earth in their home in the infinite blackness of space. In the first section, "Somewhere Else: The Black Cosmic Tradition and the Transmolecularization of Herman 'Sonny' Poole Blount," I trace Sun Ra's participation in a Black cosmic tradition that places flight, movement, and technologies of travel at the core of Black liberation politics. I read Ra's desire for an off-Earth destiny alongside Reverend A. W. Nix, the Afro-Baptist futurist, whose 1927 race record "The White Flyer to Heaven" imagined Black people traveling on a gospel-train through outer space to heaven, an early way of imagining a Black future that advanced a radical kinopolitics concerned with mobility justice as its primary aim. I offer a reading of Ra's Black alien identity and consider how his descriptions of his transmolecularization can also be seen as extended meditations on what Tina Campt has described as the *future real conditional,* a grammar of possibility that actively creates the conditions for a desired future now.

In the second section, "potential impossible potential potential potential: Le Sony'r Ra's Cosmic Black Do-It-Yourself (DIY) Textual Futurism," I explore Sun Ra's Black alien cosmology as an extension of Reverend Sutton E. Griggs's do-it-yourself (DIY) radical Black textual futurist tradition. I offer a history of Ra's intellectual work with Thmei Research, a secret society he founded with Alton Abraham while living in Chicago in the 1950s, and explore how Ra's DIY futurism, which centered owning the means and modes of publication and distribution, and communicating with Black audiences directly, was also a complex cosmic diasporic literary poetics. I make the case that Ra's construction of cosmic potential—what he described as the "potential impossible"—must be understood as an extension of his investments in the written word, speechifying, and street preaching. More specifically, I analyze several Thmei broadsides, and trace the contours of Ra's argument that, as a result of the transatlantic slave trade, Black people in the US were actually an amalgamation of cosmic and spiritual beings, Indigenous Africans and their descendants, and ancient Egyptians and Ethiopians whose rightful alter-destiny was in the stars, the truth of which had been intentionally and systematically hidden in order to keep them planet-bound. I analyze Ra's argument that the potential impossible journey of the "American negro" was to leave the planet behind, which, in his view, was a textual-sonic vibrational reality that could be (and must be) brought into being. Finally, in "Astro Black Is Cosmo Dark: The Poetics of Sun Ra's Cosmic Diaspora," I offer an extended reading of several of Sun Ra's poems and outline how his futurist poetics synthesized and extended Nix's Black cosmic tradition and Griggs's DIY textual futurism. Through a reading of the development of Ra's literary poetics in the 1950s and 1960s, I consider how his shift from polemical writing to poetry led to his construction of Astroblackness, or his vision that Black people would inevitably extend the diaspora into outer space, joining together in a new spacetime free from the gravitational constraints of antiblackness. I argue that Astroblackness can be understood as a cosmic diasporic poetics, a sound-text-vibration that was designed to awaken Black people to their alter-destiny, and help them navigate their way to an extraplanetary, intergalactic off-Earth future that would unfold in the cosmo dark of outer space.

Somewhere Else: The Black Cosmic Tradition and the Transmolecularization of Herman "Sonny" Poole Blount

In 1927 Reverend A. W. Nix recorded "The White Flyer to Heaven," a counterpart to his famous 1926 sermon "The Black Diamond Express to Hell," in which a train gathers souls from various locations—Liars Avenue, Drunkardsville, Gambling Tower, Fight Town—on its descent to Hell. Nix recorded more than fifty sermons and gospel songs between 1927 and 1931, when US record companies produced large numbers of three-minute 78 rpm recordings by Black artists. These race records, Terri Michelle Brinegar explains, "promulgated the sounds of popular music, jazz and blues, gospel and recorded sermons, allowing for the widespread dissemination of the music and voice of black folk, separate from Euro-centric art music." Marketed to Black consumers, race records amplified sounds that "historically had been ignored or dismissed, including the voices of African American ministers," which outsold popular blues artists of the day because they "offered urban black communities a down-home alternative to the arranged spirituals and other European-influenced musical repertoires favored in some churches," and performed by the Fisk Jubilee Singers, among others; Nix's recordings integrated familiar Black sonic forms, including call-and-response, group chanting, interjections from congregants, moaning, whooping, shouts, and singing. Though his sermons represented African vernacular traditions rooted in slavery, Brinegar notes that Nix's embrace of technologies—train machinery, mechanical recording, phonograph and radio equipment—and "his vocalizations on phonographs also created new traditions and new conceptions of modernity." Emergent Black modernities in the decades post-Reconstruction were, however, beset by "racial setbacks and injustices that instigated race riots throughout the US from small, rural communities of former slave states in the South to large, urban metropolises in the North. Reverend Nix's hometown of Longview, Texas, and Chicago, where he recorded his sermons, both experienced race riots in 1919."[4] Fixed jointly in the planetary and supraterrestrial domains, Nix enmeshed spiritual and political matters by asking his listeners to consider how flight from Earth would mean everlasting reprieve from racial injustice.

"The White Flyer to Heaven" tells the story of a holy congregation who travel aboard a gospel-train ("God is the engineer / The Holy Ghost is the headlight / And Jesus is the conductor") as it ascends from Earth through outer space to heaven. The White Flyer's passengers pause briefly at Mt. Calvary to visit the site of Christ's crucifixion, before they "pass on through the first heaven / the heaven of the clouds / and through God's machine shop."[5] The shift from Earth's atmosphere to outer space is seamless; as the train flies "higher and higher! and higher! / We'll pass on to the Second Heaven / The starry big Heaven, and view the flying stars / and dashing meteors / And then pass on by Mars and Mercury, and Jupiter and Venus / And Saturn and Uranus, and Neptune with her four glittering / moons."[6] Eventually, the White Flyer moves "up beyond the sun, moon, and stars / back behind God's eternal word" to Heaven, climbing "higher and higher / higher and higher, / until we / bid farewell to every tear / and wipe our weeping eyes."[7] Nix's cosmic gospel-train is analogous to the chariot, a repeating symbol in Black spirituals for escape from slavery. Horace J. Maxile Jr. explains that the "train and mothership" rest alongside the chariot as Black cultural "tropes of transit [. . . that] signif[y] freedom and liberation, by creating a modern meeting [s]ite that travels to outer space." On its face, Nix's White Flyer is a metaphor for the Christian spiritual journey, but its interplanetary flight is also evidence of the desire of Black Americans to

---

4. Brinegar, "Recorded Sermons of Reverend Andrew William (A. W.) Nix," 37, 37, 29, 29–30.

5. Brinegar, "Recorded Sermons of Reverend Andrew William (A. W.) Nix," 355; and Nix, "White Flyer to Heaven."

6. Nix, "White Flyer to Heaven."

7. Nix, "White Flyer to Heaven."

escape the intolerable pressures of Jim Crow; the White Flyer's passengers are, after all, transported from the South, from America, from the planet, from the galaxy into a liberated plane of existence. By configuring outer space as a material domain free from the quotidian violence, misery, and suffering of life on Earth, Nix also illustrates the tendency in "Afro-Baptist discourse," as John Szwed frames it, of "almost matter-of-fact perception of their place in the cosmos and the possibility of spiritual travel within it."[8]

Reverend Nix and his interplanetary sermon, alongside John Jasper, the nineteenth-century Virginia preacher whose popular 1882 sermon "The Sun Do Move" argued against heliocentrism, and Harriet Powers, the formerly enslaved folk artist from Georgia whose 1898 Pictorial Bible Quilt told her life story through astronomical images of the 1833 Leonid meteor shower, evidence an early "shared vision of a Black sacred cosmos, a spiritualized vision of the universe, where the pilgrim is comfortable where he or she may travel." Szwed describes this as a uniquely "Black cosmic vision" that explicitly embraced "the theme of travel, of journey, of exodus, of escape which dominates African-American narratives: of people who could fly back to Africa, travel in spirit, visit or be visited by the dead; of chariots and trains to heaven, the Underground Railroad, Marcus Garvey's steamship line, Rosa Parks on the Mobile bus, freedom riders"—and, the subject of this chapter, Sun Ra's intergalactic alien imaginary. This Black cosmic tradition, Szwed notes, "praised the technology of motion and travel, where trains, cars, airplanes, buses—even transmission systems ('Dynaflow')—were celebrated as part of African-American [. . .] mobility."[9] Though Black mobility has historically been restricted via slave codes, Jim Crow, and de facto and de jure segregation, for example, Black folks have also resisted those mechanisms of control through various means of transport and escape, such as jumping overboard the slave ship, following the North Star, leaving the South during the Great Migration, or marching in mass protest.

I read the centrality of travel and movement to this Black cosmic tradition as meditations on what Mimi Sheller terms "mobility justice," or "an overarching concept for thinking about how power and inequality inform the governance and control of movement, shaping the patterns of unequal mobility and immobility in the circulation of people, resources, and information." Sheller argues that "the management of mobilities under post-slavery and postcolonial regimes in the liberal West is fundamental to the making of classed, racial, sexual, able-bodied, gendered, citizen, and non-citizen

---

8. Maxile, "Black Musical Tropology," 602; and Szwed, *Space Is the Place*, 134.
9. Szwed, *Space Is the Place*, 134, 134–35.

subjects." Thinking through the logics of US kinopolitics requires us to consider how calls for mobility justice have been central to "embodied movements for social justice (combining class, race, gender, disability, and sexuality), struggles for transport justice and accessibility, arguments for the right to the city and spatial justice, movement for migrant rights, Indigenous rights, and decolonial movements, and even dimensions of climate justice and epistemic justice."[10] I argue that the Black cosmic tradition's dream of unfettered galactic movement invokes a kinopolitical counterpower that actively transitions toward increasingly just worlds. I read this desire for mobility justice as an example of what Tina Campt describes as "a grammar of futurity realized in the present," a

> grammar of possibility that moves beyond a simple definition of the future tense as what *will be* in the future. It moves beyond the future perfect tense of *that which will have happened* prior to a reference point in the future. It strives for the tense of possibility grammarians refer to as the future real conditional, or *that which will have had to happen* for the future to be realized. The grammar of Black feminist futurity is a performance of a future that hasn't yet happened but must. [. . .] It's the power to imagine beyond current fact, to envision that which is not but must be. Put another way, it's a form of prefiguration that involves living the future now, as imperative rather than subjunctive, as striving for the future you want to see.[11]

The Black cosmic tradition is an imperative futurist concern—and, indeed, many scholars read Nix as among the first Afrofuturist thinkers, insofar as movement through galaxies and the physics of velocity, acceleration/deceleration, and "movement time," or the amount of time it takes an object/subject to complete a specific motion, bend spacetime; by "living the future now," Black cosmicists "imagine beyond current fact," even as they enact *"that which will have had to happen"* in order to bring about very real conditions for a radically different future. As an adherent of Black cosmic tradition, Graham Lock argues that Ra turned to "outer space as a metaphor for both the actual scientific future and the inner space of fantasy and imagination," in which the cosmos becomes "the site of a mythic future that he proposed as the alter(native) destiny."[12] In other words, Ra's Black cosmic kinopolitics centered intergalactic space travel as imperative if the conditions of freedom were to ever be truly met for Black peoples on Earth.

---

10. Sheller, *Mobility Justice*, 14, 16, 17.
11. Campt, "Black Feminist Futures."
12. Lock, *Blutopia*, 34.

Many scholars have incorrectly claimed that Nix was born in Birmingham, Alabama; Lock goes so far as to imagine that Ra, who was actually born and raised there, might at some point have heard him deliver his galactic sermon at Tabernacle Baptist Church, which he attended each Sunday with his family. Nix never even visited Alabama, but it makes good sense that scholars would want to attach him to a state known for innovations in train travel, nascent space exploration, and powerful forms of Black resistance. Sun Ra was born Herman Poole Blount on May 22, 1914, to Cary and Ida Blount in Birmingham; his mother named him after the Black Afrocentric mysticist and magician Black Herman, who claimed to be an immortal Zulu and a direct descendant of Moses, though he went by the name "Sonny" (and his family referred to him as "Snookum"). After his parents separated, Ra and his siblings were raised with his maternal grandmother, Margaret Jones, and his great-aunt, Ida Howard, in a commercial district of Birmingham, within a block of the train station. Eleven railroad lines converged at the Beaux-Arts Terminal Station, the largest in the South at the time, moving passengers from Birmingham to Chicago, New Orleans, Memphis, Atlanta, New York City, Kansas City, St. Louis, Jacksonville, and Miami. Visitors were greeted by an enormous, twinkling ten-thousand-light sign that read "Welcome to Birmingham, the Magic City." The station served as a hub for Black Birminghamians, who gathered daily to work in the restaurant, shops, or on the line, or to collect spare coal or food from the Black railroad workers; Ra himself often took his meals at the station kitchen, where his mother and great-aunt were employed.

Ra's formative years were spent in the midst of constantly shifting machine dynamics. As a modern industrial city, Birmingham attracted migrant labor from across the South, nation, and globe to work in its factories, iron and steel plants, coal mines, and railroad station, and maintained a thriving business class of journalists, professionals, and small businessmen; it was one of the first Southern cities to construct a grid capable of powering skyscrapers and build roads for electric streetcars and motor vehicles. Birmingham was also deeply segregated, with some of the strictest residential zoning laws in the nation, requiring rigid separation of white and Black neighborhoods, in addition to separate streetcars, railroad cars, restaurants, theaters, schools, and public facilities. Though Black folks made up nearly half the urban population, Black neighborhoods were relegated to "areas of undeveloped land bypassed for more pleasant sites by industry and white neighborhoods," and therefore "generally situated along creekbeds, railroad lines, or alleys [. . .] suffer[ing] from a lack of street lights, paved streets, sewers, and other city services. The houses usually resembled the tattered and loosely constructed sharecropper cabins of the rural districts from whence almost"[13] all the city's Black workers had arrived. The tensions between Alabama's investments in technological and industrial development and its total neglect of Black living spaces only deepened over the course of Ra's life. For example, after Ra left his university studies in Huntsville, a short distance from Birmingham, the US government launched Operation Paperclip, and brought the Nazi rocket scientist Wernher von Braun to the city to develop the National Aeronautics and Space Administration (NASA)—today, the Marshall Space Flight Center outside of Huntsville, focused on rocketry and spacecraft propulsion, is the US government's largest NASA center and has recently been named the primary location for the United States Space Force. At the time, *Ebony* magazine reported on the gap between US space exploration and its intentional neglect of Black life on Earth, noting with disdain that Black people were living without running water or electricity within ten minutes of the Huntsville space lab.[14]

There was also a powerful current of resistance to Jim Crow segregation, white supremacy, and economic violence in Alabama; in 1963 Birmingham was the site of the Southern Christian Leadership Conference's (SCLC) successful civil rights campaign, animated by grassroots networks of Black folk in the city. Ra grew up middle-class in a close-knit Black quarter of the city, where he was well educated, well fed, loved, and cared for by his family, including several cousins, aunts, and uncles, and family friends, both in his neighborhood and at church; he later described his as "a protected childhood [. . .] free from violence and even the sting of race" because he "had little contact with white people." Ra was a model student and obsessive reader who went to great lengths to check out books from the segregated library (Black patrons were not allowed to enter the building and had to rely on Black aides to slip them books out of the back entrance); his Baptist childhood was animated by his reading of theosophists who, Szwed explains, had "kept alive ancient notions of the cosmos."[15] Birmingham's Black community cohered around and was suffused with the sounds of Black music: church gospel choirs; big bands playing nightly at dance clubs; Black orchestras with clashing symbols and call-and-response; social club performances for the Black elite; theater stage shows; and weekly dance bands for local organizations. His older brother, Robert, had a phonograph and many albums—perhaps a copy of Nix's sermon or one of the many

---

13. Brownell, "Birmingham, Alabama," 28–29.
14. Szwed, *Space Is the Place*, 134.
15. Szwed, *Space Is the Place*, 9, 135.

other race records was in his collection—and Ra developed an intense love for musical forms at an early age.

On what he described as his eleventh "arrival day,"[16] Ra's great-aunt gifted him a piano; he had already learned to read music by studying the notes in hymnals at school and church, and he displayed an extraordinary ability to play by ear. Ra performed in school with other children in his neighborhood, and began to arrange and compose his own music. Each week, his great-aunt would take him by streetcar to a different Black theater to see stage shows, where they watched performances by Ethel Waters, Duke Ellington, Fletcher Henderson, Fats Waller, and Bennie Moten, among others. As a teenager, Ra

> never missed a band, whether a known or unknown unit. I loved music beyond the stage of liking it. Some of the bands I heard never got popular [. . .] but they were truly naturally black beauty. [. . .] The music they played was a natural happiness of love, so rare I cannot explain it. It was fresh and courageous; daring, sincere, unfettered. It was manufactured avant-garde, and still is, because there was no place for it in the world, so the world neglected something of value and did not understand. And all along I could not understand why the world could not understand. What happened is that, in the Deep South, the black people were very oppressed and were made to feel like they weren't anything, so the only thing they had was big bands.[17]

At the root of his understanding of Black potential was Ra's perception that Black music was a collective response to oppression, neglected by the larger white world which "did not understand" it (and did not want to), and also an otherworldly, avant-garde expression of a people who fundamentally do not belong to the nation (or planet) where they found themselves.

As Ra entered adulthood and witnessed firsthand how Jim Crow delimited Black movement in Birmingham, he began to contend with the feeling that he had "never been part of this planet. I've been isolated from a child away from it. Right in the midst of everything and not a part of it. Them troubles people got, prejudices and all that, I didn't know a thing about it, until I got to be about fourteen years old. It was as if I was somewhere else that imprinted this purity on my mind, another kind of world."[18] Ra's perception that he was from "another kind of world" was, importantly,

---

16. Szwed, *Space Is the Place*, 12.
17. Szwed, *Space Is the Place*, 17.
18. Szwed, *Space Is the Place*, 11.

not a rejection of his Blackness or his sense of connection and obligation to Black communities. As I noted above, Ra believed that Black folk were a uniquely oppressed peoples with "unfettered" potential and ability. Rather, Ra rejected white supremacist political cultures, the neglect and exploitation of Black life and labor, incarceration and war-mongering, segregationist policies at home, and imperialist projects abroad. Even so, central to Ra's cosmology was his claim that he had *never been born*, but had arrived on Earth from another place:

> I came from somewhere else, but it [the Creator's voice] reached me through the maze and dullness of human experience. [. . .] I came from somewhere else, where I was part of something that is so wonderful that there are no words to express it. . . .
>
> I was there but I wasn't there . . . I remember things—images and scenes and feelings. I never felt like I was part of this planet. I felt that all this was a dream, that it wasn't real. And suffering . . . I just couldn't connect . . . My mind would never accept the fact that is like it's supposed to be. I always felt that there was something wrong. I couldn't explain it. My people kept saying, "Why are you unhappy? You never seem to be happy." And that was true. I had this touch of sadness in the midst of other people's parties; other people were having a good time, but it would have a moment of loneliness and sadness. It puzzled me, therefore I had to analyze that, and I decided that I was different, that's all. I must have come from somewhere else. I wasn't just born; I had been somewhere before I was born.
>
> I'm not a human. I never called anybody "mother." The woman who's supposed to be my mother I call "other momma." I never call anybody "mother." I never call anybody "father." I never felt that way. [. . .] I don't remember when I was born. I've never memorized it.[19]

Ra's off-Earth origins, centered on movement and forgetting, are resonant with the African enslaved and their descendants in diaspora—he "arrived" on the planet from "somewhere else," where he was "a part of something" important, but what, when, where, or with whom he can no longer clearly remember, beyond scant "images and scenes and feelings." I read Ra's mystical "arrival" as akin to moving through a "Door of No Return," or what Dionne Brand theorizes as "that fissure [. . .] that place where our ancestors departed one world for another; the Old World for the New. The place

---

19. Szwed, *Space Is the Place*, 5–6. The Creator is often synonymous with the universe in Ra's cosmology and should not be confused with the Christian God.

where all names were forgotten and all beginnings recast." And yet, Brand argues that this transitional location also functioned as "the creation place of Blacks in the New World Diaspora at the same time that it signified the end of traceable beginnings."[20] This is, of course, paradoxical; Ra's arrival is also a decampment, a beginning that is also a permanent end.

John Corbett explains that Ra's "discursive galaxies utilize a set of tropes and metaphors of space and alienation, linking [. . . a] common diasporic African history to a notion of extraterrestriality." His claims to a cosmic elsewhere are also an embrace of Black collectivity, and the potential of Black being when enjoined in an off-Earth intergalactic reality. The process of transitioning from "somewhere else" to planet Earth resulted in the total loss of connection to his genealogic kin, and therefore to any clear sense of who he was as a being, spiritual or otherwise. Ra's spatiotemporal unmooring would form the basis for his later analysis of African diasporans, whom he argued had been similarly altered by the transatlantic slave trade. Ra categorized his experiences on Earth as a rupture of self (he loses his former off-Earth identity), spacetime (after his arrival, Ra and "time never got along so good"[21]), and kinship (he never called anybody "mother" or "father"). Ra, who "was there and [. . .] wasn't there," suffered a double alienation; like Arnus of Terminus, whom I discuss in chapter 2, he arrived as a Black infant to a planet that constructs Black people as nonhuman objects, forced to mask his extraterrestrial alienness behind a human façade.

Unlike Nix, however, Ra's cosmic tradition heeded no Creator other than the universe. Ra's galactic shift from the cosmic unknown of somewhere else to the terra firma of planet Saturn commenced after he began his studies at the two-year Alabama State Agricultural & Mechanical Institute for Negroes in Huntsville in the fall of 1935. Ra's journey to Saturn heralded what he called a cosmic Black "alter destiny," or his perception that Black folk were ordained for a celestial, intergalactic reality beyond planet Earth. Ra was recruited to Alabama A&M to study music but enrolled in the teacher's college, which offered the broadest curriculum. He excelled academically, enjoying the easy access to books and knowledge, but struggled to relate to his peers, who found him bookish and odd. Early in the spring semester in 1936, those feelings of isolation were hardened when one afternoon he returned to the dormitory to discover his roommates laughing at a diary entry describing his recent visitation with extraterrestrial aliens from Saturn. Though Ra destroyed the diary after the encounter with his roommates, he still retained

---

20. Brand, *Door of No Return*, 5, 5.
21. Corbett, *Extended Play*, 7; and Szwed, *Space Is the Place*, 5.

the memory, in there I said that these space men contacted me. They wanted me to go to outer space with them. They were looking for somebody who had that type of mind. They said it was quite dangerous because you had to have perfect discipline . . . I'd have to go up with no part of my body touching outside of the beam, because if I did, going through different time zones, I wouldn't be able to get that far back. So that's what I did. And it's like, well, it looked like a giant spotlight shining down on me, and I call it transmolecularization, my whole body was changed into something else. I could see through myself. And I went up. Now, I call that an energy transformation because I wasn't in human form. I thought I was there, but I could see through myself.[22]

Szwed describes Ra's experience as a "classic UFO-abduction" narrative, but there are critical differences between those and his journey. Ra does not describe the event as an abduction at all but rather an invitation from beings who "wanted me to go to outer space with them" because he "had that type of mind"—a mind from "somewhere else"—that could accommodate and make sense of contact with aliens. Ra would describe his encounter elsewhere as an "initiation," which, in his words, "means that I was on this planet and I was selected to go somewhere also to study something else."[23] The vast majority of reported alien abductions take place by surprise and without consent, and abductees report feelings of terror; by contrast, Ra was not afraid or physically threatened, and the aliens neither subject him to testing nor take samples from him. Rather, their interest in Ra is intellectual and political, an identification of his potential to become a life-changing source of wisdom for humans on Earth. Ra's is not a captivity narrative but an odyssey, a transformation, and a radical awakening.

His story is nevertheless resonant with alien contact narratives in other important ways. According to Jacques Vallée's study, close encounters of the third kind work on three primary levels: *physical, biological,* and *social.* Vallée argues that, like Ra's "spotlight," the UFO physically "behaves like a region of space, of small dimensions [. . .] within which a very large amount of energy is stored," often by way of "pulsed light phenomena." Ra would describe his mode of interstellar transport as an "energy corridor," in which "you go up at the speed of light, or the speed of something else, to your destination. That's what happened to me. Recently, I've seen some people on TV that had sort of similar experiences. Only they were taken without warning, I was given a chance." Though Ra's physical body moves through spacetime

---

22. Szwed, *Space Is the Place,* 29.
23. Szwed, *Space Is the Place,* 30; and Ra, "Master Plan," viii.

in this initial instance, he would later recall visiting other planets via "psychic planes," in one interview describing how a "guide [...] something like a shadow" took him to Jupiter: "And that's why I'm always singing about Jupiter: I was actually there looking at this planet. So I been there. Now people might not believe it, but I went there and I know I went there."[24] When Ra reports moving from one corporeal reality to an embodied elsewhere, whether traveling by energy field, psychic plane, or spaceship, he argues he *is*, in a manner of speaking, *physically* there.

Vallée notes that witnesses who come into contact with extraterrestrials often suffer from "all kinds of psychophysiological effects," such as "visions, hallucinations, space and time disorientation, physiological reactions (including temporary blindness, paralysis, sleep cycle changes), and long-term personality changes."[25] These effects are often not the result of spacetime travel itself but from extraterrestrial intervention and experimentation. Unlike other alien encounters that leave the traveler with lasting physical and emotional harm, Ra's experience of biological change, or what he calls his "transmolecularization," is positively transformational. As he leaves planet Earth in the energy beam, Ra is decorporealized—he could "see through myself" and "wasn't in human form"—and rapidly remade. Ra continues to look the same (he is still visibly Black, and recognizable as his former self), but after his transmolecularization, his "whole body was changed into something else." Ra is altered by the process of transition *in and of itself*; it is the *movement* that changes him, the "going through different time zones," the journey through the energy beam of light. Ra's construction of a cosmic Black diaspora, both for himself and for other Black folks, was predicated on his perception that people could be permanently altered through locomotion. In other words, Ra perceived that traversing spacetime *in any capacity* could shift or change a subject from a human being to an alien (or nonhuman object), or from an alien of unknown origin to a Saturnian. According to Ra's kinopolitics, transatlantic diasporic movement and extraterrestrial spaceflight were equally transformative—the former by transforming the blend of peoples trafficked in slavery into "American negroes," and the latter by transforming him into "something else" "somewhere else."

Vallée notes that close encounters of the third kind are also experienced at the level of the social, in which "expectations about life in the universe [are] revolutionized"[26] through the sharing of stories about spaceflight

---

24. Vallée, *Dimensions*, xii; Sun Ra, "Master Plan," viii; and Corbett, *Extended Play*, 310.

25. Vallée, *Dimensions*, xii.

26. Vallée, *Dimensions*, xii.

and extraterrestrial encounter. Alien encounters provide incontrovertible evidence that human beings are not alone in the universe: the truth is, in fact, verifiably out there. Immediately following Ra's transmolecularization, he is greeted by small extraterrestrials, each with "one little antenna on each ear [. . . and] a little antenna over each eye," who journey with him in and out of the present and future (though importantly *not* the past). Ra recollected that he "landed on a planet that I identified as Saturn. First thing I saw was something like a rail, a long rail of a railroad track coming out of the sky, and landed over there in a vacant lot."[27] As I discussed earlier, the tropes of the train and mothership represent freedom and the power of flight-as-resistance in the Black cosmic tradition—Ra's alien sky-train signifies on Nix's galactic gospel-train as a mode of liberation from the constraints of the antiblack Earth. As a cosmic reference to the Birmingham Terminal Station, and therefore also to his childhood network of modern movement and transition, Ra's celestial train is also a technological marvel, a way to transverse spacetime quickly (even in outer space), and a symbol of transportive connective tissue for Black folk in diaspora. Like Nix's White Flyer, Ra's cosmic railroad track "coming out of the sky" is an early gesture toward his broader mission of bringing Black folks from Earth to the cosmos where he believed they belonged.

While on Saturn, the aliens "teach" Ra that the world will trend toward chaos, but that he "would speak, and the world would listen." The next part of his initiation involves rapid travel through spacetime—both the present and the future—in brief snatches of scenes; at every juncture, however, Ra serves as communicative interlocutor between extraterrestrial aliens and human beings. After an unknown amount of time on Saturn, Ra "found himself back on planet Earth in a room with them [the Saturnians]," at the back of an apartment with a balcony and large courtyard in a city he determines is a future Chicago. The Saturnians insist that Ra approach the balcony and speak to the people milling around in the courtyard; though initially reticent (the people seem to him to be "angry," though the Saturnians insist they are merely "bewildered"), as he approaches the edge of the balcony and the people turn their gaze to him, he "saw that I was laying down on a park bench, a stone park bench, near a river. There was a bridge. I knew it was New York City." Ra observes that "the sky was purple and dark red, and through that I could see the spaceships, thousands of them. And I sat up to look, then I heard a voice [say,] 'You can order us to land. Are conditions right for landing?' I think I said yes. They started to land, and there were

---

27. Szwed, *Space Is the Place*, 30, 29.

people running to come to the landing." Many years later, when Ra eventually arrived in New York, he returned to the site of his earlier visitation: "I was up near Columbia University. I saw the bench, I saw the bridge, so those things have been indelibly printed on my brain."[28] I read Ra's journeys to Chicago and New York, in particular, as slippages through and in spacetime, and as examples of the power of the future real conditional to enact the necessary things in order to bring about a desired future; following Campt, Ra's initiation can be seen as "a form of prefiguration that involves living the future now." Indeed, everything about his life would change as a result of his initiation.

Ra's initiation was an extraterrestrial spacetime-bending extension of the Black cosmic tradition, in which alien contact, physical transmolecularization, and spaceflight become models for radical transformative change. At its root, his visitation to Saturn transformed his relation to himself, to Black folk, the US, and the planet: "I know something they [people on Earth] don't know from equational matter and from what I learned of planet Saturn. I know what happiness looks like from a planetary point of view, because I've been on other planets. I've seen things the average person has not seen. I've seen colors that are indescribable. I've been in darkness that cannot be described. [. . .] I have been there! I have seen it. [. . .] I've got the keys. I got them on planet Saturn. And I know what it means." Ra's initiation gave him a new point-of-origin that was also paradoxically a point-of-departure: "Well you said, 'Where am I from?' Well, I'm not on this planet because I'm on it. The last place I can say where I was from is planet Saturn. If you were to say, 'Are you from planet Earth?' I would say no. [. . .] If I went back to planet Saturn, I can say I'm from planet Earth. But I can't say I'm from here, not really."[29] No longer from the mysterious realm of "somewhere else," Ra's initiation provided him with a vision for helping other Black people fulfill their destinies by transitioning from the violent Earth to potential new worlds. As I explain in the next section, Ra's intellectual and political work in Chicago as a street preacher and head of a grassroots research group expanded his Black alien cosmic tradition into a full-blown galactic, transtemporal cosmic diaspora. In the years after his transmolecularization, as his cosmic tradition took on new shape, Ra began to push for a "planetary view of happiness" from his perspective as a Black alien, one that remained fundamentally kinopolitical, centered on movement-as-transformation, and increasingly blurred the boundaries of spacetime, here and there, then and now.

---

28. Szwed, *Space Is the Place*, 30, 30, 30, 30.
29. Ra, "Master Plan," xiii, ix.

"potential impossible potential potential potential": Le Sony'r Ra's Cosmic Black Do-It-Yourself (DIY) Textual Futurism

In 1921 the board of the National Baptist Convention, on which Reverend A. W. Nix served as member, distributed to each of its attendees a pamphlet by Reverend Sutton E. Griggs; Brinegar notes that the men, both Afro-Baptist public intellectuals, "appeared to have known each other" through their mutual work with the Convention. If Nix inaugurated a Black cosmic tradition, as I discussed in the previous section, Griggs modeled a do-it-yourself (DIY) ethic that was equally futurist in its aims. Over the course of his life, Griggs self-published more than thirty novels and pamphlets, including the 1899 Black nationalist alternate history *Imperium in Imperio*, which Melissa A. Wright argues is "an important precursor in Afrofuturism [. . .] [that] presents a suspended space-time in which alternatives to governance [. . .] can be imagined." Griggs also recorded six race records. Unlike Nix's melodious cosmic gospel-sermons, however, his were academic lectures delivered without musical accompaniment, reflecting his belief that Black cultural reliance on oral-musical traditions resulted from broader systems of disenfranchisement that had condemned Black people to illiteracy by criminalizing education during slavery, and denying equal access in its aftermath. That said, Griggs's efforts to build a Black narrative counterpublic was anti-assimilationist in its aims; in his view, an emergent "national Negro literature"[30] would have more expansive political utility than sermons or songs.

Griggs was an early pioneer of Black futurist writing, Caroline Levander explains, "because he sought to harness the publishing industry's powerful role in transforming how reading audiences understood race." As cofounder and publisher of the *Virginia Baptist* newspaper (1894–98), Griggs understood well that while the new print technologies of the late nineteenth century had fueled the popularization and readership of textual media, his options for publication and distribution were limited as a Black man in a Jim Crow economy; for that reason, Griggs "undertook to control all aspects of publication and marketing by operating his own publishing company and promoting the sale of his novels among black communities during his travels as minister and orator." Griggs's literary economy was also keenly kinopolitical, and his methods for distribution embraced both alternative

---

30. Brinegar, "Recorded Sermons of Reverend Andrew William (A. W.) Nix," 302; Wright, "Future of History," 32; and Levander, "Sutton Griggs," 30.

mobile and print technologies. Harnessing his ability to locomote through Black communities, Griggs sold his books out of a suitcase by walking door-to-door, visiting segregated schools and universities, and drumming up support at churches, revivals, and on the street—and he was successful, enjoying a broader readership than both "[Charles] Chestnutt and [Paul Laurence] Dunbar."[31]

I read Sun Ra's Black alien cosmology as an intergalactic accompaniment to Nix's evangelist Black cosmic tradition, and Griggs's DIY investment in Black readership, textuality, and self-owned artistic/political circulation. In this section, I examine Ra's Thmei Research broadsides and explore how he constructed Black alienness and the cosmic diaspora as a literary poetics. Ra's construction of what he called the "potential impossible" cannot be separated from his intellectual investments in writing, speechifying, and public sermonizing, narrative forms that existed in harmony with his musical productions. Unlike Griggs, Ra emphatically believed in the value of oral Black traditions, viewing them as equally important as the written word—as he explained, "my music is words and my words are music [. . .] my words are music and my music is words." In the same vein as Nix's sonic Black cosmicism, Ra and his Arkestra invoked call-and-response, group chanting, whooping, speaking, and singing in their recordings and live performances. Ra was also equally invested in the power of the written word; he maintained a daily journal, and over the course of his life wrote hundreds of poems (which I discuss in the following section), in addition to essays and lectures, extensive album and liner notes, and dozens of broadsides. Like Griggs, Ra believed literary poetics were key to creating an "image of a better world: the alter-life for the alter-life is different from the life of this world."[32] As he argued elsewhere, "words are seeds you plant in the ground," forms of expression that, according to Brent Hayes Edwards, can be seen as "*the phonetic-dimension of words* in action: an impossible grammar, an impossible or *immeasurable* equation between grapheme and phoneme."[33] As we will see, Ra's construction of the impossible grammar of a galactic "alter-life," or his perception that Black people were destined for "other dimensions [. . .] in the infinity of the universe,"[34] evolved from a grassroots DIY textual practice.

Ra fully developed his cosmic alien narrative praxis after moving to Chicago in 1946, but its earliest philosophical roots were in Birmingham. After

---

31. Levander, "Sutton Griggs," 30, 30, 30.
32. Ra, "My Music Is Words," 27, 30, 27.
33. Edwards, "Race for Space," 35, emphasis in original.
34. Edwards, "Race for Space," 27.

leaving college on the advice of the Saturnians, Ra returned to Birmingham where he worked as a musician-for-hire, put together his own band, and lived with his elderly great-aunt Ida in his childhood home by the Terminal Station, which served as the epicenter for rehearsals that eventually "became virtual lectures, illustrated and inspired by music, and often filled with rhetorical shock tactics to focus his musicians." Ra kept the details of his transmolecularization to himself, but it was clear that he was unusual: he slept very little; refused to smoke, drink, or use drugs; took vitamins and supplements; eschewed meat; and ate unusual vegetables and the skins of fruit. As his former bandmate Frank Adams recalled, however, "no one said Sonny Blount was crazy: he was different, they said, and no one had approached his degree of difference. Birmingham could tolerate a lot of strangeness. And even in slavery there were some blacks who defied all kinds of rules."[35] And Ra was, indeed, defiant.

Birmingham struggled through the Depression but rebounded as wartime demand for mortars, bombs, and shells turned abandoned and faltering factories into defense plants. The increased demand for labor did not anneal racial tensions, and Jim Crow remained in full force even as Black men were conscripted into service. Sun Ra was one such man. In September 1941, he received an induction notice, addressed to Herman P. Blount (col.), though Ra initially refused to honor it, arguing that he did not "have the right to go and fight with those people." On the advice of the Fellowship of Reconciliation (FOR), a pacifist Christian organization, he requested a hearing with the draft board, and, against all odds, was granted a 4-E classification as a conscientious objector opposed to both combatant and noncombatant military service. Ra asked to be sent to a Civilian Public Service (CPS) camp instead of prison; in his questionnaire for the National Service Board for Religious Objectors, which assigned objectors to work detail, he described himself as a skilled poet, composer, and pianist, and, under "physical defects," explained that he suffered from a severe hernia due to cryptorchidism that restricted his movement, and made it impossible to perform strenuous physical activity. Ra was assigned to CPS Camp 48 in Marienville, Pennsylvania, a forestry service that he feared would demand hard labor; when he was denied a deferment to receive an emergency corrective operation, he refused to go. In December of 1942, after Ra failed to appear at Camp 48, a local judge ordered that he be held forty miles away from Birmingham at the Walker County Jail, in Jasper, Alabama, while they resolved the circumstances of his case, even though he was the sole caretaker for his great-aunt, and still had

---

35. Szwed, *Space Is the Place*, 36, 36.

not received adequate medical care for his condition. During his incarceration, Ra became sick with headaches, progressive numbness, and muscle weakness, which he attributed to his hernia, and grew increasingly enraged by the lackluster medical treatment he was receiving in the jail; in one letter to the National Service Board from jail, he argued that Black people in the South were "not living in a part of the U.S. but more a section which seems a member of the Axis and which is determined that no Negro will ever receive justice." Letter-writing became the primary means by which Ra advocated for himself; after much back-and-forth with the National Service Board and the judge in charge of his case, he was released from jail on February 6, 1943, put on a train, and sent to the integrated Camp 48 in Marienville, where he was assigned to play the piano. Though Camp 48 was an improvement from jail, Ra insisted that he be seen by the camp physician, who took note of his hernia, and the psychiatrist, who diagnosed him as a "well-educated colored intellectual" with a "psychopathic personality."[36] They jointly recommended that he be immediately given a 4-F classification for reasons of physical disability.

On March 22, Ra returned to Birmingham, picking up where he had left off with his band—however, Szwed observes, "ask anyone who knew him then and they'll tell you he came back changed. They had never seen him angry, but now he was furious, enraged at the city, the government, and at his family and friends for not visiting him." His imprisonment and protracted struggle with the US government were an inverse of his Saturnian initiation, experiences that revealed to him the power of antiblackness and ableism to malform Black life on Earth. And yet his embrace of narrative political activism, including public speaking, letter-writing, and legal self-advocacy, served as powerful vernacular models for future struggle. After his great-aunt's death in late 1945, Ra was suddenly in a position to join the throng of Black folks in search of other planets of possibility. Ra had known for many years that in order to bring about the future he had seen during his initiation and fulfill his alter-destiny he would eventually leave the South; indeed, as Adams remembered, in his last days in the city Ra "hated Birmingham, yes, and never got over Birmingham for racial reasons . . . but that's not why he left."[37] In early spring 1946, Ra walked to the Terminal Station, bought a ticket, and boarded the train to Chicago.

Ra was immediately hired to play with Fletcher Henderson at the Club DeLisa, an all-Black venue that could seat eight hundred patrons; at the

---

36. Szwed, *Space Is the Place*, 40, 43, 46.
37. Szwed, *Space Is the Place*, 46, 50.

time, he was known as Sonny Blount, occasionally stylized as H. Sonne Bhlount. As part of the second wave of the Great Migration to Chicago, Ra was joined by more than twenty thousand other Black folk who moved to the city that year. William Sites explains that Chicago offered "a future-oriented musician like Sonny Blount [. . .] the sight and sound of modern development in motion," including Webster-Chicago, the manufacturer of the first wire recorders, sound systems, and electronics, and elevated train lines that "push[ed] majestically through the Black Belt neighborhoods, a new kind of limited access 'urban freeway' called the Outer Drive, its name an exotic promise. [. . .] If Birmingham was the modern city with a future that never fully arrived, in Chicago the future [. . .] seemed all around him." Ra once more lived in close proximity to locomotive and sonic technologies in a city suffused with the sounds and shape of Black life. Though by no means completely free from racism and northern Jim Crow, Chicago offered Ra opportunities to participate in civic and social life. Dozens of clubs, venues, and theaters attracted players from the South. And yet, the Chicago jazz scene was deeply segregated; Black musicians (even famous ones, like Duke Ellington and Roy Eldridge) were denied access to lucrative North Side/Loop venues and restricted to South Side clubs. After Henderson left Chicago, Ra made do with gig work, playing nightclubs in the famous DuSable and Pershing districts and strip clubs and parties in nearby Calumet City. He quickly became a central player in the musical marketplace. And yet, as in Birmingham and Huntsville, Ra was notably introverted and isolated; when he was not in rehearsal or performing, he spent his time perusing Chicago's used bookstores and reading. Szwed notes that visitors were shocked to discover piles of books stacked to the ceiling, each one "marked up [. . .] in copious notes of red, green, and yellow ink, circling, underlining, arrowing, echoing what he read with comments and cross-references, sometimes with arcane symbols."[38] While these early Chicago years were sonically formative, Ra did not make it known to anyone that he was a Saturnian.

This would change in 1951, when Ra met Alton Abraham, a young radiology technician, at Washington Park on the South Side, known for its "soapbox gathering sites," and "cluster of unorthodox religious groups competing for adherents," including the Nation of Islam, Garveyites, Rastafarians, and Communists, as well as loosely affiliated spiritualists, mystics, and holiness preachers. The park was a microcosm of 1950s Black Chicago, with its vibrant political and intellectual community, albeit on the whole

---

38. Sites, *Sun Ra*, 60; and Szwed, *Space Is the Place*, 63.

"nationalist, spiritually oriented, and deeply critical of black community leaders."[39] Abraham had formed a study group with several men who were also interested in philosophy, spiritualism, and the occult; he recalled that he and Ra "had a lot of things in common, because at that time [my group] was already doing ancient biblical research and research in astrology and researching the origin of mankind—that means black, white, and everybody." Abraham was the first person in Chicago Ra told about his extraterrestrial alien origins, transmolecularization, and ongoing communication with the Creator of the universe; Abraham not only took Ra at his word but encouraged him to change his name and live publicly as a Saturnian. On October 20, 1952, at the circuit court in Cooke County, Illinois, he legally changed his name to Le Sony'r Ra, which he identified as his "vibrational name."[40]

Together Abraham and Ra founded a secret society called Thmei Research, named after the Egyptian goddess of truth, justice, law and righteous conduct, and began to study ancient history, astrology, hermeneutics, alternatives to Darwinian evolutionary theory, and "the hidden origins of black Americans and their implications for the future." As Abraham explains,

> the main purpose of this organization [. . .] was to do some things to prove to the world that black people could do something worthwhile, that they could create things, they could do things that other nations would take notice of. [. . .] We wanted to save the United States, and in order to do that, we needed to drop the old ways and seek new ones which worked. Southern blacks were still living in the past, because the future was hard on them: Blacks would have to become disciplined and prepare for the Space Age to come. [. . .] Sonny wanted to do things not the right way, but *another way*, a *better* way. The possible had been tried, and failed; now it was time for the impossible.[41]

Thmei Research gave Ra his first opportunity to share what he had learned of spacetime, the cosmos, and the future for Earthlings. Ra and Abraham met at Washington Park to exchange ideas with passersby and other interested parties; Abraham notes that "we had our own tree that we used to stand by. People came to our tree." Corbett explains that "street-corner preaching was one of the primary outlets for Ra's findings, both on his own and as

---

39. Sites, *Sun Ra*, 94, 95; 94.
40. Sites, *Sun Ra*, 97; and Szwed, *Space Is the Place*, 86.
41. Sites, *Sun Ra*, 97; and Szwed, *Space Is the Place*, 76.

part of Thmei. [. . .] Ra's preaching was accompanied by writings—booklets, pamphlets, and broadsides which were mimeographed and handed out to people on the street as well as members of the band. They were sometimes unsigned, sometimes signed 'Ra' or 'Sun' or 'El.'"[42] Thmei's public-facing work offered Ra the chance to fulfill his alter-destiny as it was presented to him during his initiation. Washington Park can be read as an iteration of the Chicago courtyard full of "bewildered" souls, his soapbox the balcony he was initially reluctant to approach, his speechifying a fulfillment of the Saturnian imperative to overcome his introversion and speak directly to the people.

The Thmei broadsides reflected the Black cosmic tradition's investments in off-Earth destinies and origins, and the Black DIY textual futurist praxis that encouraged Black readership, self-publication, and political action. Typewritten on 8x11 sheets of office paper, the undated broadsides were likely written in the early 1950s, each composed as a narrative composite of strident capitalized letters, Bible passages, Socratic exchanges, poems, and essays; of those that survived, some have handwritten titles, marginal notes, clarifications, or other observations in Ra's neat, cursive script. Though there is evidence that some were written collectively (occasionally they are signed "We—Ra"), each was also the direct result of Ra's thinking about the cosmic diaspora, the function and role of Black people in the future, and his special role as Black alien teacher and truth-teller. Of particular interest here, too, is the broadsides' narrative form, which comprise the foundations of Ra's poetics, including

> close examination of language through wordplay and the scrutiny of homophones or near homophones (God/good/cod/code; Phi Beta/far better; sine/sign/sin [Latin] without; Teutonic/two-tonic; Akneaton/a-not-tone) and etymology (treatise/treaty), especially as those words relate to music; the effects of *sounds* of words (beyond their meaning); Biblical exegesis combined with a skeptical eye to Christianity as it is popularly understood; the cross-referencing of folk and pop culture [. . .]; the mysteries and transcendent orderliness of numbers; and the importance of duality, secret knowledge, authority (certification, passport), and the affirmation of life over death.[43]

---

42. Sites, *Sun Ra*, 97; and Corbett, *Wisdom of Sun-Ra*, 5.
43. Szwed, *Space Is the Place*, 78.

Ra's broadsides are meant to be both read *and* heard (at times a word's meaning correlates to the way it appeared on the page, at others to how it sounds when spoken aloud), encourage talk-back and call-and-response, and help Black listeners and readers confront the mythic reality of their place on Earth and in the universe and ultimately embrace their impossible potential as intergalactic beings.

The contents of the Thmei broadsides defy easy summation. They cover broad and often contradictory intellectual terrain, drawing on Egyptology, biblical prophecy and hermeneutics (though sharply critical of Christianity), numerology, the occult, alchemy and magic, theosophy, linguistic etymologies, and Afrocentric philosophy that "focused on the specifically African or black characteristics of antique civilizations, along with their hidden but powerful influence on subsequent European culture." Like Griggs, Ra and Abraham were politically nationalist. Ra's Black nationalism, however, was additionally influenced by his understanding of himself as an extraterrestrial being, of Earth as a galactic vessel that was in no way singular in the universe, and of the expansive dimensions of spacetime, including universal deep time, the Now, the far future, and all points in-between—as Edwards explains, "Ra refigures the so-called black nationalist *land question* [. . .] into the *space question*."[44] In the Thmei papers and elsewhere, Ra extended the diaspora into the cosmos, and placed the planet itself in intergalactic relation by demanding that we expand our spatiotemporal register from the microcosm of nation-state to the macrocosm of the universe. As he would write later in an essay published in *The Cricket*, the jazz magazine founded in 1968 by A. B. Spellman, Larry Neal, and LeRoi Jones, "Freedom to me means the freedom to rise above a cruel planet. [. . .] When I speak of freedom, I do not speak of the freedom of the land of liberty or the freedom of any land of this plane of existence, for this plane of existence is only a temporary illusion . . . shadow and images that sometimes intermingle." Ra's embrace of the Black cosmic tradition, or his articulated desire to find "freedom," to "rise above" and escape the "cruel planet," was configured as an escape into "the potential impossible":

> Alas and happily, at last I can say this world is an unfortunate planet. [. . .] The future is obvious, but the potential impossible is calling softly and knocking gently [. . .] There are other dimensions and the equation of it is every other world in the infinity of the universe. [. . .] Yes, the truth is that the truth is *bad* as far as this planet is concerned. The neglected mathematics

---

44. Sites, *Sun Ra*, 103; and Edwards, "Race for Space," 32, emphasis in original.

of MYTH is the equation differential potential impossible potential potential potential otherness alter-isness.⁴⁵

In typical Raian rhetorical fashion, evident in his neologisms and language repetition, he shifts the conditions for freedom from the "unfortunate planet" to the "infinity of the universe," configuring the potential impossible as a grammar of possibility in which diasporic movement eclipses any "obvious" future by moving into "other dimensions," or regions of universal spacetime typified by "otherness," "potential," "alter-isness," and "infinity." Ra's triadic "potential potential potential" represents the force of his embrace of technologies of freedom from planetary boundaries, including space flight, psychic and spiritual travel, transmolecularization, teleportation, and journey by cosmic-train, each capable of offering Black sojourners an "alter-fate," or access to alternative realities (and myths) outside of, beyond, in spite of Earth—an "elastic spiral potential infinity discipline other planes myth reality."⁴⁶

Ra's cosmic diaspora also reconfigured the genealogy of the "American negro" by troubling Black folks' planetary origins and ongoing entanglements with the US empire, and by reframing Black Americans as a diverse intergalactic community of not-necessarily-human organisms who must leave not only America but the spatiotemporal boundaries of the planet itself in order to become truly liberated. I frame Ra's cosmic diaspora here as a Black kinopolitics that imagines travel to other planets and dimensions as a combination of technologies of flight, forms of authorization (including passports), and sonic-linguistic imaginaries. According to Ra, the "American negro" is a "myth," which, Edwards contends, refers paradoxically to the "historical erasure of African Americans, as a group [. . .] (*I come to you as the myth, because that's what black people are*)," and to a spatiotemporal imaginary of "possibility, an openness that even breaks syntax [. . .] in its insistence on something new, on something radically different."⁴⁷ According to Ra, the American negro's potential paradoxically arises from their mythicism—their unknowability occludes and yet makes possible their latent ability to go anywhere, do anything, or become anyone. In this context, "myth" contains both its originary denotative meaning (erasure), its opposite meaning (possibility), and all other potential connotations, a clear example of the way that a single word for Ra could describe multiple contradictory concepts at the same time.

---

45. Ra, "My Music Is Words," 28–29, 28–30.
46. Ra, "My Music Is Words," 29.
47. Ra, "My Music Is Words," 33.

In the Thmei broadside entitled "Why Don't You Turn Again!," Ra confirms that Black people's mythic origins were derived from the genealogical violence of the slave trade, which deprived them of any sense of deep time: "It is really a terrible thing to be in complete darkness concerning oneself and one's ancestors. To be in ignorance, past, present, and future is beyond belief, yet such a state of mind is actually present among people called negroes. [. . .] IT IS THE SHAME OF THE UNIVERSE. These people have been used with most callous non-consideration and the worst part of it is, they are without help as far as bettering their condition."[48] According to Ra, the persistent violations of Black diasporic kinship and memory in the afterlife of slavery were cosmic concerns, violence so profound it was unique in the "UNIVERSE," an irrecoverable galactic trauma that rendered "past, present, and future" unknowable, miring the newly formed "negro" in permanent "ignorance." Ra understood well the "complete darkness" that attended an uncertain origin. But he also understood that Black life and being—incorporated as the "Negro" in the US—was a national myth, a death-haunted illusion. In the broadside entitled "Jesus Said, 'Let the Negro Bury the Negro,'" Ra mounts a proto-Afropessimist claim about the degradation of Black life:

> Jesus said, "Let the Negro bury the Negro." [. . .] But according to Genesis C and G are interchangeable and for this reason the word of Jesus also reads, "Let the Necro bury the Necro." . . . In present day language, the sentence just quoted reads: "Let the dead bury the dead." The original Greek and Ancient Hebrew definition of Negro or Necro is dead body. Many people think that Negro means Black but if it really meant Black only black people would be called Negro . . . Unfortunately for the Negro the word Negro means dead body . . . The Cemetery itself is named after the word Negro: Necropolis or City of the dead. [. . .] If you like death and like being one of the Living dead then call yourself a Negro and continue to be rejected by the world as firstclass citizens.[49]

Through an inventive use of biblical hermeneutics, homophonic paronomasia, and political analysis, Ra explains that to be interpellated as a "Negro" in the US is to experience social death, as Orlando Patterson has described it,[50] an experience akin to zombification or being an animate "dead body." As genealogical isolates without access to histories that make "oneself and

---

48. Corbett, *Wisdom of Ra*, 110.
49. Corbett, *Wisdom of Ra*, 66.
50. For a more in-depth discussion of Patterson's construction of social death, see chapter 1.

one's ancestors" spatiotemporally intelligible, Black people in the US are the "Living dead" confined to a planetary tomb.

As he explained in "It is time to discuss," one of the few broadsides featuring a direct address from Ra that clarifies that from his soapbox he is "SPEAKING TO WHITE PEOPLE AS WELL AS TO BLACK, I AM SPEAKING TO THE WORLD," the Negro was "TOO BUSY TRYING TO BE LIKE SOMEONE ELSE'S IDEA OF LIFE TO STOP AND BE WHAT IT IS RIGHT THAT HE SHOULD BE. IT IS RIGHT THAT THE NEGRO SHOULD FREE HIMSELF OF IGNORANCE, THE IMPORTANT [sic] IS TO FACE REALITY." In order to face reality and deconstruct the myth of their origins, the Negro would have to contend with their linealogy: "IT IS A KNOWN FACT THAT THE AMERICAN NEGRO SPEAKS AND ACTS DIFFERENT FROM ANY OTHER NATION OF THIS EARTH. SOME PEOPLE TRY TO BELIEVE THAT THE NEGRO IS NOT A PEOPLE APART AND SEPARATE BUT EVEN THE MUSIC OF THE NEGRO IS DIFFERENT FROM EITHER THE WHITE MAN OR BLACK MAN OF ANY OTHER COUNTRY. WITNESS: SWING, DIXIELAND, SPIRITUALS, BOP, BLUES." Ra knew well that Black people were more complex than they appeared to be, given that his own Blackness masked his extraterrestrial origin. In his view, many more beings than "black people" had been aggregated under the category of "Negro," beginning with the transatlantic slave trade. Ra's genealogy of Blackness in the broadside entitled ". . . . . . . there are two ethiopias . . . . ," troubles the planetary origins of the "American negro," whom, he claims, is "not an original inhabitant of America. The American negro is likewise not an original inhabitant of Africa." Rather, the American negro has no originary space or place because "NEGROES ARE ALL NATIONS." In other words, the American negro is a diasporic aggregate, a mythic being whose identity was forged by and through moving through the Middle Passage:

> You have to realize this planet is not only inhabited by humans, it's inhabited by aliens, too . . . and mixed up among humans you have angels. The danger spot is the United States. You have more angels in the country than anywhere else. [. . .] Never in the history of the world has there been a case where you take a whole people and bring 'em into the country in the Commerce Department . . . It happened here . . . It was possible for aliens and angels and devils and demons to come in this country. They didn't need no passport. So then they'd come as displaced people. Perfect setup . . . They could come here and act like poor people, they could come here and act like slaves because [the authorities] didn't keep up with what was happening.[51]

---

51. Corbett, *Wisdom of Ra*, 115, 116, 81, 97; and Corbett, *Extended Play*, 17.

Black Earthlings in the US are therefore a cosmic mixture of different ethnicities, nations, and beings, human and nonhuman, extraterrestrial and celestial, an interuniversal collectivity whose origins had been deliberately occluded by capitalist and imperialist power structures; the slave trade transformed this diverse assemblage into the single confluence of the "American negro," eradicating the power and truth of their peculiar origins, transforming them into objects, and denying them future knowledge of other dimensions. Ra's cosmic diaspora is therefore a composite of "displaced people" from Africa and Asia, including the descendants of ancient Nubians, Egyptians, Indians, and Ethiopians, peoples Thmei Research contended directly influenced Greek and Roman cultures, as well as angels, demons, and aliens who were merely "act[ing] like poor people . . . like slaves" in order to gain access to the US, alongside Indigenous African ethnic groups, such as Igbo, Wolof, Yoruba, Makua, Kongo, or Akan. Though the US nation-state had systematically flattened and denied the intergalactic richness of Black origins, it would not be successful in dispelling the potential of their power if Black folk were to embrace the truth of their impossible origins, and begin to imagine other planetary realities. This, Ra explained, was his mission on Earth—to convince the American negro of their simultaneously unknowable potential and nevertheless very real intergalactic and celestial heritage, "something so impossible [. . .] it can't possibly be true. But it's the only way the world's gonna survive, this impossible thing. I'm talking about impossibilities."[52]

In his capacity as a street preacher, Ra felt compelled to let the masses know about the potential of their secret origins and alter-destiny: "It has been demonstrated that anywhere a Negro goes is not home, no matter how hard you work you are not going to be appreciated. [. . .] To such a people, I bring a message, 'Turn Again, Turn Again,' and you will be forgiven. Ye cannot hide any longer. Ye are the light of the world. A city on that is set on a hill cannot be hid." By "turn[ing] again" and again beyond the boundaries of the planet, embracing the truth of their origins, and creating new, off-Earth communities in outer space, the American negro was also a "light," both as an aggregate of cosmic beings and as a representation of the potential impossible. If aliens, angels, demons, Indigenous Africans, and ancients, among many, many others, were transmogrified into Negroes through the movement of the slave trade, Ra believed they could and would transform yet again once they moved into outer space—just as he had gone from being of uncertain provenance to being from Saturn, so too could the American negro

---

52. Corbett, *Extended Play*, 311.

be remade through cosmic locomotion. Ra's cosmic diaspora was inherently intergalactic, which, Edwards contends, "evidences Ra's continual vigilance toward the impossible, the un-thought, the un-conceived, the *not*, the *alter*, as he liked to say." As Ra explained in *The Cricket*, "I have a gift to offer this planet. [. . .] I am doing what I am supposed to do, I am doing what I came here to be. [. . .] All that I am is a visitation and that is the meaning of the natural alter-self. If you are dissatisfied with yourself in the scheme of things and the altar has not changed conditions, perhaps you should consider the alter. After all if anything changes, it will be through the word alter/alternation/alternative because how can you dare to speak of change if you do not have an alternative? The alterative to limitation is INFINITY."[53]

Ra continued his DIY Black cosmic tradition, rooted in the power of the "word" to bring about "alternatives" and effect necessary planetary and intergalactic "change" until 1961, when he decided to fulfill the remainder of his alter-destiny by leaving Chicago for New York. Ra's work with Thmei Research and his street-corner preaching had transformed him into the public extraterrestrial alien Le Sony'r Ra from Saturn; as Szwed notes, his time in the city had taught him "that there was something greater than Birmingham, than Chicago, greater even than the earth itself"[54]—that is, preparing Black folk to embrace their destinies as beings whose alter-destiny was to join interplanetary forces in outer space, to leave the confines of the antiblack and mismanaged planet for the unknowable known of the cosmos. As I discuss in the next section, Ra continued to develop his conception of the cosmic diaspora into what he described as the "Astroblack," a cosmic being with interplanetary access to other planets, worlds, and dimensions, in his poetry, album notes, and album covers. Both cosmic and DIY, Ra's conception of Astroblackness imagined Black folk as capable of being transformed into galactic beings through technologies of space flight, imagination, language, and sound, enjoining them with other entities in an outer space freed from the limitations of Earth.

Astro Black Is Cosmo Dark: The Poetics of Sun Ra's Cosmic Diaspora

In 1957, while Sun Ra was still in Chicago working with Thmei Research, the USSR launched *Sputnik*, the first satellite in outer space. The launch

---

53. Corbett, *Wisdom of Ra*, 109; Edwards, "Race for Space" 34; and Ra, "My Music Is Words," 34.
54. Szwed, *Space Is the Place*, 109.

inaugurated what came to be known as the "space race," as the US government sought to be the first to achieve spaceflight supremacy and ballistic dominance and to lead the globe in extraplanetary landings. When asked about the "race for space" in an interview, Ra argued that because global forces of antiblackness had made Earth uninhabitable for Black people, the only option left was to escape the planet entirely: "According to my research, the governments of this world have conspired to destroy the nations of black people. [. . .] And all other nations have helped with it; some by just holding off and doing nothing. The consequence though has been that there now exists a separate kind of human being, the American Black man. And I should say that he doesn't belong on Earth." Rather than work toward a national or global culture of harmony with other human beings, Ra claimed that Black people, "the only people who stand apart," were called "to live in harmony with the Creator of the cosmos." Ra believed that outer space was not only the rightful domain of American Black people, but, as he well knew, intergalactic travel could be achieved without the support of either Soviet or US war technologies. Rather than view the space race as yet another sign of thwarted Black progress, Szwed explains that Ra instead regarded "space as both a metaphor of exclusion and reterritorialization, of claiming the 'outside' as one's own, of tying a revised and corrected past to a claimed future."[55]

And yet, Ra's belief in a cosmic alter-destiny for Black people was not a metaphor at all. Interplanetary travel was, in his view, both necessary and possible; his childhood realization that he had arrived on the planet from "somewhere else," his visitation with Saturnians, his transmolecularization, and his journeys to Jupiter had taught him that human beings could prioritize space travel on their own terms by shifting their perspectives about their place in the universe. Rather than work within the bounds of extant Earth systems, or advocate for ways to improve planetary conditions for Black folk, Ra wanted to remind Earthlings that they belonged to a sprawling galactic community, in part by issuing an interplanetary passport to every person at the moment of birth. When asked what he would do if he had "Donald Trump's money," Ra explained that he would "develop a space program that would have legality from the interplanetary council of other planets. [. . .] I'd give everyone on the planet an interplanetary passport with the right to go into outer space. I wouldn't let a single astronaut go up there without an interplanetary passport." In Ra's view, the issuance of universal interplanetary passports would circumvent and destabilize state,

---

55. Szwed, *Space Is the Place*, 140, 140, 140.

national, and global politics by credentializing all Earthlings in the same way, thereby shifting formerly planet-bound political systems to those governed by councils in outer space. More importantly, Ra insisted that Earth did not belong to white humans, who pretended to own it outright, but to the universe: "This planet belongs to someone else, and the landlord sent me here. The tenants here are not treating the property good. [. . .] And if they get evicted, where are they goin'? No other landlord gonna let them come on their planet. So I'm tellin': 'Look, this is not your planet. You're staying here. It belongs to somebody, the landlord.'" Ra's criticism of the planet's "tenants," and his perception of our right relation and obligation to planet Earth, might be seen as examples of what Gayatri Chakravorty Spivak has described as "planetarity," or a mode of relation to the planet that reads Earth as a "species of *alterity*, belong[ing] to another system; and yet we inhabit it, on loan." By "thinking planet-thought in this mode of alterity,"[56] Ra constructed Earth as a species in its own right, as a separate entity entangled with human life, and yet importantly distinct from it; though Earth is important to human beings, it is simultaneously "not your planet," or an object to possess.

I have argued so far in this chapter that Ra's Black cosmic tradition and DIY textual futurism were informed by his perception that Black people in the US were a descendental amalgam of extraterrestrial aliens, Indigenous Africans, ancient peoples, and spiritual entities (angels and demons) whose alter-destiny was to leave the planet and join with other cosmic beings in an off-Earth intergalactic reality. In the remainder of this chapter, I explore the development of Sun Ra's construction of planetarity as a futurist poetics in late 1950s Chicago and 1960s New York. Through a reading of the textual and sonic development of his Arkestra and several of his self-published poems, I analyze how these projects synthesized and expanded Nix's cosmicism and Griggs's DIY textual futurism, pushing into a new Astroblack cosmic terrain that imagined outer space as an omnidirectional home for Black people. I consider how, in his textual shift from street preaching and writing broadsides to performing jazz with the Arkestra and writing poetry, he came to develop his conception of an Astroblack poetics, or an extraplanetary, intergalactic, and mythic textual community of Black beings in outer space.

In addition to pushing Ra to publicly embrace his identity as an extraterrestrial alien through their mutual work with Thmei Research, over time Alton Abraham also convinced him to further develop his sonic performance

---

56. Ra, "Master Plan," xvi; Corbett, *Extended Play*, 316–17; and Spivak, "'Planetarity,'" 291, emphasis in original; 291.

by forming a big band. Ra believed that a combination of textual forms, music, sound, and performance was key to convincing Black people of their alter-destiny. Ra had played with a trio and quartet for many years in Chicago, but he struggled to find musicians willing to endure his demanding rehearsals (as in Birmingham, he lectured his way through practice), learn his complex and unusual musical arrangements, or follow his strict rules for dress and behavior. By the mid-1950s, however, Ra had put together a band featuring a rotating cast of anywhere between fifteen and seventeen musicians, including several sets of drummers (often as many as three played at once), baritone saxophone, alto saxophone, tenor saxophone, euphonium, acoustic bass and electric bass, trombone, timbali, and tympani. In addition to composing and arranging each piece, Ra himself bounced between organ, acoustic piano, and electric piano, all while singing, chanting, and speechifying. He also instructed his band to play a collection of homemade and international instruments he renamed, including the flying saucer, space-gong, space harp, space-dimension mellophone, space master piano, intergalactic space organ, sunhorn, boom-bam, mistro clarinet, cosmic tone organ, and cosmic side drum. Ra's compositions represented a fusion of earlier jazz forms, including big band, post-bop, exotica, funk, and Latin sounds, while drawing on a wide range of global musical traditions. As he pushed his music to reflect his desire for a technological sonic future of his own making, Ra was one of the first jazz musicians to embrace electronic instruments, including the bass and piano, clavioline, celeste, synthesizer, and Hammond organ.

Ra named his band an Arkestra, a word that played on the sound of "orchestra," signified the Egyptian God Ra's solar barque and the biblical Ark of the Covenant, and echoed the sounds of his name: "Arkestra has a 'ra' at the beginning and the end. [. . .] Ra can be written as 'Ar' or 'Ra,' and on both ends of the word it is an equation: the first and the last are equal . . . That's phonetic balance."[57] In their nightly performances, Ra altered the name—the Myth Science Arkestra, the Intergalactic Research Arkestra, the Power of Astro-Infinity Arkestra, the Cosmo Discipline Arkestra, the Space-age Jetset Arkestra, the Intergalactic Astro-Infinity Arkestra, and the Alter Destiny 21st Century Omniverse Arkestra, among many others—each iteration signifying his investments in outer space, the incipient Space Age, and what he would come to describe as Astroblackness. With the help of Abraham, Ra established his own record company, El Saturn Research, and registered it with the Musicians Union in 1956. Ra had already seen in Chicago

---

57. Szwed, *Space Is the Place*, 94.

that it was possible for him to produce his own work on his own terms for himself. His Arkestra and El Saturn Research were extensions of those early investments in a Black DIY futurist tradition; like Griggs, Ra would control his artistic flow through the recording, production, and distribution of his music and poetry.

The Arkestra was also, however, a cosmic signification on Noah's Ark, which represented an interstellar spaceship and intergalactic collective capable of transporting Black people to the impossible potential of outer space through sound, spaceship, and word. Arkestra drummer Tommy Hunter recollected that, in their earliest days, Ra "thought of the band as a 'space orchestra'; space was the central idea. He began with the idea that the earth was traveling in space, so that the planet was like a spaceship. What he had in mind was an orchestra that was traveling together in space . . . And, really, anyone can travel in space in their dreams and imagination."[58] If Earth was a spaceship, then space travel was a mundane facet of everyday existence, the reality of which Ra felt had been intentionally hidden from the people by unscrupulous politicians and false leaders who were invested in exploiting Black labor forever. To Ra, because the Arkestra was an always-ready interplanetary happening, he believed that his musicians would need to live their lives and perform their music as though it were so. The Arkestra's job was to bring the reality of the Earth-as-space-vessel to the people, equipping them with the tools to challenge the myth that inhabitants of the globe are planet-bound, or that flight from Earth was impossible without the aid of global extractive technologies designed by the USSR and the US.

As his investments in Thmei Research gave way to his work with El Saturn Research, Ra and his Arkestra performed gigs around Chicago before being booked to play five nights a week at the Wonder Inn in 1958. In addition to arranging the music, Ra designed the band's clothing, recruiting band members to sew the fabric he had selected together; the band became known for their brightly colored, glittered costumes, and instruments decorated with symbols of outer space—stars, moons, planets, spaceships. As Ra later recalled while living in New York, "we started [wearing space costumes] back in Chicago. In those days I tried to make the black people, the so-called Negroes, conscious of the fact that they live in a changing world. And because I thought they were left out of everything culturally, that nobody had thought about bringing them in contact with the culture. [. . .] That's why I thought I could make it clear to them that there are other things outside their closed environment. That's what I tried with my clothes." Ra's

---

58. Szwed, *Space Is the Place*, 141.

space costumes were designed to introduce "so-called Negroes" to alternative cultures and modes of cosmic being, but they were also an expression of his belief in the interconnectedness of forms; just as he argued that "words are music," which I discuss earlier in this chapter, he also claimed that "costumes are music. [. . .] Colors throw out musical sounds." In his work with El Saturn Research, Ra became increasingly focused on performing cosmic sounds, or, as Szwed explains, creating a sonic-textual-material system of interstellar escape in order to "relocate himself so as to embody all time and nature and to escape the confines and limits of life on earth. Space to him was not empty, cold, and lifeless, but the container of the cosmos, and his true home, the greater reality, rich with potential, alternative, and promise." After watching the Arkestra's first musical performance on the West Coast, reviewer Joe Gonçalves wrote that the band represented a re-evaluation of outer space as an accessible dimension and played music that expanded the boundaries of spacetime by inviting Black audience members to join them on the journey: "It's us in outer-space, sitting down, tired, with Universe charts, not clear where we are but sure of getting there. [. . .] What we never had for so long, space, outer space. Or no space at all. Squeezes so tight. From the slaveship to the shack to the tenement. No space to really move. No space to really function. Sun Ra & Co. herald Space to Come, Freedom, to move, to live again as ourselves. Expansion. [. . .] Sun Ra is future/ALTER/what's coming."[59] Ra's re-presentation of outer space as a place for Black folks—a space of "Freedom, to move," a future "Space to Come," and space to "live again a ourselves"—is an echo of Nix's gospel-train, in which flight to outer space was structured as a reprieve, an escape from an antiblack planet that "squeezes so tight," offering Black folk "no space to really move." Ra's cosmic diaspora extends the historical trajectory of the confinement of Africans and their descendants in the hold of the "slaveship," the plantation "shack," and the urban "tenement" far beyond the gravitational hold of the planet into the broad unchartable terrain of the cosmos. As Flow Motion makes clear, Sun Ra's "tradition of conceiving of the cosmos as [. . .] a sonic dimension of spiritual transcendence" can also be seen "as a history of the cosmos as the darkness into which black music projected its quest for freedom, from slave ships to sun ships, segregation to postcolonialism."[60] To that end, in the manner of the Afro-Baptist kinopolitical futurist traditions that informed him, Ra's was a "liberationist aesthetic."[61]

---

59. Szwed, *Space Is the Place*, 173, 11, 130, 140.
60. Flow Motion, "Astro Black Morphologies," 23.
61. Flow Motion, "Astro Black Morphologies," 23.

Ra argued that his music was "*not* earth music" but "music that's from a celestial plane, it's not part of the planet." Ra's performances and their riot of sound, color, costuming, singing, chanting, and call-and-response reflected those ideas, and they were carefully designed to transport the audience to outer space. Each Arkestra performance was a sonic attempt to "play space," as he framed it: "A musician actually feels about space, outer space—he can really take people out there—because he expresses that feeling and the vibrations of it will just put them over in the sound and the sound becomes like a spaceship and lift 'em on out there, you see. And they're there." Music was a kinopolitical reality for Ra, a locomotive sound-action with the power to move subjects through spacetime; indeed, as Jayna Brown explains, "music, for Sun Ra, is a form of travel through which our material bodies transfigure past time and the human form into other worlds." Because sonic forms had the power to materially transport Earthlings to the cosmos, Ra argued that the Arkestra's function was to sonically target Black audiences—recall that at this time the music scene in Chicago was segregated—and "prepare them for space. It can prepare them for the [. . .] multiplicities of time." Following Campt, I read Ra's insistence that he "prepare" Black listeners for the multiplicities of time and space through his sound, performance, and language as another example of the future real conditional, or "a form of prefiguration that involves living the future now." If, at the moment of its creation on Earth, Ra's transformational, transportational sound was "this impossible thing," it was simultaneously "the only way the world's gonna survive. [. . .] I'm talking about impossibilities. So I have to play things that are impossible [. . .] and get these folks on this planet in order."[62]

In 1957 Ra and select members of his Arkestra (Art Hoyle, John Gilmore, Pat Patrick, John Herndon, Robert Barry, Julian Priester, Richard Evans, Wilburn Green, Dave Young, and James Scales) recorded his debut album, *Jazz by Sun Ra*, distributed by the well-known Black producer Tom Wilson's Transition Records; Wilson would go on to produce records by Bob Dylan, Frank Zappa, Simon & Garfunkel, the Velvet Underground, Cecil Taylor, and the Animals, among many others. In the years leading up to the record release, Ra had turned his attention away from the street-preaching aims of Thmei Research and their polemical broadsides and began to focus exclusively on creating music and writing poetry, narrative forms he saw as inextricable. Informed by his investments in the Black cosmic tradition and Thmei's DIY textual futurism, *Jazz by Sun Ra* was originally released with a twelve-page

---

62. Corbett, *Extended Play*, 311, 309; Brown, *Black Utopias*, 10; and Corbett, *Extended Play*, 309, 311.

pamphlet that included photographs of the band, poems, philosophic micro-essays, and song notes written by Ra. In one such micro-essay, entitled "THE AIM OF MY COMPOSITIONS," Ra clarified that the record was intended to "co-ordinate the minds of peoples into an intelligent reach for a better world, and an intelligent approach to the living future."[63] Ra explained that he had developed his own unique "sound doctrine," in which he "use[d] notes like words in a sentence, making each series of sounds a separate thought."[64] According to this sound doctrine, the borders and boundaries between sound and language, song and poetry, were permanently blurred: "Some of the songs I write are based on my poems; for this reason, I am including some of them with this album in order that those who are interested may understand that poems are music, and that music is only another form of poetry. I consider every creative musical composition as being a tone poem."[65] The blurring of tone poems, textual poems, costumes-as-music, and poems-as-music in his performance and on his albums offered listeners a "SOUND ORIENTATION," designed to awaken their senses to "the future . . . in this album we present FUTURE . . NEW HORIZONS . . TRANSITION . . SUN SONG . . BRAINVILLE."[66] Ra's tone and textual poems trace materialist imaginaries that conjure flight to outer space. In the poem "ENTICEMENT," for example, the poem's speaker explains that "IMAGINATION IS A MAGIC CARPET / UPON WHICH WE MAY SOAR / TO DISTANT LANDS AND CLIMES; / AND EVEN GO BEYOND THE MOON TO ANY PLANET / IN THE SKY. / IF WE ARE HERE, WHY CAN'T WE BE THERE?"[67] Ra's alter-destiny was both imaginary and literal, a real place and a fantasy, a sound vibration and a way of seeing the cosmos. Unlike his polemical Thmei broadsides, which were strident in their efforts to convince Black people that they were cosmic beings, Ra's poetry tended to stress the "happiness, as well as pleasure and beauty" that could come from embracing an interplanetary reality in which "MUSIC AKIN TO THOUGHT" ushers us "STRAIGHT TO THE HEART OF TOMORROW."[68] This was, in some ways, a utopian impulse. Ra was certain, as was Nix, that the cosmos would offer certain relief from the antivibrational violence of Earth. This impulse was simultaneously bolstered by his certainty that tone and textual poems were "LIKE A FIERY LAW / LOOSING THE CHAINS THAT BIND /

---

63. Sun Ra and His Arkestra, *Jazz by Sun Ra*.
64. Sun Ra and His Arkestra, *Jazz by Sun Ra*.
65. Szwed, *Space Is the Place*, 156.
66. Sun Ra and His Arkestra, *Jazz by Ra*.
67. Sun Ra and His Arkestra, *Jazz by Ra*.
68. Sun Ra and His Arkestra, *Jazz by Ra*.

ENOBLING [sic] THE MIND / WITH ALL THE MANY GREATER DIMENSIONS / OF A LIVING TOMORROW."[69] Ra retained his earlier interests in homophones, wordplay, alternative meanings, and obscure etymologies, structuring his poems as thought exercises, prompts, and psychic alarms that he hoped would awaken Black people to their impossible potential.

As Ra continued to develop his poetic vision, pushing his Arkestra to "play space" and prepare listeners for the (im)possibility of leaving Earth behind, the space race accelerated; in 1958 President Eisenhower created NASA with the help of the Nazi scientist Wernher von Braun who, as I discuss in the first section of this chapter, worked out of Alabama, while in 1959 the Soviet space program launched Luna 2, the first probe to land on the moon. By 1961, as it became increasingly clear to Ra that Earthlings would no longer be able to avoid the cosmic reality of outer space, he fully shifted his energies to the creative miasma of El Saturn Research. In April of that year, the same month Soviet cosmonaut Yuri Gagarin became the first person to orbit the planet in space, Ra and several members of his Arkestra packed their instruments and headed to New York City, following the same rural backroads that Barney and Betty Hill would travel six months later when they met their own extraterrestrial aliens. Ra's arrival in New York City was the final culminating experience he had witnessed during his Saturnian initiation. As his vision of his future had made evident, he knew he would eventually be responsible for connecting Earthlings to extraterrestrials in a material, social, and public way. Ra was excited by the potential he saw for himself in New York, which offered a decidedly futurist yet stranger, less organized, and socially freer version of civic life than Chicago or Birmingham. Ra decided to no longer mask his alienness behind a veneer of Black human respectability, choosing to wear his stage costumes on the street, telling people whenever they asked that he was an extraterrestrial from Saturn who had arrived to save the planet from itself with the vibrations of sound and poetics.

Ra and his Arkestra struggled to find steady gig work in New York City until 1962, during which time members came and went; as he waited to establish their footing, Ra's poetry became his primary method for identifying the sounds and vibrations of the galactic elsewhere, and getting Black people off the planet. So central were poetics to Ra's overall vision of Black life that Szwed claims he "on occasion said that poetry was the most important part of his work, and that music was just a pretext to make it possible and to get people's attention." Over the course of his life, Ra composed

---

69. Sun Ra and His Arkestra, *Jazz by Ra*.

hundreds of poems; between 1970 and 1995 alone he self-published twenty volumes of poetry, including *The Immeasurable Equation* (1972). Ra's poems were unique because their structures, which were not expressly rhythmic, had little in common with earlier forms of jazz poetry or the more vernacular poetics of 1960s and 1970s Black resistance poetry. As Edwards notes, Ra moved away from the *"pure formalism of a concrete poetry* and towards a poetics that reaches for [. . .] *vision of consciousness,* arousing it through language—through what Sun Ra calls the *multi-self of words.* [. . .] For Sun Ra [. . .] languages are broken, intermingled," and therefore "must be read to tease out or stitch up the fabric of *mystery.*"[70] Ra's investment in language was at root a *"poetics of exegesis,* from the Greek *exegeisthai* (to explain, to interpret), from *ex-* and *hegeisthai* (to lead): thus, *to lead out or away.* A poetic where sound-equations mark an impossible exit, a way out of no way."[71] Ra's poetics were intended to be revisional, open-ended, and ever-shifting; he often rewrote poems, some several times over a decade, and included poems as album notes and as spoken word performances often read, sung, or chanted by Arkestra member June Tyson, who shifted the spacetime of textual poetics to a sonic vibration. Most generally, Ra's poetics were intended to outline in careful detail Black folks' possible trajectories to outer space by describing the fulfillment of their potential impossible alter-destinies.

If poems are music, and songs are tone poems, and if music is a locomotive, spacetime-bending vibrational happening that can transport listeners, then Ra's poems were also intended to incite an Astroblack diaspora capable of going to the stars. In his undated poem "The Cosmo Man," Ra urges readers to "Get on the Cosmo-train / Run while you can / The Cosmo-train is a word-express." The poem is an echo of the Black cosmic tradition's investments in modern technologies as a means for escape from the antiblack Earth—remember again Nix's gospel-train—and a nod to the cosmic-train Ra witnessed during his journey to Saturn. As a "word-express," the "Cosmo-train" is also an extension of Ra's perception that language and sound were innately kinopolitical. In this case, however, the train's destination is not to Heaven, Hell, or any particular planet, but the infinite non-directionality of the blackness of space: "Black is blackness every way / . . . It's darker than the night / Eyes that see always the light / Is not accustomed to the night / . . . But rays of light are sometimes dark, / And lights of dark are sometimes black." In opposition to popular conceptions of outer space that imagined its darkness as a representation of infinite nothingness—a corollary to earlier

---

70. Szwed, *Space Is the Place,* 319; and Edwards, "Race for Space," 52, emphasis in original.

71. Edwards, "Race for Space," 52, emphasis in original.

imaginaries of "darkest Africa"—Ra constructed space as an unfolding and enfolding of "blackness every way," a proliferate blending of darkness and light, a space of potential and possibility. Light and dark operated as a metaphor for Ra's cosmic diaspora and his perception that Black people were an amalgamation of cosmic beings. As he wrote in the poem "BLACK ON BLACK," "White is an echo of black in a / different direction. Black is all of / everything because of its endless acceptance / like a black bottomless pit. [. . .] / Light is an inversion / of blackness or black in a different / dimensional frequency. All colors / have different frequencies. Black is / the storage house of all colors. / White is a reflector [. . .] / White rejects, black / accepts."[72] Blackness-as-race and blackness-as-frequency, or "all of everything," are quantified by an "endless acceptance" as "storage house[s]" for the community of angels, demons, aliens, Indigenous Africans, and their descendants, aggregated together by the state and violently codified as that "black bottomless pit" of nonbeing. As on Earth, so it is in space—whereas Blackness operates as a racial "inversion" of whiteness, in outer space it is a "different dimensional frequency," one that "accepts" rather than "rejects."

As Ra further explained in "The Outer Darkness (1972, version 1)," "Black is space: THE OUTER DARKNESS / the void direction to the heavens. / [. . .] The music of the outer darkness is / the music of the void. / The opening is the void; but the / opening is the synonym to the / beginning." The void of space, awash in blackness, is an "opening," a "beginning," or intermingled confluences of light and dark signifying the simultaneity of absence and a presence, a spacetime that is an escape and a homegoing all at once. In "The Outer Darkness (1972, version 2)," Ra directly shifts the meaning of blackness from the "void" of space to the expansive potential of Blackness in the cosmic diaspora: "Intergalactic music is of the Outer Darkness / Therefore it is of the greater Blackness / And from that point of view / It is Black Infinity / [. . .] It is unlimited in scope / Immeasurable in it's multiplicities and potentialities. / I speak of a different kind of Blackness, the kind / That the world does not know, the kind that the world / Will never understand."[73] The "Outer Darkness" of space is also a form of "greater Blackness," a "Black Infinity" "unlimited in scope," and therefore markedly different from the "bottomless pit" that traps Blackness on the planet. The infinite immeasurability of space, made manifest as "multiplicities and possibilities" of Blackness in blackness, is both a secret knowledge

---

72. Ra, *Immeasurable Equation*, 116, 116, 80.

73. Ra, *Immeasurable Equation*, 294, 295. As is often the case in his poetry, in this poem Ra plays with the punctuation and meaning of words by interchanging "its" or "it's" in the final line.

and a material reality, a "different kind of Blackness," and therefore a different "kind of world." As a form of "intergalactic music," Blackness is impossibly entangled in the Outer Darkness.

Ra's poetics reflected his thinking that he was responsible for bringing Black people into a relation with the Outer Darkness through sonic and linguistic vibrations, and for that reason might be read as prophetic. I read his poetics, however, as an expression of his sincere belief that movement through space was possible and necessary for Black people who must change their relation to Earth, embrace their celestial multiplicity, and turn toward the open void of the Black Infinity. In the short poem "The Cosmic-Bypass," Ra describes his vision of a cosmic diaspora: "Out of every nation / They shall rise. . . . / With the invitation of the sun / To journey through the Outer Darkness / To the Outer Heavens / Of the Intergalactic dawn." Ra's vision of Black flight from Earth signifies on the cosmic tradition's perception of upward and outward mobility; Black people "out of every nation" "shall rise," joining together in "the Outer Darkness" and pushing beyond its boundaries to a new "Intergalactic dawn." In this poem, Ra is framed as the "sun," or the extraterrestrial alien charged with the responsibility of inviting Black people into the light of the darkness of space. In "The Fantasy," Ra further explains that his "name is the sun / I am the stranger / From the sky / Far away further than the eye can see / Is my paradise / A mythical world / In Outer Space." Anticipating that his audience would reject his claims to a "mythical world" beyond the boundaries of the planet, in "If I Told You," Ra challenges Black listeners to accept the conditions of his offer by rethinking their "right" to leave the planet: "If I told you, 'I am from outer space,' / You wouldn't believe a word I said. / Would you? . . . Why should you? / You've lost your way. . . . . . / You should have nothing to say. / You've lost your rights / To walk on Jupiter and Mars. / And even other worlds unknown among the stars / Among the stars. / [. . .] You've lost your rights, / Your cosmo-interplanetary-intergalactic / Eternal-rights of Celestial being."[74] By reminding Black people of their "Eternal-rights" to access the Outer Darkness, or their "cosmo-interplanetary-intergalactic" rights that grant them access to all dimensions of spacetime, Ra positions Black people as a priori cosmic beings and challenges them to reclaim their access to the galaxy, as well as their right to possess an otherwise reality somewhere—anywhere—else.

Ra came to describe the fulfillment of these rights by Black people and their inevitable embrace of their cosmic potentiality as *Astroblackness*. In the

---

74. Ra, *Immeasurable Equation*, 109, 163, 200.

poem "Astro Black," chanted by June Tyson on the 1973 record of the same name, Ra begins by delineating the spatiotemporal parameters of the concept: "Astro-Black Mythology / Astro-Timeless Immortality / Astro-Thought in Mystic Sound / Astro-Black of Outer Space / Astro Natural of Darkest Stars / Astro Reach Beyond the Stars / Out to Endless Endlessness / Astro-Black American." Astroblackness is an orientation in space "Beyond the Stars," a mode of "Thought" imbricated with "Mystic Sound," a position in "Outer Space" among the "Darkest Stars," and a form of "Timeless Immortality" located in the depths of "Black Mythology." Astroblackness is also, importantly, a post-US configuration; even as the "Astro-Black American" is signified by their planetary entanglement, they are directed toward "the Dawn / [. . .] and Other Worlds / Listen While You Have the Chance / Find Your Place among the Stars." Astroblackness must therefore also be understood by its participation in a galactic system of "Rhythm, Multiplicity / Harmony, Equational / Melody Horizon / Astro Black and Cosmo Dark / Astro Black and Cosmo Dark / Astro Black and Cosmo Dark." To be an Astro Black is to become aware of one's potential, as impossible as it is, and accept that in order to survive one must be enjoined in the Outer Darkness of space and embrace the potential of the Cosmo Dark. According to Ra, the cosmic alter-destiny of the American negro was to become an Astro Black by being transpositioned, transmolecularized, or locomoted to the Black Infinity of the cosmos. As Ra wrote of the Astro Black in his poem "The Cosmic Age (1968)," "This is the Space Age / The age beyond the earth age: / A new direction / Beyond the gravitation of the past. / [. . .] Prepare for the journey! / [. . .] Your new course is the Cosmic Way— / Your new vehicle is the Cosmic plane; / You will learn to live the Cosmic Way, / You will learn to journey with courage— / With the fiery aim to reach / The even greater day / of the even greater tomorrow / The greater tomorrow of the Cosmic Age."[75] Astroblackness therefore also signified a passage away from the "gravitation of the past" and into the future of "tomorrow." In other words, the Astro Black signified the promise of the Cosmic Age, a time yet to come but that *will* come, a new epoch that, by embracing the pure potential of cosmic Blackness/blackness, will shift the planetary limitations of the Space Age to the future. Ra's construction of the cosmic diaspora drove his perception that Black people, moving together in a "new direction," would and could create the conditions for themselves to leave the planet.

Sun Ra did not live in New York City long. In 1968 the Arkestra moved to Philadelphia, and then to California, and from there traveled to Europe, to

---

75. Ra, *Immeasurable Equation*, 74, 74, 74, 106.

Egypt. During his time in Chicago and New York, however, Ra had seemed to fulfill his alter-destiny; he had overcome his shyness and spoken as a street preacher, worked to convince Black people to see themselves as the descendants of celestial beings who were calling them home to the stars, and publicly embraced his identity as Le Sony'r Ra, the extraterrestrial alien from Saturn who in his infancy had arrived on the planet from somewhere else. Ra continued to expand his vision of the cosmic diaspora and build upon the Black cosmic tradition until his death in 1993. As a testament to Ra's profound influence, the Arkestra still performs to this day under the direction of now-100-year-old saxophonist Marshall Allen, who has lived since 1968 at the Arkestral Institute, a living community founded by Ra, in Germantown, Philadelphia. Over the years, the Arkestra has maintained a DIY futurist and Black cosmic tradition of recording, producing, and distributing their own record albums, designing their costumes, and playing otherworldly instruments of their own frequency.

At no point during his life did Ra deny his alienness or suggest that it had been an elaborate performance. Rather, as he explained in the revision to "The Fantasy (1980)," "I am not a fantasy in a real sense / [. . .] Alien I? . . . . Why? / Stranger I? . . . . Why? / How can I be an alien to you unless I feel that / You are alien to me? / Yes . . . I am a spirit-stranger from the sky / Far away. . . . farther than the eye can see." Though Ra had a hopeful, and at times utopian, vision of an Astro Black future, he maintained an emotional distance from Earth; his interest was in helping Black people come to know themselves so they could leave once and for all. Though an "Alien I" and "Stranger I," Ra was also the cosmic Black "spirit-stranger" who was not a stranger or alien at all but a cosmic sibling, an Astro Black kin from the past-present-future who would lead them all out of the bottomless pit to the Outer Darkness on an intergalactic Cosmo-train. As Ra wrote in an unpublished essay, likely composed sometime in the 1980s, "I am not of this planet. I am another order of being. [. . .] I never wanted to be part of planet Earth, and I did everything not to be a part of it. I never wanted their money or fame, and anything I do for this planet is because the Creator of the Universe is making me do it . . . If I can just void it, then you have a clean spot in the Universe where Earth once was, and if I have my way I'll void it. [. . .] I would tell people on this planet that there are forces: their job is to slow you up. And you supposed to keep moving." Ra's desire to "void" the Earth—to destroy it, unmake it—can also be read as a desire to ameliorate the planet into the black "void" of space, to obliterate its antiblackness, and remake it as a new cosmic Black tabula rasa. Ra believed that being trapped on Earth was a violation of the collective Black spirit, and, to that end, his life had been a sacrifice, a seventy-nine-year effort to reach for a world in the stars. As he wrote in the poem that Trudy Morse read to him on his deathbed, "This world / Is not my home. / This world, is not my home / My home is / Somewhere better."[76]

Ra was an interplanetary emissary, a spirit-stranger from beyond the stars whose reach "expanded ever outward, from a black South to urban North, to the nation, Earth, Saturn, the universe, the omniverse; from Southern Baptist to ancient Egyptian to the Angel race." So, too, did Ra challenge our perceptions of Blackness and humanness, of alienness and kin, of diasporas of water and the diaspora of the void, and of our impossible potential to leap beyond the Space Age into the cosmic future of tomorrow. Ra's poetics embraced the radical kinopolitical potential inherent in new visions of mobility and escape, in new understandings of self and other, and new ways of imagining the relation between self and other. Ra's Black alien cosmic diaspora restructured Earth relations by orienting Black folk toward the outer space of their home, playing a tone poem to bring them home, singing a sonic-chant destined to bring about the conditions of the future: "Oh we sing this song to / A brave tomorrow / Oh we sing this song to / Abolish sorrow. / The satellites are spinning / A better day is breaking / The galaxies are waiting / For planet Earth's awakening."[77]

---

76. Ra, *Immeasurable Equation*, 163, 461, 381.
77. Szwed, *Space Is the Place*, 388; and Ra, *Immeasurable Equation*, 331.

CODA

Earth Is Ghetto

Let me set the scene again. It is December 2020, and I am sitting in front of my computer, searching for Black aliens. There is little else to do. COVID is surging everywhere, and the pressures of terrestrial spacetime are closing in on me. Gravity heaves, and everything feels dangerous: the air I breathe, the touch of my friends and family, being Black anywhere on Earth. Earlier that year, I had watched helplessly as George Floyd was murdered; for weeks, the 8 minute and 46 second video of his dying played on an endless loop on the evening news, impossible to escape from the confines of my home. It is hard to sleep, hard to think, hard to keep moving forward. The summer's global uprisings—their promise and fury and intensity—remain a small bright spot in the midst of it all, a glimpse of hope on a planet that most days feels like a bottomless pit or a bear trap. I have never been so disconnected from Earth, from the terra firma itself. All I can seem to see anymore are the ways the planet's systems unrepentantly reap Black life, refuse to embrace change, insist upon precarity, isolation, boundedness.

I scroll through the internet looking for something I am certain I will never find—evidence that other Black people are looking for a way off the planet—when I stumble upon Aliah Sheffield's music video "Earth Is Ghetto." The caption reads: "This song is for anyone is who is sick of earth."¹ Like me, Sheffield is confined to her home, holding a microphone connected to her computer, when she begins to sing.

•

Sheffield begins her song with a simple statement of desire: "Earth is ghetto / I wanna leave." In the song, she makes a direct appeal to extraterrestrial aliens to help her escape the planet: "Can you beam me up? I'm outside on the street / By the corner store, you know, the one on 15th / Got a bright shirt on, so I'm easy to see / I been down here stranded indefinitely / I can't reach my planet but I need to leave."² Sheffield imagines her home *somewhere else* because Earth is not her home—she is "down here," "stranded indefinitely," unable to "reach my planet." In other words, Sheffield is a Black alien, desperate to return to the cosmos and escape the meanness and treachery of life on Earth.

To Sheffield, Earth is *ghetto*: a run-down planet, segregated, restricted, impoverished, a snare, a site of confinement with limited possibility for escape. Sheffield's use of the word hinges on its meaning in African American Vernacular English (AAVE), where the word *ghetto,* in addition to naming a place, also connotes something that is broken down, busted, dilapidated, wrecked. To Sheffield, Earth's ghettoness is a direct function of humanity's lack of special connection and their steadfast refusal to provide care for one another: "They got the hungry starving, nothing to eat / And the homeless living out on the street / And the sick are dying, crooked police / Politicians lying, criminals on the street."³ As an alien, Sheffield finds no safe community on a planet riddled with economic inequity, homelessness, untreated illness and disease, police brutality, political ineffectiveness, and rampant interpersonal violence. Earthlings, she argues, are too disconnected from one another, too willing and able to harm one another, too narrow-minded, too planet-bound.

Sheffield also trades on the popular (mis)conception that predominantly Black urban ghettos are crime-ridden, inherently dangerous spaces. She is not asking to flee the urban ghetto, but the antiblack Earth; in other words, the *real* ghetto is the very planet itself. To this point, Sheffield offers her extraterrestrial rescuers "five on fuel," volunteering to "sit in the back if we riding too deep," cautioning them to "lock the doors, these people lie, steal,

---

1. Sheffield, "Earth Is Ghetto."
2. Sheffield, "Earth Is Ghetto."
3. Sheffield, "Earth Is Ghetto."

and cheat," in yet another echo of the common perception that you have to protect and barricade yourself from harm in poor urban areas. In this instance, however, it is *true*—Earth-as-ghetto *is* dangerous for aliens. As an alien herself, Sheffield can vouch that her extraterrestrial kin will have to "leave" as soon as they arrive, that Earth is not a place to linger or explore or *be* if you are Black. In the end, Sheffield urges her extraterrestrial ride to "roll the windows up, so we can head out in peace,"[4] an articulation of her desire to be entirely cut off from the stuff of Earth life, to become a fugitive in spacetime.

•

In 2023 Aliah Sheffield released a music video for "Earth Is Ghetto," directed by Mac Grant, to accompany the release of her record *These Songs Are for Anyone Sick of Earth* (2023). In the video, a young Black terrestrial girl is beamed up to a spaceship and entangled in a cosmic Black diaspora with extraterrestrial Black kin. The video begins with the girl asleep on a couch with her mother; in her dream, she swings freely in a hammock, gazes up at the sky through the trees, lovingly draws a picture of a green alien. These images correlated together speak to her desire to move effortlessly against gravity into the heavens, to meet with extraterrestrials in a galactic elsewhere, to be free to move through space. The girl is suddenly awakened by the television, which spontaneously turns itself to the news; the chyron reads "DEATH! DESTRUCTION! POVERTY! DISEASE! POLITICS!" As the images on the television flit between ravaged war landscapes, out-of-control wildfires, the police intimidating peaceful protestors, and raging ecological disasters, the news anchor asks, "Can we save ourselves? Or is Earth just *doomed* to be ghetto? This, and more, when we return."[5]

The girl leaves her mother behind on the couch, puts on a bright yellow sweatshirt, and heads outside to the corner store to buy a popsicle. She notices an elderly Black woman sitting on the porch at the house next door and waves at her, but when the woman, seemingly blind, does not respond or wave back, the girl walks away discouraged. On her short walk, the girl bears witness to social dysfunction and strife everywhere: her neighbors, a white man and Black man, fight over the placement of a political sign at the boundary of their property lines, pushing and screaming at one another; a homeless man, covered by cardboard and newspaper, sleeps on a bench

---

4. Grant, "Earth Is Ghetto."
5. Grant, "Earth Is Ghetto."

alone; a man in a car, presumably a drug dealer, menacingly drops a lit cigarette in the street at her feet. As she walks alone through her broken and isolated community, however, she consistently orients herself to the sky; the camera frequently reflects her perspective as she gazes up through the trees in an echo of her dreams.

While the girl purchases her popsicle from the store clerk (played by Sheffield), the television plays a newscast featuring an image of a flying saucer: "This just in. We've received multiple reports of a large object flying over the metro area."[6] As the girl walks home, she sees the elderly Black woman—now, apparently, able or willing to see her—standing alone some distance away in the middle of the street. The girl moves tentatively but steadily toward her, seeking an acknowledgment to make up for their earlier missed connection. As she walks, the people she passed by earlier now begin to look at the sky themselves, and a giant spaceship floats by in the reflection in the windshield of the drug dealer's car, in the fighting neighbor's sunglasses. As the girl approaches the elderly Black woman and stands before her, the spaceship hovers above them, pulling them up in a beam of light.

As the screen fades to white and back to reality, the girl looks around, surprised and confused to discover that she has been transported to the spaceship; as she looks through a window at her feet, she can see Earth far below, a southern place now, soon to be a pale blue dot in the ship's rearview mirror. As she becomes oriented to her surroundings, she discovers that she is not alone—the elderly Black woman and Sheffield, the store clerk, stand before her, beaming with joy and recognition.

In the end, the girl's escape from the confines of the Earth-as-ghetto is framed as a form of Black alien kinship. She is joined by aliens who *look like* her, who offer her a future where she, too, can grow old on another planet, in otherworlds and with intergalactic beings who can and will ensure her survival as they have ensured their own. We know that the girl has family on Earth, that she is human—again, at the beginning of the video she is sleeping on the couch with her mother—but in this galactic imaginary, the girl is entered into a *new* relation, a cosmic diaspora where extraterrestrials become kin and humans become strangers, a promise of becoming entangled somewhere else with something else.

•

6. Grant, "Earth Is Ghetto."

Why does Sheffield conjure this vision of Black cosmic kinship? Like Oprah, she articulates a desire to be enjoined in an infinite Black cosmos with *your people*, to be given a new direction, reorientation, and escape from the ceaselessness of the now and the incomprehensibility of the past. I share this same desire—I have always been captivated by the possibilities proffered by extraterrestrial aliens. As a young girl growing up in the space-obsessed 1980s, I was fascinated by and terrified of the universe, by the knowledge that it was constantly expanding outward into nothingness, creating itself; that its boundaries were totally unknown to us; of the certainty that *we are not alone*. I was raised by a reverend, and in my world, angels, demons, an eternal afterlife, and a blameless god roaming the Earth as man were commonplace, everyday realities—it was *taken for granted* that the world I interacted with was not all there was. In the midst of that, it was not too difficult to imagine that aliens might also exist, that God's love would be magnanimous enough to cover the universe, that in His hunger for life He would *have* to have created cosmic kin, our extraterrestrial siblings.

Much of my childhood imaginary, I am not ashamed to admit, was influenced by *Star Trek* and its many Black aliens: Nyota Uhura, Geordi La Forge, Guinan, Tuvok, Benjamin and Jake Sisko, Worf. Even then, I could see how these figures were alien *to* and *from* the places they found themselves. But I was also inspired by their promise and the way they gestured toward the possibility of all-Black planets, where things might be better, where I might not be so despised, where I would be with an interstellar family moving toward the promise of space exploration and discovery and community. There was no more appealing future, it seemed to me, than floating through streams of cosmic spacetime with Black aliens *as* a Black alien. What I wanted, and what I believe Oprah and Sheffield want, is to be *in community* with Black aliens, to *join them* as a family, to *become part of their future*. If doing so requires becoming fugitive to the antiblack Earth—perhaps losing your mother, or leaving your brother on Earth—then it is still a risk worth taking, a sacrifice worth making.

I wanted to be the little girl who finds herself in outer space with alien kin because, more than anything, *I wanted a future*. And it seemed so difficult to have one on Earth.

•

My early vision of an intergalactic Black alien future was as invested in narrative as it was in art or culture or media. I wanted to see aliens who looked Black, but I was equally drawn to the way *Star Trek* bent spacetime by reinventing itself, threading futures and pasts and presents together. I was always searching for the way Black alien futures were represented in literature, how they shifted the boundaries of narrative spacetime in order to tell their stories, built worlds that promised our survival and imagined that we were important in the future. I have never stopped looking for and finding those narratives. This book is an attempt to explain why these Black alien narratives matter, what they have to offer us as readers and thinkers, and why I love them.

There are a number of Black alien kinship futures that I do not discuss here: Nalo Hopkinson's *Midnight Robber* (2000); Nnedi Okorafor's *Lagoon* (2014) and her *Binti* trilogy (2015, 2017, 2018); N. K. Jemisin's *Far Sector* (2019–21); Robyn Smith and L. L. McKinney's *Nubia: Real One* (2021); Cadwell Turnbull's *The Lesson* (2019); or Rivers Solomon's *An Unkindness of Ghosts* (2017), to name a few. These texts move in and beyond the planetary south to Lagos, the US Virgin Islands, New Half-Way Tree, the invisible floating island of Themyscira, the confines of the Matilda, the metal planet powered by Baby Sun, adrift in space. These imaginaries and those of the writers I explored in this book—Octavia E. Butler, Maisy Card, Dwayne McDuffie and M. D. Bright, and Le Sony'r Ra—offer us exciting and important ways to conjure narrative spacetime, to imagine ourselves in kin-community together in another future, on another planet, in another time and space altogether. This book offers one possible direction for studying kinship in the cosmic diaspora, my own Black alien line of flight. But these texts remind me (or, rather, I hope they remind *us*) that there are many other places yet to go, other peoples to make our kin, other worlds to imagine or explore. *Black Aliens* is my effort to chart a star map to other systems of relation, networks of belonging, and ways of being in the world. It is, above all else, an archive of the promise and potential inherent in Black alien kinship futures.

•

Let me set the scene one last time. It is July 2024, and I am in Roswell, New Mexico, attending the UFO Festival. I have no clue what to expect, but I have a pass that covers admission to various talks and grants me access to the International UFO Museum. I know what I hope to find. I am looking for stories about Black aliens, but I would settle for narratives about alien abduction, or living with or befriending aliens, like *E.T.* (1982) or *Flight of the Navigator* (1986). I want to meet SETI enthusiasts who claim to have evidence of close encounters of every kind, any kind; I want to see their evidence, and take it seriously, and be taken seriously when I ask *if they believe too*. More than anything, I want to find and be in community with people who *love* aliens. I assume that there will be no better place to be than Roswell to do that work.

I am, however, bitterly disappointed—and, given my high hopes, somewhat traumatized by the experience. Almost every alien I see as I walk through the festival grounds is torn apart, crash-landed, battered, *dead*. After a time, even my son asks, as we pass yet another corpse, if we are likely to see any *living* aliens, any possibility of tracking down an alien who is doing anything other than dying. I tell him I am not so sure that we will. As I entered the UFO museum, I counted no fewer than eight alien corpses—tiny, gray-skinned, big-eyed bodies on the ground, in the window display, painted on a mural on the side of a wall. At the back of the museum, in a long display, is a yet another alien corpse, this one undergoing autopsy by a group of humans; it is ghastly, hideous, terrifying, and I can barely stand to look at it. We are surprised by how death-haunted the entire experience is, how alien bodies are treated as threats, or as refuse, or as punchlines in a bad joke. Amid so much death, there is also plastic kitsch everywhere like a taunt: bright green aliens adorn everything imaginable, from hats to wallets to keychains, all of it for sale. I buy myself a pair of sunglasses molded in the eyes of a Gray, one of the few non-green items I discover while there; when I put them on my face, it is as though I have been somehow changed by them, as though I cannot quite recognize myself.

I am struck by how painful I find the reverberations between the degradation of Black life on Earth and the dead alien bodies on display in Roswell, utterly alone and disconnected from their homelands, their families, their *selves*. I tell myself not to take it too seriously, but that turns out to be impossible. I had traveled to Roswell hoping to find my kin, and it was terribly sad to think that perhaps I *had*, that Black folk and extraterrestrial aliens are united not in our aliveness or cosmic potential but in our absence, our *missingness*. I look for a way out or a way forward or any way to reconnect, but I never find it there.

•

I hope this book provides us (you, me) with an antidote to the terror and sadness of Black death, alien death, human death; that it offers us a way to reconnect and reimagine our obligations to one another as cosmic kin. I want us to rethink the boundaries of terrestrial spacetime entirely, to disintegrate and renew the borders between here and there, then and now, Black and human, human and alien, Black and alien. I offer this book as an invitation to another planet, an opportunity to imagine ourselves elsewhere, together forever, with our Black alien kin in the cosmic diaspora. I hope that we can fashion from these Black alien revisions of narrative spacetime an inertial stellar compass continuously locating us anew in the stars, a textual gyroscope guiding us together to a new home, away from the Earth.

I conclude here with a poem from Sun Ra, whose intergalactic journey through the cosmos arrives at the end of the book. I urge you to read this poem as a lyrical vector magnetometer offering us directions off the planet, a way to imagine ourselves belonging elsewhere together: "'Imagination' is a magic carpet / Upon which we may soar / To distant lands and climes / And even go beyond the moon / To any planet in the sky / If we came from nowhere here / Why can't we go somewhere else?"[7]

If we came from nowhere here, why can't we go somewhere else?

Why can't we go somewhere else?

Let's go somewhere else.

---

7. Ra, *Immeasurable Equation*, 206.

ACKNOWLEDGMENTS

This book was a long time coming; its origins are in my childhood, watching *X-Files* and the director's cut of *Dune* and *The Arrival* (the one with Charlie Sheen) with my brothers. I want to thank the other triumvirs of The Mighty Triumvirate—Matthew Davis and Daniel Davis—for shaping and indulging and molding my earliest visions of what was possible, potential, or allowable in the universe. If anyone is hanging out on Saturn right now, it's you, Matty. Thank you, Danny, for your brothership—main damie, best friend, tightest homes. Thank you to Nora and Jun just for being—you're the coolest kids I know, and I love you so much. Thank you to my father, Don Davis, for your insatiable curiosity, your deep love for amazing stories, your impeccable ethical and forward-thinking intellectual example. Thank you to my mother, Beth Davis, for instilling in me a deep love of reading, and for having absolutely perfect taste in all things literary. Without you, mama, I would not be a scholar at all. And thank you to Molly Freeman, my sister, for *being there,* for believing in aliens (and so many other things, too), and for always, always, always making me laugh, even when I'm crying.

Thank you to my partner, Colin Davis-McElligatt, for so many things: for taking care of house and home and kid while I wrote and traveled and researched; for all of the fact-checking and background information about jazz, without which this book could not have been written; for listening to me and always being on my side; for encouraging me and supporting me with everything you've got; for loving me; for letting me love you back. To my son, August Davis-McElligatt—thank you for keeping it real always, and for making me laugh so hard I cry, and for being kind and gentle but also fierce and fearsome when you want to or have to be. I love you so much, and I'm proud of you.

Thank you to my editor, Ana Jimenez-Moreno, for your steadfast and enthusiastic support, and constant encouragement; to Addie Tsai for the endless chats and always knowing exactly what I mean; to TJ Tallie for your everlasting friendship and having-my-back-ness; to Aja Martinez, Priscilla Ybarra, and Anna Hinton for the realness—seriously, I appreciate y'all more than I can say; to John Edward Martin, for being the most supportive librarian on Earth, and for being cool enough to know how important comics and aliens are. Thank you to folks who have read or listened to portions of this book, offered friendship and support, and broadened my horizons in countless ways: Vincent Haddad, Regina Bradley, Mark Bould, Matthew David Goodwin, Maia Butler, Megan Feifer, Jim Coby, Peter Coogan, Frederick Luis Aldama, Sasha Sanders, D'Arcee Neal, Kristen Reynolds, Anthony Boynton, Julia Brown, Jeremy Carnes, Kiana Murphy, Christian Hines, David A. Davis, Michał Choiński, Frédérique Spill, Solveig Dunkel, Beata Piątek, Rebecca Hains, Dennis (for the laughs), Sara Chirchirillo Carter, Kai Chirchirillo, Jacqueline Foertsch, Devin Garofalo, Daniel Peña, Tarfia Faizullah, Qiana Whitted, Rebecca Wanzo, Jonathan Gray, John Jennings, Stacey Robinson, Susana Morris, Kinitra Brooks, Michelle Wright, Hosam Aboul-Ela, Kate Polak, Andrew Kunka, Sam Langsdale, Graham Barnhart, Marissa Zerangue, Emily Fontenot, Paria Rahmani, Robert Tate Morrison, Jasmyn Huff, Aletha Dale, Kaitlyn Coalson, DeAnna Daniels, Sheri Marie Harrison, Aletha Dale, Brannon Costello, Maria Seger, Jennifer Gómez Menjívar, Justin Wigard, Haley Fedor, Christy Welles, Patricia Eamon, Adam Villalobos, Jasmyn Huff, Marshall Armintor, Deb Armintor, Megan Morrissey, Suzanne Enck, Bryan Conn, Kathleen Hobson, Adriane Bezusko, Yosra Bouslama, Ed Ankomah, Bird Sellergren, Wesley Cornett, Ethan Wood, Jennifer Ho, and Corey Creekmur (thanks for the issues of *Icon*!).

This book was supported by a generous Scholarly and Creative Award from the University of North Texas College of Liberal Arts and Social Sciences, which made it possible for me to spend a week at the Huntington Library in Pasadena, California, looking through Octavia E. Butler's archive, and a week at Michigan State University in Lansing, Michigan, examining the Comic Art Collection in the Stephen O. Murray and Keelung Hong Special Collections. The research presented in this publication was supported in part by the "Memory and Trauma in American Studies" grant, founded by the program "Excellence Initiative—Research University" at Jagiellonian University in Kraków, Poland. Thank you to Jacque Vanhoutte for finding course releases and funds when there seemed to be none available, and for being an all-around one-woman support system for junior faculty. Thank you to Nicole Smith and the English Department at the University of North Texas for providing me with material support for researching, writing, and completing the manuscript.

BIBLIOGRAPHY

Al-Saji, Alia. "Glued to the Image: A Critical Phenomenology of Racialization Through Works of Art." *The Journal of Aesthetics and Art Criticism* 77, no. 4 (2019): 475–88.

"alien, adj. and n." *OED Online*, December 2022, Oxford University Press, https://doi.org/10.1093/OED/6235244187 (accessed February 23, 2023).

Anatol, Giselle. *The Things That Fly in the Night: Female Vampires in Literature of the Circum-Caribbean and African Diaspora*. New Brunswick: Rutgers University Press, 2015.

Bachollet, Raymond, Jean-Barthelémi Debost, Anne-Claude Lelieur, and Marie-Christine Peyrière. *NégriPub: L'image des Noirs dans la publicitè*. Paris: Somogy, 1994.

Bakhtin, Mikhail. *The Dialogic Imagination: Four Essays*. Edited by Michael Holquist. Translated by Caryl Emerson and Michael Holquist. Austin: University of Texas Press, 1981.

Barr, Maureen. *Lost in Space: Probing Feminist Science Fiction and Beyond*. Chapel Hill: University of North Carolina Press, 1993.

Beal, Frances M. "Double Jeopardy: To Be Black and Female." *Meridians: Feminism, race, transnationalism* 8, no. 2 (2008): 166–76.

Bennett, Joshua. *Being Property Once Myself: Blackness and the End of Man*. Cambridge, MA: Belknap Press of Harvard University Press, 2020.

Bhattacharya, Kakali. "Foreword: Methodology Is Connectivity." In *Decolonial Feminist Research: Haunting, Rememory and Mothers*, by Jeong-eun Rhee, xi–xvi. New York: Routledge, 2020.

Bindman, David. *Race Is Everything: Art and Human Difference*. London: Reaktion Books, 2023.

Brand, Dionne. *A Map to the Door of No Return: Notes to Belonging.* Toronto: Vintage Canada, 2002.

Brinegar, Terri Michelle. "The Recorded Sermons of Reverend Andrew William (A. W.) Nix: Black Voices and the Creation of Modernized Tradition." PhD diss., University of Florida, 2019, ProQuest Dissertations & Theses (28289306).

Brown, Jayna. *Black Utopias: Speculative Life and the Music of Other Worlds.* Durham, NC: Duke University Press, 2021.

Brownell, Blaine A. "Birmingham, Alabama: New South City in the 1920s." *The Journal of Southern History* 38, no. 1 (1972): 21–48.

Butler, Octavia E. Papers. The Huntington Library, Art Collections, and Botanical Gardens, Pasadena, California.

Butler, Octavia E. *Kindred.* Boston: Beacon Press, 2003.

Butler, Octavia E. *Lilith's Brood.* New York: Grand Central Publishing, 2000.

Butler, Octavia E. "The Monophobic Response." Published in *Partial Correction to the Representations of Earth Culture Sent Out to Extraterrestrials on the United States 1977 Voyager Interstellar Space Probes,* edited by Connie Samaras, 5. San Francisco: New Langton Arts, 1994.

Butler, Octavia E., and Stephen Potts. "We Keep Playing the Same Record." *Science Fiction Studies* 23, no. 3 (1996): 331–38.

Butler, Octavia E., and Charles H. Rowell. "An Interview with Octavia E. Butler." *Callaloo* 20, no. 1 (1997): 47–66.

Campt, Tina. "Black Feminist Futures and the Practice of Fugitivity." Helen Pond McIntyre '48 Lecture, Barnard College, October 7, 2014, https://bcrw.barnard.edu/black-feminist-futures-and-the-practice-of-fugitivity/.

Campt, Tina. *A Black Gaze: Artists Changing How We See.* Cambridge, MA: MIT Press, 2021.

Capers, I. Bennett. "Reading Back, Reading Black." *Hofstra Law Review* 35, no. 1 (2006): 9–14.

Card, Maisy. *These Ghosts Are Family.* New York: Simon & Schuster, 2020.

Card, Maisy, and Greg Mania. "Living with Our Ghosts: A Conversation with Maisy Card." *The Rumpus,* March 30, 2020. https://therumpus.net/2020/03/23/the-rumpus-interview-with-maisy-card/.

carrington, andré m. *Speculative Blackness: The Future of Race in Science Fiction.* Minneapolis: University of Minnesota Press, 2016.

Carter, Jimmy. Voyager Spacecraft Statement by the President. Online by Gerhard Peters and John T. Woolley, The American Presidency Project. https://www.presidency.ucsb.edu/node/243563.

Ching, Jacqueline, and J. J. Birch. "Icon in the 20's." *Icon* 37. DC Comics, 1996.

Cohn, Neil, and Hannah Campbell. "Navigating Comics II: Constraints on the Reading Order of Comic Page Layouts." *Applied Cognitive Psychology* 29 (2015): 193–99.

Corbett, John. *Extended Play: Sounding Off from John Cage to Dr. Funkenstein.* Durham, NC: Duke University Press, 1994.

Corbett, John. *The Wisdom of Sun-Ra: Sun Ra's Polemical Broadsheets and Streetcorner Leaflets.* Chicago: WhiteWalls, 2006.

Crawford, Margo Natalie. "Black Aesthetics Unbound." *Journal of Contemporary African Art* 29 (2011): 8–21.

DelConte, Matt. "Why *You* Can't Speak: Second-Person Narration, Voice, and a New Model for Understanding Narrative." *Style* 37, no. 2 (2003): 204–19.

Deleuze, Gilles, and Félix Guattari. *A Thousand Plateaus: Capitalism and Schizophrenia*. Translated by Brian Massumi. Minneapolis: University of Minnesota Press, 1987.

Devitt, Amy J. "Re-Fusing Form in Genre Study." In *Genres in the Internet: Issues in the Theory of Genre*, edited by Janet Giltrow and Deiter Stein, 27–47. Amsterdam: John Benjamins Publishing, 2009. Accessed February 3, 2023, ProQuest Ebook Central.

Donadey, Anne. "'Y'a bon Banania': Ethics and Cultural Criticism in the Colonial Context." *French Cultural Studies* 11, no. 31 (2000): 9–29.

Druyan, Ann. "The Sounds of Earth." In *Murmurs of Earth: The Voyager Interstellar Record*, edited by Carl Sagan, F. D. Drake, Ann Druyan, Timothy Ferris, Jon Lomberg, and Linda Salzman Sagan, 149–60. New York: Random House, 1978.

Drysdale, David. "Alienated Histories, Alienating Future: Raciology and Missing Time in *The Interrupted Journey*." *ESC* 34, no. 1 (2008): 103–23.

Edwards, Brent Hayes. "The Race for Space: Sun Ra's Poetry." In *Sun Ra: The Immeasurable Equation: The Collected Poetry and Prose*, edited by James L. Wolf and Hartmut Geerken, 29–55. Glasgow: Waitawhile, 2005.

Fanon, Frantz. *Black Skin, White Masks*. 1952. Translated by Richard Philcox. New York: Grove Press, 2008.

Ferreira da Silva, Denise. *Unpayable Debt*. Cambridge, MA: Sternberg Press, 2022.

Ferris, Timothy. "Voyager's Music." In *Murmurs of Earth: The Voyager Interstellar Record*, edited by Carl Sagan, F. D. Drake, Ann Druyan, Timothy Ferris, Jon Lomberg, and Linda Salzman Sagan, 161–209. New York: Random House, 1978.

Fields, Karen E., and Barbara J. Fields. *Racecraft: The Soul of Inequality in American Life*. London: Verso, 2014.

Flagel, Nadine. "'It's Almost Like Being There': Speculative Fiction, Slave Narrative, and the Crisis of Representation in Octavia Butler's *Kindred*." *Canadian Review of American Studies* 42, no. 2 (2012): 216–45.

Flow Motion. "Astro Black Morphologies: Music and Science Lovers." *Leonardo* 39, no. 1 (2006): 23–29.

Fuller, John G. *The Interrupted Journey: Two Lost Hours "Aboard a Flying Saucer."* New York: Dial Press, 1965.

Genette, Gérard, and Marie Maclean. "Introduction to the Paratext." *New Literary History* 22, no. 2 (1991): 261–72.

Gilroy, Paul. *The Black Atlantic: Modernity and Double-Consciousness*. Boston: Harvard University Press, 1994.

Glissant, Édouard. *Poetics of Relation*. Translated by Betsy Wing. Ann Arbor: University of Michigan Press, 2010.

Goodwin, Matthew David. *The Latinx Files: Race, Migration, and Space Aliens*. Newark, NJ: Rutgers University Press, 2021.

Grant, Mac, dir. "Earth Is Ghetto." Music video featuring Aliah Sheffield, produced by Trae Hawkins. June 9, 2023, YouTube, 3:41. https://www.youtube.com/watch?v=CYlHuaTMWIQ.

Groensteen, Thierry. *The System of Comics*. Jackson: University Press of Mississippi, 2007.

Gumbs, Alexis Pauline. "m/other ourselves: a Black queer feminist genealogy for radical mothering." In *Revolutionary Mothering: Love on the Front Lines*, edited by Alexis Pauline Gumbs, China Martens, and Mai'a Williams, 19–31. Oakland, CA: PM Press, 2016.

Halberstam, Jack. "The Wild Beyond: With and For the Undercommons." In *The Undercommons: Fugitive Planning & Black Study*, 5–12. by Stefano Harvey and Fred Moten. Wivenhoe, UK: Minor Compositions, 2013.

Haraway, Donna. *Staying with the Trouble: Making Kin in the Chthulucene*. Durham, NC: Duke University Press, 2018.

Hartman, Saidiya. *Lose Your Mother: A Journey Along the Atlantic Slave Route*. New York: Farrar, Straus and Giroux, 2008.

Hartman, Saidiya. *Scenes of Subjection: Terror, Slavery, and Self-Making in Nineteenth-Century America*. New York: Oxford University Press, 1997.

Hartman, Saidiya. "An Unnamed Girl, A Speculative History." *New Yorker*, February 9, 2019. https://www.newyorker.com/culture/culture-desk/an-unnamed-girl-a-speculative-history.

Hartman, Saidiya. "Venus in Two Acts." *small axe* 26 (2008): 1–14.

Hartman, Saidiya. *Wayward Lives, Beautiful Experiments: Intimate Histories of Social Upheaval*. New York: W. W. Norton, 2019.

Harvey, Stefano, and Fred Moten. *The Undercommons: Fugitive Planning & Black Study*. Wivenhoe, UK: Minor Compositions, 2013.

Hatfield, Charles. *Alternative Comics: An Emerging Literature*. Jackson: University of Mississippi Press, 2005.

Hauman, Nicholas. "Heavenly Bodies: Scientific Racism and the Taxonomy of Extraterrestrial Life." *borderlands* 20, no. 2 (2021): 124–54.

Heath, R. Scott. "The Other Side of Time: Theorizing the Planetary South." *PMLA* 131, no. 1 (2016): 170–73.

Hill Collins, Patricia. *Black Feminist Thought*. New York: Routledge, 2009.

Holsey, Bayo. *Routes of Remembrance: Refashioning the Slave Trade in Ghana*. Chicago: University of Chicago Press, 2008.

hooks, bell. *Black Looks: Race and Representation*. Boston: South End Press, 1992.

Jackson, Zakiyyah Iman. *Becoming Human: Matter and Meaning in an Antiblack World*. New York: New York University Press, 2020.

Johnson, Charles. "Foreword." In *Black Images in the Comics: A Visual History*, by Fredrik Strömberg, 6–19. Seattle, WA: Fantagraphics, 2003.

Kenan, Randall. "An Interview with Octavia Butler." *Callaloo* 14, no. 2 (1991): 495–504.

Kilgore, De Witt Douglas. *Astrofuturism: Science, Race, and Visions of Utopia in Space*. Philadelphia: University of Pennsylvania Press, 2003.

Koerner, Michelle. "Line of Escape: Gilles Deleuze's Encounter with George Jackson." *Genre* 44, no. 2 (2011): 157–80.

Koski, Jessica, Hongling Xie, and Ingrid R. Olson. "Understanding Social Hierarchies: The Neural and Psychological Foundations of Status Perception." *Social Neuroscience* 10, no. 5 (2015): 527–50.

Lavater, Johann Kaspar. *Essays on Physiognomy*. Translated by Thomas Holcroft. London: William Tegg, 1853.

Le Guin, Ursula K. "American SF and the Other." *Science Fiction Studies* 2, no. 3 (1975): 208–10.

Levander, Caroline. "Sutton Griggs and the Borderlands of Empire." In *Jim Crow, Literature, and the Legacy of Sutton E. Griggs*, edited by Tess Chakkalakal and Kenneth W. Warren, 57–84. Athens: University of Georgia Press, 2013.

Lock, Graham. *Blutopia: Visions of the Future and Revisions of the Past in the Works of Sun Ra, Duke Ellington, and Anthony Braxton*. Durham, NC: Duke University Press, 1999.

Lomberg, Jon. "Pictures of Earth." In *Murmurs of Earth: The Voyager Interstellar Record*, edited by Carl Sagan, F. D. Drake, Ann Druyan, Timothy Ferris, Jon Lomberg, and Linda Salzman Sagan, 71–121. New York: Random House, 1978.

Maxile, Horace J. Jr. "Extensions on a Black Musical Tropology: From Trains to the Mothership (and Beyond)." *Journal of Black Studies* 42, no. 4 (2011): 593–608.

McCoy, Beth A. "Race and the (Para)Textual Condition." *PMLA* 121, no. 1 (2006): 156–69.

McDuffie, Dwayne, and M. D. Bright. "Brother from Another Planet?" *Icon* 8. New York: DC Comics, 1993.

McDuffie, Dwayne, and M. D. Bright. "Extra-Sized Anniversary Action!" *Icon* 25. New York: DC Comics, 1995.

McDuffie, Dwayne, and M. D. Bright. "The Final Fate of the Earth." *Icon* 36. New York: DC Comics, 1996.

McDuffie, Dwayne, and M. D. Bright. "Mothership Connection 1: Icon Go Home!" *Icon* 17. New York: DC Comics, 1994.

McDuffie, Dwayne, and M. D. Bright. "Mothership Connection 2: Coming for to Carry You Home." *Icon* 19. New York: DC Comics, 1994.

McDuffie, Dwayne, and M. D. Bright. "She's Got Your Hero Right Here." *Icon* 1. New York: DC Comics, 1993.

McDuffie, Dwayne, and M. D. Bright. "Stop! Do Not Hop on Cop!" *Icon* 2. New York: DC Comics, 1994.

McDuffie, Dwayne, and M. D. Bright. "World's Collide: Icon vs. Superman." *Icon* 16. New York: DC Comics, 1994.

Meinhardt, Micki. "Maisy Card: 'There Is This Hazy Quality to My Family History That No Amount of Research Can Clarify.'" *Guernica*, April 28, 2020. https://www.guernicamag.com/miscellaneous-files-maisy-card/.

Mitchell, Angelyn. *The Freedom to Remember: Narrative, Slavery, and Gender in Contemporary Black Women's Fiction*. New Brunswick, NJ: Rutgers University Press, 2002.

Mitchell, W. J. T. *Picture Theory: Essays on Verbal and Visual Representation*. Chicago: University of Chicago Press, 1994.

Modriag, Hannah. *Comics as Language: Reimagining Critical Discourse on the Form*. Jackson: University Press of Mississippi, 2013.

Moffit, John. *Picturing Extraterrestrials: Alien Images in Modern Mass Culture*. Amherst, NY: Prometheus Books, 2003.

Morrison, Toni. *Beloved*. New York: Vintage, 2004.

Moten, Fred. "The Case of Blackness." *Criticism* 50, no. 2 (2008): 177–218.

Muñoz, José Esteban. *Cruising Utopia: The Then and There of Queer Futurity*. New York: New York University Press, 2009.

Nix, A. W. "The White Flyer to Heaven, Part I." 1927, Document Records, Track 5 on *Rev. A. W. Nix: Complete Recorded Works in Chronological Order, Vol. 1, 1927–1928,* 1995, Spotify app.

Nuzum, K. A. "Historic Time: The Uses of Mythic and Liminal Time in Monster Literature." *Children's Literature Association Quarterly* 29, no. 3 (2004): 217–27.

Oka, Cynthia Dewi. "Mothering as Revolutionary Praxis." In *Revolutionary Mothering: Love on the Front Lines,* edited by Alexis Pauline Gumbs, China Martens, and Mai'a Williams, 51–58. Oakland: PM Press, 2016.

OWN. "Oprah Winfrey Delights at the Thought of Black Aliens." *The Oprah Winfrey Show,* September 11, 2015. YouTube Video, 1:50, https://youtu.be/tIxAsorNbHg?si=-cLFxPocFE9ZAho6.

Palmié, Stephen. *Wizards and Scientists: Explorations in Afro-Cuban Modernity and Tradition.* Durham, NC: Duke University Press, 2002.

Patterson, Orlando. *Rituals of Blood: Consequences of Slavery in Two American Centuries.* Washington, DC: Civitas/Counterpoint, 1998.

Patterson, Orlando. *Slavery and Social Death: A Comparative Study.* Cambridge, MA: Harvard University Press, 1982.

Pechurina, Anna. "Researching Identities Through Material Possessions: The Case of Diasporic Objects." *Current Sociology* 68, no. 5 (2020): 669–83.

Prince, Gerald. "The Disnarrated." *Style* 22, no. 1 (1988): 1–8.

Ra, Sun. "My Music Is Words." In *The Cricket: Black Music in Evolution, 1968–1969,* edited by Amiri Baraka, A. B. Spellman, and Larry Neal, 27–34. Brooklyn: Blank Forms Editions, 2022.

Ra, Sun. *Sun Ra: The Immeasurable Equation: The Collected Poetry and Prose.* Edited by James L. Wolf and Hartmut Geerken. Glasgow: Waitawhile, 2005.

Ra, Sun. "Sun Ra Has a Master Plan." Interview by Phast Phreddie Patterson, in *Prophetika,* Sun Ra. New York: Kicks Books, 2014.

Reed, Lizzie, and Milou Stella. "'To Raise a Village, Fall Far from the Tree': Methods for Queer Kinship Pasts, Presents, and Futures." *Sexualities,* October 18, 2024. https://doi-org.proxy.lib.ohio-state.edu/10.1177/13634607241293933.

Rhee, Jeong-eun. *Decolonial Feminist Research: Haunting, Rememory and Mothers.* New York: Routledge, 2020. Accessed May 15, 2023. ProQuest Ebook Central.

Ricœur, Paul. *Time and Narrative: Volume 3.* Chicago: University of Chicago Press, 1985.

Robertson, Benjamin. "'Some Matching Strangeness': Biology, Politics, and the Embrace of History in Octavia Butler's *Kindred.*" *Science Fiction Studies* 37, no. 3 (2010): 362–81.

Russell, Heather. *Legba's Crossing: Narratology in the African Atlantic.* Athens: University of Georgia Press, 2009.

Sagan, Carl. "For Future Times and Beings." In *Murmurs of Earth: The Voyager Interstellar Record,* edited by Carl Sagan, F. D. Drake, Ann Druyan, Timothy Ferris, Jon Lomberg, and Linda Salzman Sagan, 1–43. New York: Random House, 1978.

Samaras, Connie. *A Partial Correction to Representations of Earth Culture Sent Out to Extraterrestrials on the United States 1977 Voyager Interstellar Space Probes.* San Francisco: New Langton Arts, 1994.

Schalk, Sami. *Bodyminds Reimagined: (Dis)ability, Race, and Gender in Black Women's Speculative Fiction.* Durham, NC: Duke University Press, 2018.

Sheffield, Aliah. "Earth Is Ghetto." YouTube, December 16, 2020, music video, 2:30, https://www.youtube.com/watch?v=vr2xMRSObto&list=RDvr2xMRSObto&start_radio=1.

Sheller, Mimi. *Mobility Justice: The Politics of Movement in an Age of Extremes.* London: Verso, 2018.

Sites, William. *Sun Ra: Afrofuturism and the City.* Chicago: University of Chicago Press, 2020.

Smith, Toby. *Little Gray Men: Roswell and the Rise of a Popular Culture.* Albuquerque: University of New Mexico Press, 2000.

Soja, Edward. *Thirdspace: Journeys to Los Angeles and Other Real-and-Imagined Places.* Cambridge, MA: Blackwell, 1996.

Spiegelman, Art. "Drawing Blood: Outrageous Cartoons and the Art of Outrage." *Harper's Magazine* (June 2006): 43–52.

Spillers, Hortense. "Mama's Baby, Papa's Maybe: An American Grammar Book." *Diacritics* 17, no. 2 (1987): 65–81.

Spivak, Gayatri Chakravorty. "'Planetarity' (Box 4, WELT)." *Paragraph* 38, no. 2 (2015): 291.

Streeby, Shelley. "Radical Reproduction: Octavia E. Butler's HistoFuturist Archiving as Speculative Theory." *Women's Studies* 47, no. 7 (2018): 719–32.

Sun Ra and His Arkestra. *Jazz by Sun Ra.* Transition TRLP 10, 1957, vinyl.

Szwed, John. *Space Is the Place: The Lives and Times of Sun Ra.* Durham, NC: Duke University Press, 2020.

Töpffer, Rodolphe. *Enter: The Comics: Rodolphe Töpffer's Essay on Physiognomy and The True Story of Monsieur Crépin.* Lincoln: University of Nebraska Press, 1965.

Vallée, Jacques. *Dimensions: A Casebook of Alien Contact.* San Antonio: Anomalist Books, 2008.

Walcott, Rinaldo. *The Long Emancipation: Moving Toward Black Freedom.* Durham, NC: Duke University Press, 2021.

Wanzo, Rebecca. *The Content of Our Caricature: African American Comic Art and Political Belonging.* New York: New York University Press, 2020.

Webb, Stephen. *If the Universe Is Teeming with Aliens . . . Where Is Everybody? Seventy-Five Solutions to the Fermi Paradox and the Problem of Extraterrestrial Life.* Cham, Switzerland: Springer, 2015.

Weil, François. *Family Trees: A History of Genealogy in America.* Harvard University Press, 2013. ProQuest Ebook Central. Accessed December 28, 2022.

Whiteman, Shawn D., Susan M. McHale, and Anna Soli. "Theoretical Perspectives on Sibling Relationships." *Journal of Family Theory & Review* 3, no. 2 (2011): 124–39.

Wiese, E. "Introduction: Rodolphe Töpffer and the Language of Physiognomy." In *Enter: The Comics: Rodolphe Töpffer's Essay on Physiognomy and The True Story of Monsieur Crépin,* ix–xxxii. Lincoln: University of Nebraska Press, 1965.

Wilson, E. O. *Sociobiology: The New Synthesis.* Boston: Harvard University Press, 1978.

Winnubst, Shannon. "The Many Lives of Fungibility: Anti-Blackness in Neoliberal Times." *Journal of Gender Studies* 29, no. 1 (2020): 102–12.

Wright, Melissa A. "Sex and the Future of History: Black Politics at the Limit in Sutton E. Griggs' *Imperium in Imperio.*" *The Black Scholar* 51, no. 4 (2021): 32–46.

Wright, Michelle. "Diaspora and Entanglement." *Qui Parle* 28, no. 2 (2019): 219–40.

Wright, Michelle. *The Physics of Blackness: Beyond the Middle Passage Epistemology.* Minneapolis: University of Minneapolis Press, 2015.

Wynter, Sylvia. "Towards the Sociogenic Principle: Fanon, Identity, the Puzzle of Conscious Experience, and 'What It Is Like to Be "Black."'" In *National Identities and Socio-Political Changes in Latin America*, edited by Antonio Gomez-Moriana and Mercedes Duran-Cogan, 30–66. New York: Routledge, 2001.

Wynter, Sylvia. "Unsettling the Coloniality of Being/Power/Truth/Freedom: Towards the Human, After Man, Its Overrepresentation—An Argument." *CR: The New Centennial Review* 3, no. 3 (2003): 257–337.

Yaszek, Lisa. "'A Grim Fantasy': Remaking American History in Octavia Butler's *Kindred*." *Signs: Journal of Women in Culture and Society* 28, no. 4 (2003): 1053–66.

INDEX

ableism, 106, 172. *See also* disability
Abraham, Alton, 13, 155, 173–74, 183
Adams, Frank, 171
Adulthood Rites (Butler). See *Xenogenesis*
advertisements, 11, 78–81
African American Vernacular English, 197
Afro-Baptist, 13, 155, 158, 169, 186
Afrofuturism, 13, 155–56, 159, 169–70, 175, 183, 185. *See also* do-it-yourself politics
Afropessimism, proto-, 178
alien abductions, 1–2, 64–67, 120, 165–67. *See also* UFO sightings
alienation, natal, 3, 27–31, 35–36, 39–40, 43, 46, 142, 164, 178. *See also* genealogy: exclusion from
aliens, extraterrestrial: Black Americans in Africa as, 27–28; and Black terrestrials, 11–13, 58–59, 72, 86–108, 121–52, 156, 181–95; as celestial, 88, 91, 103, 179–80; children as, 139–40; as cosmic siblings, 121; Grays, 2, 62, 66, 90, 149–50, 202; omissions in messages to, 114–18; physical descriptions and depictions, 1–3, 62, 64–67, 73, 133–34; self as (*see* Sun Ra); violence toward, 4, 59, 88, 198, 202. See also *Icon*; Sun Ra; Superman; *Xenogenesis*
aliens, terrestrial: ghosts as (*see* ghosts); humans of the past as, 11, 14, 21, 24, 45–46; mothers as (*see* mothering: radical m/othering); outsiders as, 36, 120, 127–28 (*see also* Black bodies: and dysgenicity; migrants; othering; queerness); soucouyants as (*see* soucouyants); time travelers as, 24, 36–37; zoologically defined as (*see* animality)
Al-Saji, Alia, 76–77
alterity, 57, 64, 177, 183. *See also* Black bodies: and dysgenicity; othering
alternative history, 19n9. *See also* speculative histofiction
analepsis. *See* narrative strategies: analepsis
ancestors. *See* aliens, terrestrial: humans of the past as; genealogy; kinship
animality, 57, 61, 67, 69–72, 74–75, 78, 83, 86; frogs, 69–72, 74–75, 91, 106;

217

monkeys and apes, 67, 69–70, 83. *See also* celestiality; physiognomy
antiblackness: and ableism, 172; aliens subject to, 4–6, 61; and capitalism, 37, 128, 131; and carceral state, 12, 61, 88; cosmic diaspora as escape from, 8–9, 12–13, 61, 155–56, 167, 181–82, 186, 190, 194, 197; death-logics of, 4–5, 58; imagery, 81, 84; taxonomies of, 58–59; and under-commons, 131
Apollo, 69–72, 74. *See also* celestiality
archive, 11, 16, 19–20, 22–26, 35, 38. *See also* historiography; speculative histofiction
Arkestra. *See* Sun Ra Arkestra
Armstrong, Louis, 116
Arnold, Kenneth, 62
"Astro Black" (Sun Ra), 193
astrobiology, 64
Astroblackness, 13, 156, 181–95
astrology, 174
Aunt Jemima, 80
autonomy, reproductive. *See* mothering: and reproductive autonomy

Bakhtin, Mikhail, 43
Banania, 78–81, 85
Barr, Maureen, 36
Beal, Frances M., 36
belonging: diasporic, 2, 6, 9, 11–12, 41, 47–48, 50–51, 56, 201; exclusion from (*see* alienation, natal); and kinship, 12, 17, 28, 33, 34–35, 40–42, 109, 111, 147, 152; and nationality, 32, 33n45
Beloved (Morrison), 40–41
Bhattacharya, Kakali, 41
binaries, 31–32, 88–89. *See also* Thirdspace
Bindman, David, 81
Binti trilogy (Okorafor), 201
biological determinism. *See* sociobiology
Birmingham, AL, 153, 160–62, 167, 170–73, 181, 184, 189
Black Atlantic, 9
Black bodies: being, seeing, and being seen as, 11, 58–61, 75–77, 82, 87, 90, 108; commodification of, 30, 58, 77, 163; and dysgenicity, 4–5, 30, 33, 50,

57, 61, 67, 72, 74–75, 77, 81, 83, 88, 91, 100, 105 (*see also* animality); and suprahumanity, 58, 75, 88, 91, 180 (*see also* Astroblackness; celestiality); as zombies, 178–79
Black cosmicism, 13, 155, 158–59, 175–76, 181, 183
"Black Diamond Express to Hell, The" (Nix), 156
Black Herman (Benjamin Rucker), 160
Black liberation, 13, 98, 130, 155–60, 176–77, 180–81, 185–87, 203. *See also* fugitivity and escape; kinopolitics
Black nationalism. *See* nationalism: Black
"BLACK ON BLACK" (Sun Ra), 191
Black Skin, White Masks (Fanon), 12, 61, 77–80, 85
blood logics, 16, 34, 38, 48
"Bloodchild" (Butler), 109
Blout, Herman Poole. *See* Sun Ra
blues, 116, 156
bootstraps mentality, 95, 98–99, 104
Brand, Dionne, 163–64
Braun, Wernher von, 161, 189
Brazel, William "Mack," 62
Bright, M. D., 3, 10, 12, 85. *See also Icon*
Brinegar, Terri Michelle, 156–57, 169
broadsides, 170, 175–80
Buffon, Georges-Louis Leclerc, comte de, 71
Butler, Olivia, 3, 8, 10–12; *Kindred*, 3, 11, 14–18, 21–24, 34–37, 40–47, 51; *Mind of My Mind*, 109; "The Monophobic Response," 12, 112, 119–21, 124; Patternist series, 109, 111, 122; *Positive Obsession*, 19; rememory, 40–42; speculative histofiction, 19–21, 34–36; *Survivor*, 22; *Xenogenesis*, 3, 12–13, 109–12, 121–52

Campbell, Hannah, 90–91
Campt, Tina, 85, 155, 159, 168
cancer, 125, 130, 139–40
Capers, I. Bennett, 88
capitalism, 30, 36, 126, 128, 130
carceral state, 61, 99–102, 197. *See also* Sun Ra: incarceration
Card, Maisy, 3, 10; speculative histofiction, 21, 24–26, 34–35; *These Ghosts*

Are Family, 3, 11, 16–18, 24–27, 34, 37–42, 47–56
caricature, 70, 82, 84
carrington, andré m., 95
Carter, Jimmy, 113–15, 121, 127, 136
cartography. *See* mapping
cartoons, 11, 61–62; counterpublics, 62, 85, 88, 103, 108; layout and Z-path, 89–93, 95–97, 100, 105–8; and physiognomy, 82–84, 90–91; reading strategies, 61–62, 88–90
celestiality: and Blackness, 58, 75, 88, 91, 179–80, 183, 192–94; and extraterrestrials, 75, 91, 179; and music, 187; and whiteness, 70–71, 103. *See also* animality; Astroblackness; physiognomy
chariots, 157–58
Chicago, IL, 155, 157, 167–68, 170, 172–75, 181, 183–85, 187, 189, 194
Chthulucene, 146–49, 152
Close Encounters of the Third Kind (Spielberg), 66
Cohn, Neil, 90–91
Collins, Hill, 139
colonialism, 30, 59, 72, 76, 78–80, 84, 126, 129–30
comics. *See* cartoons
communalism and collectivism. *See* kinship: community; survival, collective systems of
conservatives, Black, 87, 94–95
Coon, Carleton S., 67
copyright law, 116
Corbett, John, 154, 164, 174
"Cosmic Age, The" (Sun Ra), 193
"Cosmic-Bypass, The" (Sun Ra), 192
"Cosmo Man, The" (Sun Ra), 190
cosmology, Black alien, 155, 164, 170, 191–94. *See also* Astroblackness
costumes. *See* rhetorical strategies: costumes
counterpublics, 62, 85, 88, 103, 108, 169
Cowan, Denys, 86
Cream of Wheat's Rastus, 80
critical fabulation. *See* narrative strategies: critical fabulation

Davis, Michael, 86
Dawn (Butler). See *Xenogenesis*
DC Comics, 86
DelConte, Matt, 49
Deleuze, Gilles, 6, 47–48
dermopolitics, 67–69, 78
Devitt, Amy J., 19
diaspora, cosmic, 2–4, 202–3; extraterrestrials seen as Black, 11–12, 80, 94–95, 106–8; and fugitivity and escape, 8, 13, 154–56, 166–68, 177, 180–81, 186, 191–93, 195, 198–99, 201; and genealogy, 9, 27–30, 37, 50, 56, 163–64, 177, 179–80, 198–99; and mothering, 12–13, 135, 137, 152; as poetics, 170, 175–77, 190–94; and speculative fiction, 9–11, 20, 141
Dingle, Derek, 86
disability, 15, 32, 114, 118, 127, 138–39, 159, 171–72
disnarration. *See* narrative strategies: disnarration
do-it-yourself politics, 13, 155, 169–70, 175, 181, 185. *See also* Afrofuturism
Donadey, Anne, 80
Douglass, Frederick, 23
Drake, F. D., 114
drawings, amateur, 11, 60, 65–66, 73–75, 91
Druyan, Ann, 114–16
Drysdale, David, 67
Dunn, Alan, 62, 74
duppies. *See* ghosts
dysgenicity. *See* Black bodies: and dysgenicity

"Earth Is Ghetto" (Sheffield), 196–200
Edwards, Brent Hayes, 170, 176–77, 181, 190
Egyptology, 155, 174, 176. *See also* Thmei Research
El Saturn Research, 184–86, 189
embodiment, 35–36, 43–44, 56, 86
Essay on Physiognomy (Töpffer), 12, 61
Essays on Physiognomy (Lavater), 12, 68–72, 74–75
eugenics, 17, 32–34, 59, 67–69, 88, 103, 134, 138. *See also* physiognomy; racism, scientific

Eurocentrism, 16–17, 32, 66, 68–70, 81, 103, 116–18, 156. See also colonialism; imperialism
exegesis, 90, 175, 190
experimentation, nonconsensual, 142. See also genetic engineering

Fairbank's Gold Dust Twins, 80
family, 12, 54, 109–10, 120, 151. See also kinship
Fanon, Frantz, 4, 82, 103; *Black Skin, White Masks*, 12, 61, 77–80, 85
Far Sector (Jemisin), 201
fear of difference, irrational, 112, 121, 124, 128–29. See also "Monophobic Response, The"; xenophobia
Fellowship of Reconciliation, 171
feminism, 12, 118–19, 159
Fermi, Enrico, 62–63
Ferreira da Silva, Denise, 34
Ferris, Timothy, 114, 116
Fields, Karen E. and Barbara J., 61, 75
Fisk Jubilee Singers, 156
Fisk University, 93
Flagel, Nadine, 42
Floyd, George, 196
flying saucers, 62–65, 184, 199. See also spaceships; UFO sightings
foster families. See kinship: foster families
freedom riders, 158
friends. See kinship: friends
fugitivity and escape, 3, 6, 9, 13, 98, 155, 176–77, 180–81, 185, 197–98, 203. See also Black liberation; kinopolitics
fusion music, 184. See also Sun Ra Arkestra
futurism. See Afrofuturism

Galton, Francis, 67
Garvey, Marcus, 158, 173
gaze: Black, 84–85, 88, 100; white, 69, 76–78, 84, 88, 90, 100, 103
genealogy, 10–12, 25; and Black folks' planetary origins, 155, 177, 180 (see also Astroblackness); colonial, 32; democratization of, 32; enslaved alien linealogy, 17–18, 27–28, 34, 39–40, 42; eugenic lineralogy, 17, 40, 57; exclusion from, 29–30, 32–33, 40, 46, 50, 52, 103, 105 (see also alienation, natal); and family history, 10, 16–18, 21, 23–27, 35, 97; and family trees, 17, 27, 32, 34; and heritable descent (see inheritance of property); horizontal vs. vertical, 17–18, 33–34, 37–38, 40, 42, 48, 50–52; interracial linealogy, 25–26, 32; kin-related, 33, 51, 146; matrilineal, 16, 37; and music, 179; and online tools and databases, 27, 38; as paratext, 27, 34, 37–39, 47; racialized, 32; rhizomatic, 17–18, 39–40, 46–48, 56, 147; root to branch, 33, 39–40, 47–48, 55–56; and Thirdspace, 32, 40
genetic engineering, 111, 122, 138–42
Genovese, Eugene, 23
Ghana, 28
ghetto, Earth as. See "Earth Is Ghetto"
ghosts, 16, 51–52, 55
Gilroy, Paul, 9
Glissant, Édouard, 48
Gobineau, Joseph-Arthur, comte de, 67
Golden Record, 12, 111, 113–21, 134
Goodwin, Matthew David, 59
Gorbachev, Mikhail, 126
Gould, Stephan Jay, 123
Grant, Madison, 67
Grays. See aliens, extraterrestrial: Grays
Great Migration, 158, 173
Griggs, Sutton E., 13, 155, 169–70, 176, 183, 185
Groensteen, Thierry, 89
Guattari, Félix, 6, 47–48
Gumbs, Alexis Pauline, 12, 110, 136, 152

Halberstam, Jack, 127
Haraway, Donna, 112, 143–44, 146
hard heredity, 68–69
Hartman, Saidiya, 4, 17–18, 20, 27–29
Harvey, Stefano, 126
Hauman, Nicholas, 59
Heath, R. Scott, 6
Henderson, Fletcher, 172–73
hermeneutics: Biblical, 174–78; cartoon, 88–89; critical, 10, 88–89

heteropatriarchy, 26, 34, 36, 48, 130
hierarchies: Black women's place in, 126, 130–31 (*see also* undercommons); communitarian rejection of, 136; destructive, 122, 124–27; as distinct from status, 126; and extraterrestrials, 59, 64; gender, 127 (*see also* heteropatriarchy; sexism); and intersectionality, 89; racial, 32, 49–50, 57–60, 67, 69–70, 82, 84, 88, 127 (*see also* eugenics; physiognomy)
Hill, Barney and Betty, 1–2, 64–67, 73–74, 91, 189
Hill Collins, Patricia, 135
historical fiction, 19n9. *See also* speculative histofiction
historiography, 16–24
holobiont, 143–46, 149–51. *See also* kinship; queerness
hooks, bell, 84
Hopkinson, Nalo, 201
Hunstville, AL, 161, 164, 173

"I am not of this planet" (Sun Ra), 153–56
Icon (McDuffie and Bright), 3, 61, 85–108
illustrations, scientific, 11
image-texts, 60, 65–66, 69–70, 72, 78–82
Imago (Butler). See *Xenogenesis*
Immeasurable Equation, The (Sun Ra), 190
imperialism, 12, 30–32, 60, 64–67, 76–82, 114–18, 126, 163, 182
Imperium in Imperio (Griggs), 169
inheritance of property, 50, 52
instruments, electronic, 184
inter-genre-ality, 17, 19–21, 23–24, 40
intersectionality, 37, 84, 89

Jackson, Zakkiyah Iman, 4, 72
Jacobs, Harriet, 23
Jamaica, 16, 24–25, 27, 38–39, 48, 52
Jasper, John, 158
jazz, 116, 156, 173, 176, 183–90
Jazz by Sun Ra (Sun Ra), 187–89
Jemisin, N. K., 201
Jim Crow, 94, 157–58, 160–63, 169, 171, 173, 187

Kardashev, Nikolai, 64
Kilgore, De Witt Douglas, 8
Kindred (Butler), 3, 11, 14–18, 21–24, 34–37, 40–47, 51
King, Martin Luther, Jr., 100
King, Rodney, 100
kinopolitics: of A. W. Nix, 157–58; mobility justice, 155, 158–59; music as, 157–58, 187, 190; of Sun Ra, 13, 155, 159, 168, 176–77, 180–83, 185–95; of Sutton Griggs, 169–70. *See also* Black liberation; fugitivity and escape
kinship: adoption, 33, 54–56, 102–3, 109, 121, 133n41, 135, 153; alienation from (*see* alienation, natal); community, 54–56, 61, 106, 153, 161 (*see also* survival, collective systems of); with extraterrestrials, 2–3, 5, 106, 133–35, 138–39, 146–54, 198–200, 202–3 (*see also* Sun Ra: transmolecularization); fictive, 7–8, 33; foster families, 33, 110; friends, 2, 26, 33, 39, 54, 109, 112, 138, 161; horizontal social structures, 18, 30, 33–35, 41; interracial, 43; neighbors, 33, 39, 135, 161; with nonhuman entities, 16–17, 39–41, 50–52, 54–56; othermothers (*see* mothering: othermothers); play cousins, 33, 110; queer family systems, 13, 54–56, 109–10, 120, 122, 130–31, 133–35 (*see also* queerness); siblings, 49, 110, 112, 120–21, 135, 138–39, 149, 151, 194. *See also* diaspora, cosmic; genealogy; holobiont; *Kindred*; mothering; *These Ghosts Are Family*; *Xenogenesis*
Koerner, Michelle, 6
Konopinski, Emil, 62
Koski, Jessica, 125–26

Lagoon (Okorafor), 201
Lapouge, Georges Vacher de, 67
Lavater, Johann Kaspar, 12, 68–72, 74–75, 82, 91
Le Guin, Ursula K., 58–59
Leonid meteor shower, 158
Lesson, The (Turnbull), 201
Levander, Caroline, 169
library science, 23–24, 38
Lilith's Brood (Butler). See *Xenogenesis*

linealogy. *See* genealogy
liner notes, 155, 170, 181, 188, 190
Lock, Graham, 159–60
Lomberg, Jon, 114, 117
Los Alamos National Laboratory, 62–64
Lose Your Mother (Hartman), 27–29

mapping, 6–8, 58, 77, 80, 115, 117, 201
Martens, China, 110
Maxile, Horace J., Jr., 157
McDuffie, Dwayne, 3, 12, 85–86
McHale, Susan M., 120
McKinney, L. L., 201
McKitrick, Eric, 23
metamorphosis, 76, 137–38, 149–50
Middle Passage, 179
Midnight Robber (Hopkinson), 201
migrants, 28, 48, 50, 82, 102, 127, 159
Milestone Media, 86, 108
Mind of My Mind (Butler). *See* Patternist series
Mitchel, W. J. T., 60
Mitchell, Angelyn, 41
mobility justice. *See* kinopolitics: mobility justice
Modriag, Hannah, 89
Moffitt, John F., 66
"Monophobic Response, The" (Butler), 12, 112, 119–21, 124
Morrison, Toni, 40–41, 97–98
Moten, Fred, 9, 126
mothering: Black mothering praxis, 12, 110, 135–36, 139, 152; bloodmothers, 134–36; combating simplified accounts of, 119; othermothers, 13, 33, 112, 134–36; and racial stereotypes, 136; radical m/othering, 12, 111–12, 134, 136–37, 141, 152; and reproductive autonomy, 136, 141–42; revolutionary mothering praxis, 110, 122, 130–31, 135–36, 139, 152; sibmothers, 134, 151; as social practice, 110, 132, 148; of Sun Ra, 160. *See also* kinship; *Xenogenesis*
motherships, 157, 167
Muñoz, José Esteban, 8
misogyny. *See* heteropatriarchy; sexism

narrative spacetime. *See* spacetime: narrative
narrative strategies, 10–11, 16; analepsis, 97; critical fabulation, 10, 17, 20–21; disnarration, 40, 42, 47, 49, 51, 53; first-person narration, 26, 37, 44, 50, 52, 77, 141; linearity and nonlinearity, 4, 10, 15, 20, 26, 37, 42–44, 47, 49, 56, 89; paratext, 27, 34, 37–39, 47; prolepsis, 95; rememory, 11, 17–18, 40–41, 44–46, 48, 53, 55; second-person narration, 49; third-person narration, 52; unnarration, 40, 42, 45–47
NASA, 64, 161, 189
natal alienation. *See* alienation, natal
nationalism: Black, 169, 174, 176; in US space policy, 114
neighbors. *See* kinship: neighbors
New York, NY, 62–63, 167–68, 181, 183, 189, 193–94
Nix, A. W., 13, 155–58, 160, 164, 170, 183, 186
Noah's Ark, 185
Northrup, Solomon, 23
Nubia: Real One (Smith and McKinney), 201
nuclear war, 124–26, 136
Nuzum, K. A., 56

obruni, 28
Oka, Cynthia Dewi, 130
Okorafor, Nnedi, 201
Olmstead, Frederick Law, 23
Olson, Ingrid R., 125–26
oral traditions, Black, 169–70
Origin of the Races, The (Coon), 67
othering, 7, 31, 36, 58, 67, 80, 128–29. *See also* alterity; Black bodies: and dysgenicity; mothering: radical m/othering
othermothers. *See* mothering: othermothers
"Outer Darkness (1972, version 1), The" (Sun Ra), 191

paratext. *See* narrative strategies: paratext
Parks, Rosa, 158

Partial Correction to the Representations of Earth Culture Sent Out to Extraterrestrials on the United States 1977 Voyager Interstellar Space Probes, A (Samaras), 12, 112, 118–21
patriarchy. *See* heteropatriarchy
Patternist series (Butler), 109, 111, 122
Patterson, Orlando, 4, 178–79
Pechurina, Anna, 50
phrenology, 68, 83
physiognomy, 11–12, 57, 61, 66–77, 82–85, 90–91, 103, 105
play cousins. *See* kinship: play cousins
poetics: Black, 13; of relation, 48–51, 53, 155–56; of Sun Ra, 170, 175, 188–95
police. *See* carceral state
Positive Obsession (Butler), 19
Powers, Harriet, 158
preaching. *See* sermons
prejudice. *See* fear of difference, irrational
Priest, Christopher, 86
Prince, Gerald, 45
prolepsis. *See* narrative strategies: prolepsis

queerness, 9, 12, 110–12, 118–22, 127, 129, 134, 143, 151–52
quilts, pictoral, 158

Ra, Sun. *See* Sun Ra
race records, 155–56, 162, 169
racecraft, 61, 75–77, 88, 105
racism, scientific, 67–68. *See also* eugenics; physiognomy
rape and sexual assault, 15, 26, 36, 133, 138
reading Black, 88–90
Reagan, Ronald, 124, 126, 136
rememory. *See* narrative strategies: rememory
reproduction, 110–11, 118–19, 122, 132–33, 138, 141, 151. *See also* mothering
Rhee, Jeong-eun, 41
rhetorical strategies: call-and-response, 156, 161, 170, 176; capitalized letters, 175, 178–79, 181, 188–89; costumes, 185–86, 188–89; etymology, 175–76, 178, 189; language repetition, 177; musical accompaniment, 155–56, 162, 170, 186–88. *See also* broadsides; poetics; race records
rhizome, 47–48, 147–48. *See also* Deleuze, Gilles; genealogy: rhizomatic; Guattari, Félix
Ricœur, Paul, 20–21
Robertson, Benjamin, 35
Roswell, NM, 62, 201–2
Russell, Heather, 10

Sagan, Carl, 64, 111, 114, 116. *See also* Golden Record
Salzman Sagan, Linda, 114, 116
Samaras, Connie, 12, 112, 118–19
science fiction. *See* speculative fiction
scientific racism. *See* racism, scientific
segregation, 94, 157–58, 160–63, 169, 171, 173, 187, 197
sermons, 156–58, 160–61, 169–70, 174, 180–81
SETI, 64, 201
sexism, 37, 88–89, 102, 106, 117, 119, 127–28, 131, 158–59
sexual assault. *See* rape and sexual assault
Sharpe, Christina, 4
Sheffield, Aliah, 196–200
Sheller, 158–59
siblings, humanity as, 120–21. *See also* kinship: siblings
sight. *See* gaze; taxonomies: visual
slavery: and advertising, 81; and diaspora, 11, 28–30, 33, 155, 164, 178–80, 186; *Icon* (McDuffie and Bright), 86, 93–95; gaze as resistance to, 84; *Kindred* (Butler), 15, 23–24, 37; and mothering, 135; and physiognomy, 72, 81; *These Ghosts Are Family* (Card), 24–27, 39
slaveships, 158, 186
Smith, Robyn, 201
Smith, Toby, 67–68
social death, 29, 103
sociobiology, 123–28, 134, 136–37
Soja, Edward, 7, 31, 140
Soli, Anna, 120

Solomon, Rivers, 201
Sömmering, Samuel Thomas von, 70
Song of Solomon (Morrison), 98
soucouyants, 53–56
Southern Christian Leadership Conference, 161
space race, 130, 182, 189. *See also* Golden Record
spaceships, 1, 62, 122, 160–61, 166–67, 182, 185, 187, 199. *See also* motherships; NASA; UFO sightings; Voyager space probes
spacetime, 3–9; alternative, 4, 13, 155–56, 177; bending, 13, 155, 159, 164–68, 200; and cartoons, 87, 97, 102; estrangement in, 147; expansiveness of, 176, 192, 200; future, 141; historical, 20–21, 26, 34, 41, 51; linear/nonlinear, 18, 37, 44, 56; and music, 186–87, 190; narrative, 4, 10, 13, 15–18, 44–45, 83, 134, 137, 152, 201–3; pressure of, 196; rememory of (*see* narrative strategies: rememory); time travel (*see* time travel); and visual systems, 60–61, 77, 87
speculative fiction: Black, 10, 19–20, 58–59; Jimmy Carter's message to aliens as, 114
speculative histofiction, 11, 16–21, 23–24, 27, 31–40
speculative history, 18, 19n9, 20
Spiegelman, Art, 82
Spillers, Hortense, 4, 33
Spivak, Gayatri Chakravorty, 183
Sputnik, 181
Stampp, Kenneth, 23
Star Trek, 200–201
stereotypes, 76, 78, 81–84, 136, 197
sterilization, forced, 142, 149
Still, William, 23
Stoddard, Lothrop, 67
"Sun Do Move, The" (Jasper), 158
Sun Ra, 3, 10, 13, 153–56, 160–68, 170–95; alter-destiny in the stars, 13, 154–56, 172, 175, 180–84, 188, 190, 193–94; "Astro Black," 193; "BLACK ON BLACK," 191; Black potential, 155–56, 162–65, 168, 170, 176–77; as conscientious objector, 171–72; "The Cosmic Age," 193; "The Cosmic Bypass," 192; "The Cosmo Man," 190; "I am not of this planet," 153–56; *The Immeasurable Equation*, 190; incarceration of, 171–72; isolation of, 164, 173; *Jazz by Sun Ra*, 187–89; Jupiter encounters, 166, 182, 192; kinopolitics, 13, 155, 159, 168, 176–77, 180–83, 185–95; "The Outer Darkness (1972, version 1)," 191; physical disability, 171–72; poetics, 170, 175, 188–95, 203; Saturn encounters, 154, 164–68, 171–75, 180–82, 189–90, 194–95; transmolecularization, 10, 154–56, 165–68, 171, 174, 177, 182, 193. *See also* rhetorical strategies
Sun Ra Arkestra, 170–72, 183–94
superheroes. *See Icon*; Superman
Superman, 100, 102
suprahumanity. *See* celestiality
survival, collective systems of, 11, 36–37, 59–61, 98, 109–12, 118, 122–52
Survivor (Butler), 22
symbiosis. *See* holobiont; sympoiesis
sympoiesis, 143, 145
Szwed, John, 13, 158, 161, 165, 172–73, 181–82, 186, 189

taxonomies: Kardashev scale, 64; visual, 12, 57, 67–72, 76, 82–84. *See also* genealogy; physiognomy
Teller, Edward, 62
These Ghosts Are Family (Card), 3, 11, 16–18, 24–27, 34, 37–42, 47–56
Thirdspace, 7–8, 10, 13, 17, 31–32, 34, 40, 56, 133, 138, 140–43
Thmei Research, 13, 155, 174–76, 180–81, 183, 185, 187–88. *See also* broadsides
time travel, 15, 23–24, 34, 36–37, 42–45. *See also Kindred*
tirailleurs sénégalais, 79–80
Töpffer, Rodolphe, 82
trains: Black access to, 160, 173; cosmic, 167, 177, 190, 194; gospel, 155–58, 167, 186, 190; and liberation (*see* Black liberation); and music, 157–58, 187; Underground Railroad, 93, 158
transit. *See* Black liberation; chariots; kinopolitics; trains; spaceships
transmolecularization. *See* Sun Ra: transmolecularization

trauma, 15, 25, 33, 104, 141, 149–50, 166, 178, 202
triple consciousness, 78, 85, 88. *See also* Fanon, Frantz; intersectionality
Tubman, Harriet, 23
Turnbull, Cadwell, 201

UFO Festival, 201–2
UFO sightings, 62, 65, 113n4, 165, 189. *See also* alien abductions
Uncle Ben, 80
Uncle Tom, 104
undercommons, 126–27, 131, 136
Unkindness, An (Solomon), 201
unnarration. *See* narrative strategies: unnarration

Vallée, Jacques, 165–67
visual systems. *See* gaze; taxonomies: visual
von Braun, Wernher. *See* Braun, Wernher von
von Sömmering, Samuel Thomas. *See* Sömmering, Samuel Thomas von
Voyager space probes, 12, 113–15, 118, 122

Walcott, Rinaldo, 8

Wanzo, Rebecca, 82, 88
Washington, Booker T., 95
Weismann, August, 67
"White Flyer to Heaven, The" (Nix), 155–58
white supremacy, 25, 36, 44, 59, 84–87, 94, 104, 154, 163
Whiteman, Shawn D., 120
Wiese, Ellen, 82–83
Wild Seed (Butler). *See* Patternist series
Williams, Mai'a, 110
Wilson, E. O., 123
Winckelmann, Johann Joachim, 70
Winfrey, Oprah, 1–2, 200
Wright, Michelle, 4–5, 49–50, 58, 169
Wynter, Sylvia, 4, 30, 57

Xenogenesis (Butler), 3, 12–13, 109–12, 121–52
xenophobia, 86, 120–24, 133. *See also* fear of difference, irrational
Xie, Hongling, 125–26

Yaszek, Lisa, 36
York, Herbert, 62

zombies. *See* Black bodies: as zombies

NEW SUNS: RACE, GENDER, AND SEXUALITY IN THE SPECULATIVE
Susana M. Morris and Kinitra D. Brooks, Series Editors

Scholarly examinations of speculative fiction have been a burgeoning academic field for more than twenty-five years, but there has been a distinct lack of attention to how attending to nonhegemonic positionalities transforms our understanding of the speculative. New Suns: Race, Gender, and Sexuality in the Speculative addresses this oversight and promotes scholarship at the intersections of race, gender, sexuality, and the speculative, engaging interdisciplinary fields of research across literary, film, and cultural studies that examine multiple pasts, presents, and futures. Of particular interest are studies that offer new avenues into thinking about popular genre fictions and fan communities, including but not limited to the study of Afrofuturism, comics, ethnogothicism, ethnosurrealism, fantasy, film, futurity studies, gaming, horror, literature, science fiction, and visual studies. New Suns particularly encourages submissions that are written in a clear, accessible style that will be read both by scholars in the field as well as by nonspecialists.

Black Aliens: Kinship in the Cosmic Diaspora
JOANNA DAVIS-MCELLIGATT

Afrofuturism and World Order
REYNALDO ANDERSON

Dispelling Fantasies: Authors of Color Reimagine a Genre
JOY SANCHEZ-TAYLOR

Reading in the Postgenomic Age: Race, Discipline, and Bionarrativity in Contemporary North American Literature
LESLEY LARKIN

Black Speculative Feminisms: Memory and Liberated Futures in Black Women's Fiction
CASSANDRA L. JONES

Anti-Blackness and Human Monstrosity in Black American Horror Fiction
JERRY RAFIKI JENKINS

Gendered Defenders: Marvel's Heroines in Transmedia Spaces
EDITED BY BRYAN J. CARR AND META G. CARSTARPHEN

The Dreamer and the Dream: Afrofuturism and Black Religious Thought
ROGER A. SNEED

Diverse Futures: Science Fiction and Authors of Color
JOY SANCHEZ-TAYLOR

Impossible Stories: On the Space and Time of Black Destructive Creation
JOHN MURILLO III

Literary Afrofuturism in the Twenty-First Century
EDITED BY ISIAH LAVENDER III AND LISA YASZEK

Jordan Peele's "Get Out": Political Horror
  Edited by Dawn Keetley

Unstable Masks: Whiteness and American Superhero Comics
  Edited by Sean Guynes and Martin Lund

Afrofuturism Rising: The Literary Prehistory of a Movement
  Isiah Lavender III

The Paradox of Blackness in African American Vampire Fiction
  Jerry Rafiki Jenkins

www.ingramcontent.com/pod-product-compliance
Lightning Source LLC
Chambersburg PA
CBHW030136240426
43672CB00005B/144